The Model
Steam Locomotive

The Model Steam Locomotive

A complete treatise on design and construction

by

Martin Evans

Nexus Special Interests

Nexus Special Interests Ltd
Nexus House
Azalea Drive
Swanley
Kent BR8 8HU
England

First published 1983
Reprinted 1986, 1987, 1989, 1991, 1994, 1998
ISBN 0 85242 817 0

Phototypesetting by M & G Studios Limited. London. N.W.10. England.
Printed and bound by Whitstable Litho Ltd., Whitstable, Kent.

Contents

The Model Steam Locomotive

Introduction

To the railway enthusiast, the steam locomotive has always been an object of veneration; the attraction of the machine itself must surely be unique, for there can be no other that has commanded so much respect and interest from the human race. Perhaps the reason for this is that unlike other machines, the steam locomotive is vividly alive, it has personality as well as grace and power, and unlike so many other inventions of mankind, it has never been used as an instrument of destruction, always it has been applied to further the wellbeing and progress of human civilisation.

I fell for the attractions of the steam locomotive at a very early age, and my interest in it has never wavered for over fifty years, but perhaps this was because I was born in an old house which overlooked the old Great Eastern Railway main line from Liverpool Street to Cambridge. This line always held tremendous interest for the steam enthusiast.

With the disappearance of the steam locomotive from Britain's railways and indeed from most of the railways throughout the world, it was at first thought that interest in the model steam locomotive would decline. However, this has not been the case, on the con-

trary, interest in the model seems to have greatly increased. There are today more enthusiasts building model steam locomotives than ever before, and throughout the country and in many countries overseas, members of model engineering societies are constructing more and more continuous tracks, especially for the popular 3½in., 5in. and 7¼in. gauges. It is not surprising, therefore, that more and more potential enthusiasts wish to try their hand at model steam locomotive construction.

Many readers will already be familiar with my original "Manual of Model Steam Locomotive Construction", which was written in 1959. Since then, there have been many technical developments in the field of the model steam locomotive, and after 24 years, I thought it was high time that my original "Manual" should be revised and brought right up to date, hence the present volume. May I draw readers' attention particularly to the chapters on brakes, lubrication and boiler fittings, where the opportunity has been taken to add new and interesting designs.

In the preparation of this work, I have drawn on the work of several well-known experts, both past and present, and I would like in this connection particularly to mention the late C. M. Keiller, the late K. N. Harris, the late L. Lawrence ("LBSC"), the late G. S. Willoughby, Mr. F. Cottam, Mr. C. R. Amsbury and Mr. D. E. (Laurie) Lawrence. My thanks also to the proprietors of the magazine "Model Engineer" for some of the photographs, and last but not least, to my wife Yvonne for many of the drawings.

If the book proves of some assistance to those who follow this most fascinating hobby, I will feel well rewarded.

Martin Evans

Eydon, near Daventry. 1983

The L.N.E.R. 4-6-0 Class B1 locomotive *Springbok in 5in. gauge is one of the author's many successful and popular designs. This example was built by N. Popich of South Africa.*

CHAPTER ONE

Gauge and Scale

THE FIRST DECISION that the prospective model locomotive builder has to take is the scale and gauge to which he is to work.

In this volume, it is proposed to deal with steam locomotives from Gauge "0" (32 mm. – 7 mm. scale) to 10¼ in. (2¼ in. to 1 foot scale). Locomotives of 15 in. gauge or larger scale, such as those which operate on the Romney, Hythe & Dymchurch Railway, or the Ravenglass & Eskdale Railway, are beyond the workshop facilities of the great majority of model engineers.

The author driving Lord Gretton's 10¼in. gauge Berkshire.

The 10¼ in. gauge has always had a certain following ever since the days of the late Henry Greenly, and it enjoys a fair popularity today. It is an ideal size for the larger passenger-carrying railways in pleasure parks, private estates, seaside resorts, and so forth. The gauge is wide enough to provide a thoroughly stable engine and passenger car. The boiler is large enough to steam for long periods without attention and firing is quite easy even with a fire-door of "scale" proportions.

9½ in. gauge seems to have lost ground in recent years, possibly because it is in the way of being a half-way house between 10¼ in. and 7¼ in., the smaller gauge being closer to the resources of the average amateur. Locomotives built for 9½ in. gauge are usually made to a scale of 2 in. to the foot, and as they may weigh anything up to 14 cwt., they are still a heavy job for the model engineer to tackle.

Coming now to 7¼ in. gauge, generally associated with 1½ in. scale, this is an excellent size for the amateur who is well equipped, and provides a powerful locomotive for use on the ground-level track. A small 7¼ in. gauge locomotive will negotiate a curve of about 30 ft. radius, but for high-speed running, a minimum radius of at least 60 ft. is recommended. It must however be remembered that even a 7¼ in. gauge locomotive (except for the very small tank types) is too heavy to be lifted by one person, so that some form of lifting tackle is essential for locomotives of this gauge.

In the U.S.A. and in certain parts of Canada, 7½ in. gauge has been adopted for locomotives in 1½ in. scale.

A 7½in. gauge 4-8-4 in California; note wheel pattern.

The next smaller gauge in general use in this country is the 5 in. gauge, and models built for this gauge are usally made to the rather cumbersome scale of 1 1/16in. to the foot. In the U.S.A. and generally in Canada, the 4¾ in. gauge is used, together with 1 in. scale.

This gauge is becoming increasingly popular, as it provides a locomotive powerful enough to haul 15 to 20 passengers, either on a ground-level track or on a raised track, while the equipment required for its construction is within the resources and capabilities of the great majority of model engineers. It may be said as a rough guide that a small 5 in. gauge tank locomotive can be lifted on to the track by one person, while two can handle a large express engine quite comfortably.

3½ in. gauge, ¾ in. scale, is one of the most popular sizes and thousands of locomotives built to this scale are today running on club and private tracks in this country and abroad. No doubt the popularity of this size of model is due to the fact that it can be built with modest workshop facilities, none of the components being particulary heavy, nor are they so small that they call for very precise work.

Given a minimum radius of curved track of about 40 ft., a ¾ in. scale locomotive can be driven at "express" speed, and will haul from 2 to 15 passengers according to its size and type. Even a large 3½ in. gauge locomotive can be comfortably handled by one person (large American or Garratt types excepted!).

The next gauge to be considered is the 2½ in. Originally, models for this gauge were built to ½ in. to the ft. scale. Nowadays, however, the scale generally

7¼in. gauge G.W.R. 4700 class 2-8-0 built by K. E. Wilson, on Ted Martin's garden railway.

Bill Carter's famous 5in. gauge G.N.R. "Atlantic".

TABLE 1
STANDARDS FOR THE DIFFERENT GAUGES

Gauge	Scale	Buffer height from rail	Weight of an average express loco.	Average train weight	Average speed	Loading gauge	Minimum radius of curves	Recommended radius for curves
1¼ ins.	7 mm.	24.2 mm.	7 lbs.	30 lbs.	2 m.p.h.	63 x 94½ mm.	4 ft.	6 ft.
1¾ ins.	10 mm.	34·6 mm.	20 lbs.	80 lbs.	3½ m.p.h.	90 x 135 mm.	5 ft.	15 ft.
2½ ins.	17/32 in.	1²⁷/₃₂ ins.	50 lbs	2 cwt.	5 m.p.h.	4¾ x 7⅛ ins.	8 ft.	25 ft.
3½ ins.	¾ in.	2¹⁹/₃₂ ins.	100 lbs	9 cwt.	7 m.p.h.	6¾ x 10⅛ ins.	14 ft.	40 ft.
5 ins.	1¹/₁₆ in.	3²¹/₃₂ ins.	2½ cwt.	18 cwt.	10 m.p.h.	9⁹/₁₆ x 14⅜ ins.	18 ft.	45 ft.
7¼ ins.	1½ ins	5³/₁₆ ins.	6 cwt.	2½ tons	12 m.p.h.	13½ x 20¼ ins.	30 ft.	60 ft.
9½ ins.	2 ins.	6⅞ ins.	10 cwt.	4 tons	15 m.p.h.	18 x 27 ins.	40 ft.	100 ft.
10¼ ins.	2¼ ins.	7¾ ins.	17 cwt.	5 tons	17 m.p.h.	20¼ x 30¼ ins.	50 ft.	150 ft.

Harry Brooks driving the late E. J. Linden's prize-winning Princess Elizabeth, ¾in. scale (3½in. gauge).

adopted is $^{17}/_{32}$ in. to the ft., which gives a slightly larger and more powerful locomotive. A large type of engine in 2½ in. gauge should be capable of hauling 2 or 3 "live" passengers, while curves for high-speed running should be 25 to 30 ft. radius. Although coal firing is generally adopted, successful models have been built with methylated spirit and paraffin firing, and in more recent years, propane or butane firing.

Descending the scale once more, we come to the 1¾ in. gauge or Gauge "1"

usually associated with a scale of 10 mm. to the ft. This size of model is generally built for use on "scenic" model railways and methylated spirit, paraffin or butane fuels are commonly used, although solid fuel is sometimes adopted. For fast running, the minimum radius of curves should be about 15 ft.

Models of gauge "O" or 1¼ in. gauge are generally built to a scale of 7 mm. to the ft. and are used on indoor or outdoor scenic railways. Spirit firing is probably the commonest method, although suc-

TABLE 2

Gauge		Scale			Conversion Factor	
Ins.	m/m	Ins. per foot	m/m per foot	m/m per 100 m/m	A	B
2½	63.5	$^{17}/_{32}$	13.50	4.43	1.124	22.59
3½	89.0	¾	19.05	6.25	1.587	16.00
5	127.0	1$^{1}/_{16}$	26.99	8.85	2.250	11.29
7¼	184.0	1½	38.10	12.50	3.175	8.00
9½	241.0	2	50.80	16.67	4.233	6.00
10½	260.0	2¼	57.15	18.75	4.763	5.33

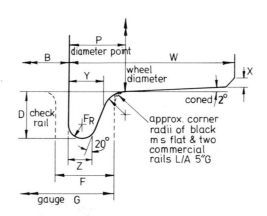

Gauge	Back to Back	Tyre Width	Flange Depth	Root Radius	Flange Radius	Chamfer	Tread Diameter Point	M/cª Dimension	M/cª Dimension	Flange Way
G	B	W	D	RR	FR	X	P	Y	Z	F
2½ in.	2.281	0.268	0.085	0.035	0.020	0.015	0.090	0.055	0.034	0.125
63.5 mm	58	6.8	2.2	0.9	.50	.40	2.3	1.4	0.90	3.2
3½ in.	3.281	0.375	0.110	0.050	0.030	0.020	0.126	0.076	0.051	0.130
89 m/m	83	9.5	2.8	1.3	.75	.50	3.2	1.9	1.3	3.3
5 in.	4.687	0.535	0.140	0.070	0.045	0.030	0.176	0.106	0.077	0.190
127 m/m	19	13.6	3.6	1.8	1.2	.80	4.5	2.7	1.95	4.8
7¼ in.	6.800	0.776	0.203	0.100	0.065	0.040	0.245	0.154	0.110	0.270
184 m/m	172	19.7	5.2	2.5	1.7	1.00	6.4	3.9	2.8	6.9
9½ in.	8.900	1.017	0.266	0.133	0.086	0.050	0.336	0.203	0.146	0.350
241 m/m	225	25.8	6.8	3.4	2.2	1.30	8.5	5.15	3.7	8.9
10¼ in.	9.600	1.097	0.287	0.144	0.093	0.060	0.363	0.219	0.158	0.380
260 m/m	244	27.8	8.0	3.7	2.4	1.50	9.2	5.55	4.0	9.7

A Mallet locomotive in gauge 0 by A. A. Sherwood.

cessful butane fired and even coal fired models have been built. The difficulty with the coal fired model in this small scale is the tiny size of the fire; unless the level of the coal and the blower are watched with the greatest care, the fire will die down. A gauge "0" steam locomotive has been known to haul a live passenger, but this should only be regarded as a stunt rather than a serious model engineering proposition! Working steam models have been built for "00" gauge and even for "000" gauge, but this is "watch-making" with a vengeance!

LOADING GAUGES.

Many model engineers, in order to gain greater power, or to obtain more clearance for outside cylinders and valve gears, increase the loading gauge beyond the normal accepted limit. There seems no objection to this provided it is not carried so far as to spoil the external proportions of the locomotive. Another way to achieve the same result is to follow "narrow-gauge" practice, and the narrow-gauge type of locomotive has always had an enthusiastic following. Some fine models of this type have been built in recent years, such as those of the old Lynton & Barnstaple Railway, the Festiniog, the Talyllyn, the Welshpool & Llanfair, and so on.

The old Broad Gauge of the G.W.R. provides a different aspect, as in this case, the model would appear small in relation to the rail gauge. On the other hand, the Broad Gauge would provide greater stability for the rolling stock.

A comparison between the average British loading gauge and that of the U.S.A. is interesting, the former measuring 9 ft. wide by 13 ft. 6 in. high, the latter 10 ft. 6 in. by 15 ft. It will be appreciated therefore that a model of the typical American locomotive is likely to be very much larger than its British counterpart.

The 2½in. gauge Ayesha, the first coal-fired locomotive built by the late LBSC.

CHAPTER TWO

Types of steam locomotive

ONE OF THE GREATEST charms of the steam locomotive is the enormous variety of types, classes and designs which have been produced since Richard Trevithick built his Pen-y-Darren locomotive in 1801. Before deciding on the type of locomotive he intends to model, the amateur engineer should consider very carefully the pros. and cons. of the various full-size designs and their suitability or otherwise as prototypes. This is most important if disappointment is not to result.

Generally speaking, the beginner or less-experienced model engineer should choose a fairly simple locomotive with cylinders outside the frames, so that complications of a crank-axle are avoided. It should not be thought that the *smallest* type of locomotive is necessarily the *easiest* to build, far from it. The very small engines often have very low-pitched boilers and short fireboxes and these features can cause trouble in arranging the connections to the cylinders, the blast pipe and the steam pipes in the smoke-box.

If a valve gear with full cab reversing and "linking up" facilities is required, it will be found that there is little to choose between Joy's, Stephenson's,

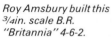

Roy Amsbury built this ³⁄₄in. scale B.R. "Britannia" 4-6-2.

Walschaerts' or Baker's as regard difficulty of manufacture, provided that the detailed design of the individual parts does not exactly follow the full-size article. In fact it is in achieving great fidelity to the prototype locomotive that real skill is required.

Locomotives can be classified under four main headings: Express passenger engines, Mixed-traffic locomotives, Goods or Mineral engines, Tank engines and small Industrial types. Let us now therefore consider the various types available to us under these headings.

EXPRESS PASSENGER ENGINES

4-6-4 type.

Only one locomotive of the 4-6-4 wheel arrangement was ever built for service in Great Britain; that was Sir Nigel Gresley's experimental water-tube boiler locomotive No. 10,000, though the type was not uncommon in some European countries and in America.

4-6-2 type.

The "Pacific" or 4-6-2 type locomotive is one which was very popular in this

A S.R. Bulleid "Pacific" in 3¹/₂in. gauge by A.R.W. Crowhurst.

country and was also much used in North America (where it originated) and in many other countries.

The first "Pacific" built in Great Britain was *The Great Bear* on the Great Western Railway, built mainly for prestige purposes and not particularly successful. Then followed the Gresley Great Northern variety and the Raven North Eastern engines. The Gresley "Pacifics" underwent considerable development, culminating in the famous streamlined "A.4" class, one of which captured the World's speed record for steam traction at 126 m.p.h.

Other British "Pacifics" included the Thompson and Peppercorn engines on the L.N.E.R., the Stanier "Pacifics" of the L.M.S., the Bulleid engines on the Southern Railway and their rebuilds, and the three types of British Railways, the light Class 6, the Class 7's or Britannias and the solitary Class 8 three-cylinder *Duke of Gloucester*.

The "Pacific" type of engine makes an excellent model, its only real drawback

Another view of Bill Carter's 5in. gauge "Atlantic", a gold medal winner.

being the fact that a fairly large radius of curved track is necessary owing to the long wheelbase. The adhesion of this wheel arrangement is generally considered inferior to the 4-6-0 owing to the weight carried on the trailing wheels and the tendency for a proportion of the weight to be transferred to these wheels when starting a load. This point probably applies more to full-size locomotives than to models.

In larger gauge models, the length of the tender usually fitted to "Pacifics" makes the locomotive a little difficult to reach for driving purpose (unless the driver is able to sit on the tender) while the majority of this type of engine had inside cylinders in addition to outside cylinders, introducing a certain amount of complication.

The boilers fitted to the L.N.E.R. "Pacifics", being of the round-top "Wootten" type, are somewhat easier to build in model form than those on the L.M.S., S.R. or B.R. engines, which had wide "Belpaire" fireboxes.

A very fine 1 1/2 in. scale G.S.R. (Ireland) 4-6-0 by the late C.R.S. Simpson.

4-6-0 Type.

This type was also very popular in Great Britain, and was used to some extent in most European countries. It originated in the U.S.A., where it was known as the "Ten-wheeler" type, but was rapidly superseded by the "Pacific" in that country.

As far as British railways were concerned, the 4-6-0 wheel arrangement provided a wonderful variety of engines. Among the express passenger types, perhaps the best known were the G.W.R. "Kings", "Castles", "Stars" and "Saints", the L.M.S. "Royal Scots" and "Baby Scots", the Southern "Lord Nelsons" and "King Arthurs", and the L.N.E.R. "Sandringhams". There were also many other interesting 4-6-0's, with two, three or four cylinders and generally speaking they make excellent prototypes for models, combining power with flexibility, though the G.W.R. 4-cylinder locomotives can prove rather troublesome as regards the latter quality, owing to the proximity of the cylinders to the bogie wheels.

4-4-2 Type.

The 4-4-2 or "Atlantic" wheel arrangement is yet another that originated in the U.S.A. It makes a very good prototype for a model locomotive, and as far as the old G.N.R. "Large Atlantics" and the very similar Southern (L.B.S.C.) "Atlantics" are concerned, quite easy to build.

In Great Britain, nearly all the "pregroup" railway companies built 4-4-2 engines. In addition to the G.N.R. and the L.B.S.C.R., the North Eastern Railway had several types, the Great Central and the North British built several, and the Great Western had a few for a short period. The Lancashire & Yorkshire Railway built some 4-4-2 engines with inside cylinders.

The short rigid wheelbase of the average "Atlantic" makes it suitable for fairly sharp curves, while the size of the boiler allows good steaming capabilities. The only possible drawback of the type would appear to be the limited adhesion weight available, but in models of up to 7¼ in. gauge, this does not count for very much as the proportion of the total engine weight carried by the bogie and trailing wheels may be very much less than in full-size practice.

4-4-0 Type.

At one time, the 4-4-0 wheel arrangement was the most popular of all for express work in Great Britain. Every major railway company possessed several varieties, and most of the minor railways also. It was used extensively abroad too.

Though the classic British 4-4-0 was an inside-cylinder machine, some engines of this type were built with outside cylinders, such as the L.S.W.R. Adams express locomotives, while in more recent years, some 3-cylinder 4-4-0's were built, such as the L.N.E.R. "Shire" and "Hunt" classes and the Southern Railway "Schools".

Although at first sight, the 4-4-0 wheel arrangement may appear a good one for model work, it suffers from the serious disadvantage of being "front-heavy". In the case of the S.R. "Schools" class

5in. gauge S.R. "Schools" 4-4-0 by Cyril Hammond.

G. M. Cashmore's 5in. gauge L.N.W.R. 4-4-0.

Silver medallist Peter Dupen with his impeccable 5in. gauge Midland 4-4-0.

A very fine 5in. gauge Caledonian 2-4-0 by Roy Amsbury.

locomotive, the weight of the three cylinders is concentrated over the middle of the bogie and a good deal of adhesion weight is lost as a result. To counteract this weight distribution problem, the rear end of a 4-4-0 model should be made as heavy as possible. A heavy cast drag-plate helps a great deal.

2-4-0 Type.

The 2-4-0 wheel arrangement was used to some extent towards the end of the 19th century, particularly on the Great Eastern and London & North Western Railways; it was also seen in Europe and North America in small numbers.

Prize-winning 3½in. gauge G.N.R. "Single" by A. G. Peacock.

Although not particularly flexible, the 2-4-0 type can make quite a successful light express engine for model work, and several examples have been built in recent years, particularly for 3½ in. gauge.

2-2-2 and 4-2-2 Type.

Many years have passed since the "Single-wheelers" were seen on our railways, yet several of the more successful designs have undoubted attractions for the model engineer. The famous Dean 4-2-2's of the old Great Western Railway were considered by many enthusiasts the most handsome locomotives ever built, while their

performance on light trains was as good as their looks. Other "Singles" of beautiful proportions were the Johnson engines on the Midland Railway, the Caledonian No.123, built for the Railway Races of the late 19th century, and the outside cylinder Stirling "Eight-footers" of the Great Northern.

From a model engineering point of view, the "Singles" make very interesting prototypes, though they cannot really be recommended to the beginner. It is most important that the scale proportions are closely adhered to, otherwise the appearance of a "Single" is easily spoilt. Although the "Single" was abandoned due to insufficient adhesion weight for any but light trains, this need not apply to a model. A relatively much higher proportion of the total engine weight may be carried by the driving wheels.

Some very fine passenger-hauling "Single-wheelers" have been built for gauges as small as 5 in. and 3½ in., and in fact a 5 in. gauge G.W.R. "Dean" 4-2-2 won the 1971 International Model Locomotive Efficiency Competition on the Southampton Society's track, and by a handsome margin.

MIXED-TRAFFIC ENGINES

4-6-0 Type.

Originally, the 4-6-0 type in this country was designed as a goods engine (the Highland Railway "Jones Goods"). It was then developed almost exclusively for express passenger work; finally, in more recent years, several 4-6-0's appeared with medium-sized driving and coupled wheels for mixed-traffic work.

Well-known and highly successful mixed-traffic 4-6-0's include the L.M.S. Stanier 5P5F class (the "Black Fives"), the G.W.R. "Halls", "Granges" and "Manors" and the L.N.E.R. Thompson B.I. class.

All these locomotives make very good prototypes for passenger-hauling models. For those who require a powerful locomotive which is not difficult to build, but which has a good reserve of power, the two-cylinder mixed-traffic type is ideal.

2-6-2 Type.

In the 1930's, Gresley on the L.N.E.R. brought out his famous "Green Arrow" class of 2-6-2 locomotives, very similar to his "Pacifics" but with 6 ft. 2 in. driving and coupled wheels, and shorter boiler. Gresley also built, shortly before his death, two lightweight 2-6-2 engines for mixed-traffic work.

No other 2-6-2 tender locomotives were built in this country, though the wheel arrangement found some favour in America and some other overseas countries.

The type is a useful one for model work as it combines a large boiler, usually with a wide firebox, and a wheelbase somewhat shorter that the average "Pacific".

2-6-0 Type.

The 2-6-0 or "Mogul" type of locomotive has been popular in many countries and all the old "Big Four" possessed several designs. Perhaps the largest and most imposing of these was the L.N.E.R. Gresley K.3 class, a three-cylinder machine with very large diameter "round-top" boiler.

Fine 3½in. gauge L.M.S. "Black Five" before painting (see page 199).

Rene Etter driving Basil Palmer's 2-8-0 in Johannesburg.

Most of the British "Moguls" had outside Walschaerts valve gear, though the L.B.S.C.R. produced a 2-6-0 with outside cylinders and inside Stephenson valve gear. The Churchward G.W.R. "Moguls" also had outside cylinders with inside valve gear, though in this case the motion was transferred to outside steam chests by rocking shafts.

The wheel arrangement is an excellent one for a model locomotive, being powerful and very compact and able to negotiate quite small radius curves, especially where the cylinders are not mounted too close to the leading wheels.

GOODS OR MINERAL ENGINES

2-8-2 Type.

The 2-8-2 type locomotive was at one time fairly common in America, and on the L.N.E.R. in this country two engines with this wheel arrangement were built for mineral traffic by Gresley. When built, they were fitted with boosters acting on the trailing wheels. Strange to say, these engines proved unnecessarily powerful as the trains they could haul turned out to be too long for the existing sidings. Later, Gresley built a few passenger engines with the 2-8-2 wheel arrangement. They were really intended for heavy express work in Scotland, but although extremely powerful, they were not altogether sucessful on the sharp curves of the Scottish lines and were rebuilt by Gresley's successor, Thompson, into "Pacifics".

The wheel arrangement produces a large and powerful model, but not one which takes kindly to sharp curves.

2-8-0 Type.

The 2-8-0 or "Consolidation" wheel arrangement originated in the U.S.A., and also achieved great success in this country and many other lands. The Great Western Railway had two distinct types which were both very good engines, though the 47xx class, with 5 ft. 8 in. driving and coupled wheels, were really mixed-traffic machines.

The Somerset & Dorset, the Great Northern, Great Central, L.N.W.R. and L.M.S. Railways all built locomotives with this wheel arrangement. During the 1914-18 War, the G.C.R. 2-8-0 was chosen by the War Department and was built in large numbers. Again, during the 1939-45 War, the L.M.S. Stanier design of 2-8-0 was adopted for service in all theatres.

From a model point of view, the 2-8-0 wheel arrangement is a good one provided radii of curves are adequate. On some models of this type, greater flexibility has been obtained by removing one or more pairs of flanges from the

19

A Caribou 3¹/₂in. gauge 0-8-0 built to the author's design by Mrs. Y. Etter.

driving and 8 coupled wheels, but this policy is not recommended owing to the danger of the wheels falling between the rails on model tracks. As a matter of fact, this minor disaster has not been unknown in full-size practice! A better way is to allow additional end play to the coupled axles, and to allow a certain amount of play in coupling rod bushes.

0-8-0 Type.

Several of the British railways had locomotives of the 0-8-0 type, the Fowler design for the L.M.S., and the Webb and Bowen Cooke designs for the London & North Western being well known. The 0-8-0 wheel arrangement has the advantage that the whole of the weight of the engine is available for adhesion. As with the 2-8-0, the type is not altogether suitable for tracks with small radius curves.

0-6-0 Type.

The 0-6-0 type of locomotive has justly been described as the "Maid-of-all-work", as engines of this wheel arrangement have been used for anything from express passenger to slow mineral work, though they are not by any means ideal for the former.

As far as Great Britain is concerned, the 0-6-0 type of locomotive was at one time most numerous of all. It was certainly a typical British type. Almost every railway possessed some goods engines with this wheel arrangement, and some had 0-6-0's with wheels as large as 5 ft. 8 in. dia. for mixed-traffic work, for instance the Ivatt engines on the Great Northern Railway. But the most numerous 0-6-0's were those with wheels around 4 ft. 8 in. diameter.

An advantage of the type for model purposes is its compactness and the fact that the whole weight of the engine is available for adhesion. As to the ability of the 0-6-0 locomotive to negotiate curves, this obviously depends on its wheelbase and here there is quite a wide choice. Some of the largest 0-6-0's were built by the Great Eastern Railway, the J.18. J.19 and J.20 (L.N.E.R. classifica-

A fine 5in. gauge 4-6-4T Remembrance by J. R. W. Heslop.

tion) classes in particular. The J.20's, designed by Mr. A. J. Hill, were the longest 0-6-0's built in this country. The Gresley J.38 and J.39 classes were also large and imposing engines.

OTHER SMALL TENDER ENGINES

Before passing on to tank engines, a few words should be said about the small tender engines of the 0-4-2 wheel arrangement. The 0-4-2 type was built by several railways in this country, though generally for passenger work. Perhaps the best known of these was the "Gladstone" class of the L.B.S.C.R., which railway also had a smaller-wheeled variety, the "Lyons" class, while the L.S.W.R. possessed a useful 0-4-2 locomotive in the so-called "Jubilee" class.

The Caledonian Railway also had a few tender engines of the 0-4-2 wheel arrangement; these had outside cylinders.

For those who prefer a small express or mixed-traffic locomotive out of the usual run of such engines, the 0-4-2 can be considered, though it has often been criticised on the grounds of lack of stability at high speeds. On the face of it, the lack of any leading wheels seems undesirable on a locomotive with any pretensions to speed.

TANK LOCOMOTIVES

Although tank locomotives have never been much favoured overseas, owing to their limited fuel and water capacity, they have always been popular in this country and were used for semi-fast passenger trains, suburban trains, short distance goods trains and for shunting.

The big advantage of the tank engine in model form is that the whole locomotive is self-contained, avoiding all flexible connections between an engine and its tender. Many of the smaller tank engines are of course rather inaccessible from the driver's point of view, due to the back of the cab and the bunker preventing access to the firedoor and backhead fittings. For this reason, many model locomotives of this type are built with part of the bunker and cab roof easily removable for driving purpose. But this disadvantage hardly applies to the larger 2-6-4 and 4-6-4 tanks which make fine prototypes for models.

For those wishing to build a powerful locomotive quickly and without meeting too many technical difficulties, there is a lot to be said for a 0-6-0 outside-cylinder tank engine, such as the ex-L.M.S. Fowler "2F" class. The complication of a crank-axle is avoided, while there are no loose carrying wheels to bother about.

For the larger tank engine models, the Fowler, Stanier and B.R. types of 2-6-2 and 2-6-4 locomotives make excellent prototypes, as do the various 2-6-2 tanks of the Great Western Railway. Then there were the handsome 4-6-2 and 4-6-4 or "Baltic" tanks built by the L.B.S.C.R. and the 4-cylinder "Baltic" tanks on the Lancashire & Yorkshire Railway.

The L.N.E.R. possessed two classes of 2-6-2 three-cylinder tank engines, and later the Thompson 2-cylinder 2-6-4 type. The Great Central also had a large inside-cylinder 2-6-4 tank locomotive. The Metropolitan and the Southern Railway also possessed some fine 2-6-4 tanks.

B.R. 2-6-4 tank locomotive, 5in. gauge, by Cyril Hammond.

G.W.R. 2-6-2 tank in 5in. gauge made principally by the author but completed by Norman Spink.

Other 4-6-4 tank engines included the "Tilbury" type, the Glasgow & South-Western engines and the Furness "Baltics", which had inside cylinders.

In these large tank engines, there should be plenty of space available for fuel and water, while accessibility for driving purpose is adequate.

Next we come to the 0-4-0 tank, built in large numbers for contractors, though many of the main line companies had a few of these engines. Example of the latter are the well-known L.S.W.R. B.4 and K.4 classes, which had outside cylinders with inside valve gears. The Great Eastern, South Eastern and many other railways had similar engines. As for the industrial tank locomotives, there were at one time enormous numbers of these with the 0-4-0 wheel arrangement built by such well-known firms as the Hunslet Engine Co., Avonside, Peckett, Manning Wardles, Andrew Barclay, etc, etc. Many of these were saddle tanks, and a large proportion had outside cylinders with inside Stephenson valve gear.

ARTICULATED LOCOMOTIVES

Under this heading comes the "Mallet", at one time very popular in the U.S.A., the "Garratt" type, the "Fairlie", the "Shay", "Climax" and "Heisler" geared locomotives, and many other special purpose types.

The principal feature of the Mallet is the large boiler supplying two sets of cylinders, motion and driving wheels, each set of which can swing in relation to the other, thus providing greater flexibility than would otherwise be possible. Generally, these locomotives were built as compounds, the leading cylinders working on low pressure steam and the rear cylinders on the high pressure.

The Garratt type generally consists of two complete "chassis", the leading chassis carrying a water container, the rear supporting a second tender holding the fuel, or fuel and water, the two units being bridged by a large boiler and cab mounted on a girder framework. This type of locomotive proved very popular and successful in South and East Africa and in Rhodesia, and at the time of writing, some of these imposing and very powerful locomotives are still in service. The Garratts were built for both standard and narrow-gauge railways.

The Fairlie, Shay, Heisler and Climax are special types of locomotive built for particularly sharp curves or for lines of indifferent level and stability.

The original Fairlie locomotive was a double-ended articulated machine of the 0-4-0 plus 0-4-0 wheel arrangement with two boilers having a large central firebox. There were also a few single boiler Fairlies, and the last development of the type was the fitting of two quite separate boilers as in the case of those supplied to the Burma State Railways.

The typical Shay locomotive had the boiler, cab and fuel carried on a single rigid frame, resting on two bogies; a vertical engine, usually a three-cylinder, was arranged on the right-hand side of the boiler and transmission was by a

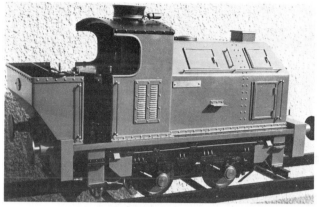

Above, a Sentinel locomotive by R. S. Spalding, right, a Tich *0-4-0T by Richard Nutt.*

horizontal shaft connected by bevel gears to each axle of each bogie.

In the Climax geared locomotive, the transmission shaft was located on the centre-line of the engine, immediately above the axles, all of which were driven by gears. The two-cylinder engines were either vertical or inclined and ran on either two or three bogies.

The Heisler geared locomotive differed from the Shay and Climax types in that the transmission was partly by gears and partly by coupling rods. The engines used were generally two-cylinder with the cylinders arranged in a 90 deg. Vee formation.

The famous Baldwin Works also built a number of geared articulated locomotives. They had four-wheel bogies driven by means of bevel gears and a longitudinal shaft from two outside cylinders on each side of the locomotive.

Some of these special types of locomotive make most interesting prototypes for the more experienced model engineer. In fact, several model Shay locomotives have been built and have proved most successful.

As far as the Mallet and Garratt types of locomotives are concerned, these are generally too large and complicated to appeal to other than a very small minor-

ity of builders, and apart from design and building problems, they are difficult to drive owing to their great length. However, there are some exceptions, notably the first Garratts built for the standard gauge. These were of the 0-4-0 plus 0-4-0 wheel arrangement, and had quite a short and small rear "Tender", so that the cab (of a scale model) would be readily accessible. These Garratts were built for the Hafod Copper Works at Swansea and were designed to operate on curves of radii as small as 90ft.

Finally, a word should be said about vertical boiler locomotives, of which the most notable were the Sentinels. The first Sentinel shunting engines used the boiler from the Super Sentinel steam wagon, with the two-cylinder high-pressure engine, horizontal, driving through chains. This design soon gave way to a locomotive with a vertical engine placed in the middle, again driving by chains, the vertical boiler being placed at one end with its grate clear of the axles. This type of Sentinel makes an unusual and interesting prototype for a model of 5 in. gauge or larger and in fact several such models have been built and have proved quite successful.

The later Sentinel-Cammell steam railcars would also make most interest-

Gauge 0 Virginian Mallet by A. A. Sherwood, Australia, who builds live steam models down to 1cm. gauge.

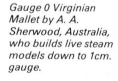

The Sentinel locomotive from the previous page with outer casing removed. Uses a S.T. Double Ten engine.

ing prototypes, though as far as is known, no models of these vehicles have been built so far. This may be due to the difficulty in gaining access to the controls owing to the greater length of the coaches.

FREE-LANCE DESIGNS

Many model engineers prefer not to build exact replicas of full-size locomotives, but design their own, embodying the features of locomotive practice which most appeal to them, This might at first sight appear an easier task than copying some particular full-size locomotive, but if the free-lance model is to be of good proportions and to have a first-class performance this is not necessarily so. However, the working out of the design and the proportioning of the various components will be found a most interesting and absorbing occupation.

The important point in free-lance designing is to keep to proportions which would be practical if enlarged to full-size, and while a strict scale "loading gauge" can be ignored to some extent, too great a liberty in this direction may well spoil the appearance if not the performance of the model.

An unusual 3¹/₂in. gauge free-lance 2-10-0 by Mr. B. H. Fogg.

CHAPTER THREE

Workshop equipment

At this stage, perhaps a few words on the question of workshop equipment for the building of model steam locomotives would not come amiss.

For the average model engineer, the important point to be decided right at the outset is the size and scale of the locomotives he wishes to build. The most important item in any amateur workshop is the centre lathe — often, and rightly, described as the "king of machine tools". Given suitable accessories, there is hardly any machining process which cannot be carried out on the lathe.

At the time of writing, there are at least two small centre lathes of centre height between 1¾ in. and 2 in. on the market, and it is often asked whether these are of any use for the machining work involved in the building of model steam locomotives. The beginner might be led to imagine that if, say, a 3¾ in. dia. wheel casting can be set up on a lathe of 2 in. centre height, then that lathe would be capable of machining it efficiently. Unfortunately, this is not necessarily so.

The ability of a lathe to machine a heavy casting lies primarily in the stiffness of its spindle, and secondly in the stiffness of its bed, saddle and slides.

However, for those who do not wish to build anything larger than Gauge "0" or "1", these miniature lathes should not be despised. For those whose ambitions lie in the direction of locomotives for 2½ in. and 3 ½ in. gauge, a lathe of at least 3 in. centre height should be chosen; one of 3½ in. centre would be even better.

Many model engineers may not have the financial resources nor the workshop space available for a milling machine, which means that essential milling operations will have to be carried out on the lathe. It is therefore sound policy to acquire a fairly heavy machine. For this reason, a used 4 in. to 6 in. centre lathe may be a better proposition for the prospective locomotive builder than a new 3 in. or 3½ in. machine. Such a lathe can often be acquired at a modest price from a firm of engineers who have no further use for it, through perhaps having purchased a more modern and sophisticated machine.

It should not however be forgotten that a centre lathe of 5 or 6 in. centre height generally requires an electric motor of about 1 h.p. to enable the operator to get the best out of it, and a 1 h.p. motor is about the largest that can be used on the ordinary domestic A.C. 1-phase supply. This point applies even more strongly to milling machines.

The next most important machine for the locomotive builder, or in fact for any model engineer, is the drilling machine. Motorised drilling machines of ¼ in., ⅜ in. and ½ in. can be purchased for considerably less than the cost of a lathe, which is perhaps why we are sometimes advised to obtain one before a lathe. As against this, most drilling operations can be done in the lathe, while even the best drilling machines make exceedingly poor lathes.

Once again, the desirable size of drilling machine depends on the size and scale of locomotives it is desired to build. Generally speaking, a ½ in. capacity machine will be useful, though not essential, for locomotives of ¾ in. scale, and invaluable for the larger scales. A ¼ in. capacity drilling machine is adequate for Gauge "1" and "0" models.

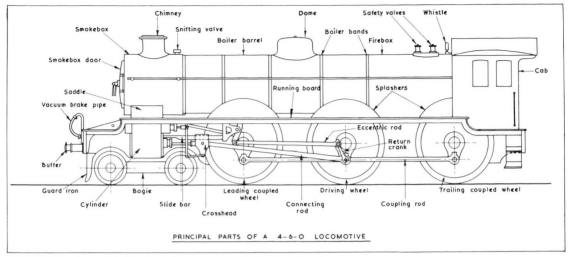

Chimney
Smokebox
Smokebox door
Saddle
Vacuum brake pipe
Buffer
Guard iron
Cylinder
Bogie
Slide bar
Crosshead
Snifting valve
Boiler barrel
Leading coupled wheel
Connecting rod
Dome
Boiler bands
Firebox
Running board
Driving wheel
Coupling rod
Safety valves
Whistle
Cab
Splashers
Eccentric rod
Return crank
Trailing coupled wheel

PRINCIPAL PARTS OF A 4—6—O LOCOMOTIVE

FIG. 1

FIG. 2

Those who are fortunate enough to be able to instal a milling machine will be faced with the age-old problem of whether to choose a vertical or a horizontal machine. There is no doubt that the vertical machine is more generally useful in the average workshop, and its cutting tools are considerably cheaper (or may more easily be home made). As against this, for model locomotive work, the horizontal milling machine is generally considered more useful. Of course a horizontal machine with vertical head is an ideal choice for those who can afford it.

Other machines which are most useful for model locomotive work (and in fact for any kind of fairly heavy model engineering) include the shaping and planing machine and the hacksaw machine. A more modest requirement is a bending rolls, for boiler work, though these

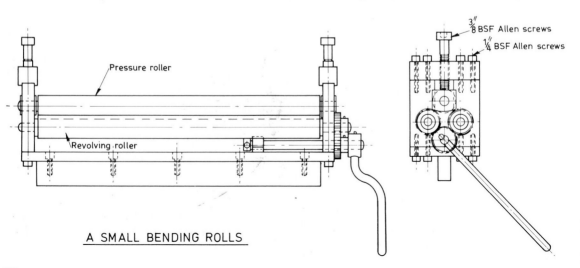

Pressure roller
Revolving roller
$\frac{3}{8}$" BSF Allen screws
$\frac{1}{4}$" BSF Allen screws

A SMALL BENDING ROLLS

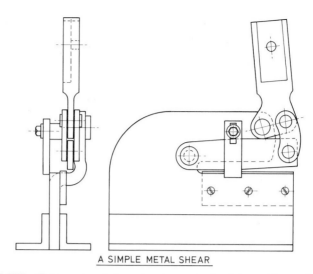

A SIMPLE METAL SHEAR

FIG. 3

Opposite, bending rolls (12in.) made especially for locomotive boiler work by the author.

are not at all difficult to make. A bench metal shear is also most useful for all kinds of sheet metal work.

Now, a few words on the equipment required for boiler work. Few model engineers possess oxy-acetylene equipment, although some of the model engineering societies possess this highly desirable apparatus.

At one time, the paraffin blowlamp was the most commonly used item for the silver-soldering and brazing of model boilers. While the largest ones (5 or 6 pint capacity) are rather frightening machines to use, they will do the job. But paraffin blowlamps can be unreliable things at times and they have now been largely superseded by the modern self-contained bottled gas burners, using propane or butane.

The propane blowpipes are to be preferred to butane, and they can be obtained in a great variety of sizes, the largest of which will provide sufficient heat to braze a one inch scale locomotive boiler, while the smallest blowpipes are ideal for the silver-soldering of small fittings, etc.

In the author's experience, the best results in the use of propane blowpipes on large boilers are obtained by using two medium-sized blowpipes rather than one of the largest size; the flame from the latter tends to be too large and diffused, making it difficult to see the job properly. With two slightly smaller burners, the operation is under better control and the total amount of heat less distressing to the operator.

An important point in brazing boilers using propane blowpipes is to ensure that there is an adequate supply of fuel; the small cylinders of gas usually supplied by the manufacturers of the burners are not large enough to cope with boilers larger than Gauge "1".

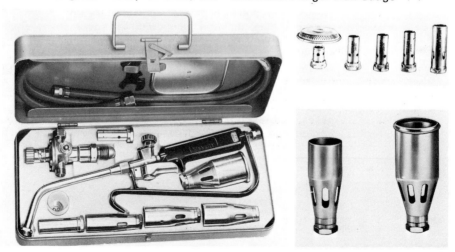

A propane blowpipe and assorted nozzles by Sievert.

27

An air-gas brazing blowpipe.

not function properly on natural gas. The Gas Board has undertaken to alter all existing gas appliances to make them suitable for natural gas, but this has not always proved successful. Evidently more experiment is needed regarding size of jets, air openings, etc., to get the best results.

After the model engineer has equipped himself with a suitable brazing torch, a brazing pan or forge will be required. For ¾ in. scale boilers, a convenient size would be about 30 in. long by 15 in. wide by 10 in. deep, the side nearest the operator being left open. A brazing pan of this type can be quickly made up from black steel sheet bolted to steel angle, the height of the bottom of the pan being made about 30 in. from ground level.

A circle of rather greater diameter than the diameter of the boiler barrels likely to be dealt with should be cut in the floor of the brazing pan for operations on the smokebox end of the boilers, and a plate will then be needed to cover this opening when not required.

The back of the pan can be lined with a few firebricks, while coke can be heaped around the job as required. Some thick asbestos sheet will also be found most useful to retain the heat from the blowpipe or to deflect it as required for a particular operation.

A suitable "pickling" tank is an essential accessory for boiler brazing, and for small boilers a rubber bucket will be found suitable. For larger boilers there are various plastic buckets and oblong receptacles which are moderate in price and which can be used, though they must be handled with care as they are generally made of very thin material. For boilers of 7¼ in. gauge and larger locomotives (built of copper) heavy gauge plastic tanks can be obtained from the trade.

Other useful tools for model boiler work include a selection of riveting punches and "dollies", hammers (ball-pein) and strong brazing tongs, that is tongs suitable for handling the boiler when hot.

Another type of brazing equipment in use is the air/town gas outfit. An air/gas torch having the burner tube 1 inch diameter and an adequate supply of air (generally supplied by an electrically-driven rotary blower) will supply enough heat to braze most ¾ inch scale boilers, and in fact many 1 inch scale boilers. The great advantage of the air/gas torch is the good control provided (assuming that the air and the gas supply are controlled by separate taps — as they should be) enabling the operator to produce a very hot flame of compact size, or a larger flame of lower temperature, which will be found most useful in model boiler work.

Many houses are now of course supplied by North Sea or other natural gases, and it will be found that air/gas torches designed for the older gas will

CHAPTER FOUR

General principles of design

In attempting the design of a model locomotive, the model engineer should beware of relying too much on accepted data and formulae which have been adopted for full-size locomotives. It may be said that in full-size practice, the power output of the locomotive depends mainly on the grate area, assuming of course that the locomotive as a whole is well proportioned. But in model locomotives up to 1½ in. scale, the power output depends mainly on its adhesion weight.

Another point which should be considered is that in full-size work, the size of the driving and coupled wheels chosen depends on the type of work the locomotive is intended for. For high-speed passenger work, the diameter of the driving wheels is likely to be around 6 ft. 8 in.; for mixed-traffic duties, a diameter around 6 ft. would be chosen, while for slow goods traffic, a diameter of around 4 ft. 10 in. would be appropriate.

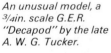

An unusual model, a ¾in. scale G.E.R. "Decapod" by the late A. W. G. Tucker.

But model locomotives are very different. On 3½ in. or 5 in. gauge, it will be found that even a goods locomotive with very small driving and coupled wheels will attain a very high speed, and the limitation to its speed is likely to be whether it can keep on the rails, rather than a question of the diameter of its wheels.

In designing his own locomotive, the amateur is usually compelled to think in terms of the capacity of his workshop, but suitable proportions of boiler and cylinders will be one of his first problems, so it is now proposed to say a few words on this subject.

TRACTIVE EFFORT

In determining the theoretical tractive effort of a model locomotive, it is most important to arrange for this to be in proportion to its adhesive weight. When possible, the tractive effort should not

be higher than one quarter of the adhesion weight, although this generally means that the scantlings of the model must be on the heavy side. But in considering the overall weight of the locomotive, the problem of handling it on and off the track should also be considered.

The formula generally employed for estimating the theoretical tractive effort of a locomotive with two cylinders is as follows:-

$$\text{Tractive effort} = \frac{B^2 \times S \times P}{W} \text{ lbs.}$$

Where B is the diameter of the cylinders in inches.
S is the stroke of cylinders in inches.
P is the effective steam pressure in lbs. per sq. in.
W is the diameter of the driving wheels in inches.

In full-size practice, it is customary to take 85 per cent of the boiler working pressure as the effective steam pressure (P) but it is better to take only 80 per cent for small models, where the drop in pressure between boiler and steam chests is likely to be greater.

For three-cylinder simple locomotives, the above formula should be multiplied by $3/2$, and for four-cylinder engines by 2.

For two-cylinder compound locomotives, the following formula (Von Borries) may be used:-

$$\text{T.E.} = \frac{D^2 \times S \times P}{4 \times W} \text{ lbs}$$

Where D is the diameter of the low-pressure cylinder, and where the ratio between the high and low pressure piston areas is between 1:2.1 and 1:2.3

For four-cylinder compounds, the following formula (Baldwin) is generally used:-

$$\text{T.E.} = \frac{2B^2 \times S \times P}{3 \times W} + \frac{D^2 \times S \times P}{4 \times W}$$

Where D is the diameter of the low-pressure cylinders.
and B is the diameter of the high-pressure cylinders.

As an example of the working of the first formula, consider a typical $3\frac{1}{2}$ in. gauge mixed-traffic locomotive of modern type. The two cylinders might be $1\frac{1}{4}$ in. bore and $1\frac{5}{8}$ in. stroke. Driving wheels $4\frac{1}{2}$ in. dia., and boiler working pressure 80 lbs. per sq. in.

Then T.E.=

$$\frac{1\frac{1}{4}^2 \times 1\frac{5}{8} \times 80}{4\frac{1}{2}} \times \frac{80}{100} \text{ lbs.}$$

$$= 36 \text{ lbs.}$$

In estimating the load which a model locomotive can be expected to haul, the tractive effort formula will only give an approximation as there as so many other factors of variable influence which have a bearing on the matter. Among these we may mention the adhesive weight of the locomotive, the actual area of contact between the wheels of the locomotive and the rails, the material and condition of the rails themselves, the internal resistance of the locomotive

Mr. F. Cottam's 5in. gauge G.W.R. 52XX 2-8-0T.

and the rolling resistance of the train being hauled. However, as a rough guide it may be said that in a model locomotive, 1 lb. of drawbar pull will haul a train of 30 lb. weight on level track.

SIZE OF CYLINDERS

If the locomotive is to be a fairly close scale model of some fullsize prototype, experience has shown that the cylinders may be made to scale size; it is also true that the dimensions of the boiler, externally at least, may be to scale, subject to certain reservations which will be discussed in a later chapter. Whether the grate area should also be to "scale" is, however, a matter of opinion.

The following table of the important dimensions of some well-known "Model Engineer" locomotive designs may be found helpful, particularly to those who wish to design a successful "free-lance" model:-

Returning to column A in the table, a high figure here suggests that the free gas area through the tubes is insufficient for the grate area; conversely, a low figure suggests that the free gas area is unnecessarily large and that the size of the grate could be increased. In practical terms, locomotives having a high figure for A will tend to work with somewhat "black" fires and may be rather shy steamers, while locomotives having a low figure for A will tend to be over driven, the fire may lift and become clinkered in prolonged steamings.

As for column B, a high figure here suggests that the locomotive would be more efficient with larger cylinders, or somewhat smaller grate area, while a low figure for B suggests that the cylinders should be somewhat smaller, or the grate area larger.

To mention some particular designs, it would seem that Simplex would benefit from a larger number of tubes in the boiler, while all three wide-box locomo-

Locomotive	Firebox heating surface sq. in.	Grate area sq. in.	No of tubes	Internal diameter of tubes	Swept Vol. of cylinders cu. in.	A	B
Dart	118	25.6	29	.428"	11.5	2.06	2.23
Springbok	120	22.3	22	.428"	10.07	2.37	2.21
Torquay Manor	121	17.9	22	.428"	10.07	1.90	1.78
Nigel Gresley	131	21.8	21	.428"	8.63	2.42	2.53
Ashford	108	21.9	20	.428"	9.34	2.56	2.34
Enterprise	90	15.8	20	.428"	10.03	1.83	1.58
Firefly 5"	106	15.2	24	.365"	7.51	1.73	2.02
Simplex	87	15.6	14	.365"	7.51	3.05	2.08
Euston	72	10.7	18	.303"	3.88	1.91	2.76
Jubilee	75	11.2	18	.303"	3.23	2.05	3.47
Rob Roy	30	7.1	9	.319"	1.90	2.47	3.74
Virginia	52	7.0	15	.319"	2.66	1.46	2.63
Caribou	66	23.4	20	.365"	4.83	3.20	4.84
Evening Star	62	21.6	17	.365"	4.30	3.48	5.02
Maisie	54	16.8	16	.319"	4.0	3.29	4.20

In the table above, column A is the fraction

$$\frac{\text{Grate area}}{\text{No. tubes} \times \text{Int. dia.}}$$

Column B is the fraction $\frac{\text{Grate area}}{\text{Swept vol. cyls.}}$

The figures for firebox heating surface are only approximate, but provide a reliable comparison. The heating surfaces of combustion chambers, where fitted, have been omitted. The number of tubes includes superheater flues, and these have been taken as very roughly equivalent to tubes as far as gas flow area is concerned.

tives might benefit from a greater number of tubes, though practical considerations may prevent this.

From column B, it would appear that Caribou could do with larger cylinders, as could Evening Star to an even greater extent.

Among the narrow-firebox locomotives, Enterprise should benefit from both a larger grate and greater firebox heating surface.

Readers will no doubt draw their own conclusions from the table, but the author's suggestion is that for a successful medium-sized narrow-firebox locomo-

A 7¹/₄in. gauge Royal Scot *driven by Ben Nixon in America; it was built in England in 1937.*

tive, capable of hauling a good load continuously, the fraction A should be around 2.4, and the fraction B should be about 2.3.

SIZE OF BARREL

When it comes to deciding the size of the boiler barrel, none of the above figures help very much, at least as far as free-lance designs are concerned. However, it is generally accepted that the most important part of the boiler heating surface is the firebox; furthermore, the longer the barrel, the longer the tubes, unless the smokebox tubeplate be set well in, to reduce the distance between firebox and smokebox tubeplate, and the longer the tubes, the greater the resistance to gas flow. All this leads one to conclude that the locomotive barrel should not be too long; this conclusion is also reinforced by the fact that the short barrel boiler is quicker to raise steam, and also quicker to recover to working pressure, should the pressure fall for any reason.

As mentioned in the later chapter on boilers, it has been appreciated for many years that there is an optimum length for the tubes for any given diameter, and this would appear to apply to both full-size locomotives and to models. The expression to take account of this, attributed to the late C. M. Keiller in model practice, is:-

$$\frac{\text{Length}}{\text{internal dia.}^2}\text{ to be between }60\text{ and }70$$

DRAUGHTING ARRANGEMENTS

In full-size locomotive design, much is made of the point that the steam line all the way from regulator port to steam chest should be of good cross-sectional area, so that there is no restriction to the steam flow, and so as to reduce as far as possible the drop in pressure between boiler and steam chest when the locomotive is at work. The passage of the exhaust gases from the cylinders to the blast pipe should be as direct as possible.

While of some importance in model locomotives up to 1 inch scale, they are negatived to some extent by the much lower piston speeds in models, and by the much shorter distance between regulator port and cylinder bores.

It has been shown in practice that even the despised inverted-tee shaped exhaust pipes in the smokebox have only a slight deleterious effect on the blast. However, this is not to suggest that a more streamlined "way out" for the steam is not worth while!

The size of the smokebox in the model locomotive is not particularly critical, though a small smokebox is undesirable as there will be less levelling out of the intermittent exhaust beat at low speeds, and also a smaller capacity to deal with the accumulation of ash etc., especially if poor quality coal is being burnt. The partial vacuum in the smokebox necessary for good combustion of the coal should not need to be more than 0.5 in. of water, nevertheless, the proportions

32

of blast pipe orifice, bore and length of the petticoat pipe and the distance between the blast pipe orifice and the bottom of the petticoat are important, and can be decided by the 1 : 3 and 1 : 6 rule, introduced by the late Henry Greenly many years ago. It is of course most important that the blast pipe is quite concentric with the petticoat pipe.

The actual diameter of the blast pipe orifice has a critical effect on steaming, and for this reason, the blast pipe cap should be made so that it can be easily removed for alteration. A variable blast pipe cap is well worth considering and should amply repay the extra work involved.

To assist the model engineer designing a "free-lance" model locomotive, the following simple formula for deciding the diameter of the blast pipe orifice is suggested (for models from ½in. to 1in. scale only):-

$$\text{Diameter of orifice} = \frac{(\text{swept volume of cylinders} + 15)^2}{1900} \text{ in.}$$

To take some examples from the previous table:-

Swept vol. cyls.

$$10.07 \text{ cu. in.} - \frac{(10.07 + 15)^2}{1900} = 0.331 \text{ in.}$$

$$9.34 \text{ cu. in.} - \frac{(9.34 + 15)^2}{1900} = 0.312 \text{ in.}$$

$$8.63 \text{ cu. in.} - \frac{(8.63 + 15)^2}{1900} = 0.294 \text{ in.}$$

$$7.51 \text{ cu. in.} - \frac{(7.51 + 15)^2}{1900} = 0.276 \text{ in.}$$

$$4.83 \text{ cu. in.} - \frac{(4.83 + 15)^2}{1900} = 0.207 \text{ in.}$$

$$4.30 \text{ cu. in.} - \frac{(4.30 + 15)^2}{1900} = 0.196 \text{ in.}$$

$$3.88 \text{ cu. in.} - \frac{(3.88 + 15)^2}{1900} = 0.188 \text{ in.}$$

$$1.90 \text{ cu. in.} - \frac{(1.90 + 15)^2}{1900} = 0.150 \text{ in.}$$

The figures above compare closely with the diameters of blast pipe orifices of well-known designs. The formula is not, however, suitable for locomotives of 1½ in. scale or larger, or to be more exact – not for locomotives with the swept volume of the cylinders over 12 cu. in.

The working pressure of the locomotive boiler is another matter which should be decided early on in the design. Generally speaking, the larger the scale of the model, the higher the working pressure. The table below shows recommended working pressures for different scales of models:-

7 mm.	(Gauge "0")	45 lb. per sq.in.
10 mm.	(Gauge "1")	60 lb. per sq. in.
17/32 in.	(2½" gauge)	70 lb. per sq. in.
¾ in.	(3½" gauge)	80 lb. per sq. in.
1 1/16 in.	(5" gauge)	90 lb. per sq. in.
1½ in.	(7¼" gauge)	100 lb. per sq. in.
2 in.	(9½" gauge)	120 lb per sq. in.
2¼ in.	(10¼" gauge)	140 lb per sq. in.

For compound locomotives, working pressure should be somewhat higher, for instance in ¾ in. scale, 100 lb. per sq. in. would be about right, 120 lb. per sq. in. for 1 1/16 in. scale.

The advantages of a high working pressure are as follows:- less liability to "prime", higher tractive effort for a given size of cylinder, higher thermal efficiency in the cylinders, improved draught for the fire. The disadvantages are: a heavier and stronger boiler is required, leakage of steam past pistons, valves and glands more likely and lubrication more critical due to the higher temperature of the steam, particularly where superheating is used.

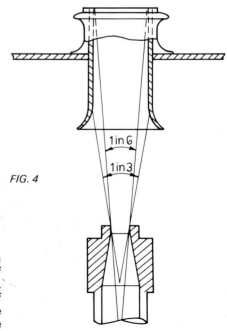

FIG. 4

1 in 6

1 in 3

BLAST NOZZLE SETTING

SUPERHEATING

The economy of superheated steam was proved conclusively in full-size locomotive practice, and practically all modern locomotives, except for shunting engines, were fitted with superheaters.

Steam is said to be superheated when its temperature has been raised above that of the water from which it is formed. The term "saturated" is applied to steam when in contact with the water in the boiler, under which conditions its temperature cannot be raised without a corresponding increase of pressure. With modern piston valves and metallic packings, a superheated steam temperature of 700 degrees F. is often reached, and the advantages gained are as follows:- greater production of steam, as a given volume of saturated steam increases in volume when superheated; reduction of losses from cylinder condensation; more efficient expansive behaviour of the steam in the cylinders.

At one time, superheating was not regarded as necessary on model steam locomotives, but when the results obtained from full-size practice were considered, it soon became apparent that similar advantages ought to be obtained in models and, in fact, this has been found to be the case. It is probable that the reason why superheaters were at first thought to be not worth the extra complication involved was that the type of superheater then in use, the so-called "grid-iron" or smokebox superheater, gave no real superheat at all, it probably did no more than dry the steam. Later, the "spearhead" or flue-tube superheater came into general use. This was an improvement, though the superheat obtained, in most cases, was very modest. The real break-through came when the late Jim Crebbin tried a firebox radiant-heat type of superheater, and superheaters of this general type are now coming into widespread use. Steam temperatures as high as 600 deg. F are now obtained (in the steam chest) using suitable firebox superheaters.

The process of transferring heat from the fire into the steam in the superheater involves three separate steps: a. the transfer of heat from the fire to the exterior surface of the superheaters. b. the passage of the heat through the metal wall of the superheater tube. c. the transfer of the heat from the inner wall of the superheater tube to the passing steam. The resistance of the actual metal of the tube to the passage of the heat is very small compared with a. and c. In full-size practice, flue tube superheaters are satisfactory because the necessary heat transfer can be obtained by convection owing to the high flue gas velocities, but in models convection transfer is not sufficient for effective superheat, hence the adoption of the firebox type superheater which utilises both convection and radiation effects.

Under construction, a Baltimore and Ohio RR D30 class switcher in ³/₄in. scale.

To obtain high superheat temperature, therefore, the elements should be carried right over the fire to the upper rear corner of the firebox (where incidentally the "return bends" will be out of the way of the firehole). The elements should not be of too large a diameter but there should be sufficient of them to ensure that the total cross-sectional area of all the elements is about 25% greater than that of the main steam pipe. It is also advantageous to flatten the elements where they are over the fire, so as to present the greater area of the tube surface to the fire while at the same time reducing the distance between the flowing steam and the walls of the element. All this means that if the superheater elements are to have a long life, they should be made of stainless steel, seamless tube of about 22 SWG being suitable. The return bends may be made from solid "blocks" of stainless steel with the joints brazed or welded.

As stainless steel is not easy to bend, it is a good plan to use brass or copper tube for the downcoming part of the element from the "wet" header, and also for that part of the tube between the superheater element proper and the steam chests. The connection between the stainless steel tube and the brass tube should be made by turning down the ends of the two tubes to somewhat less than their original thickness and slipping over a sleeve of brass tube with the ends well faired off, to eliminate completely any obstruction to the flow of the exhaust gases. The joints are then silver-soldered.

In boilers with long barrels, it may become necessary to give some support to the firebox ends of the superheater elements. One way of achieving this is to fit a small bracket, made of stainless steel sheet, inserted through the firehole and screwed to the backhead immediately above the firehole, using bronze screws. The attachment of the superheater as a complete assembly to the "wet" header should be made as strong as possible; any leak at this point would destroy the smokebox vacuum. At the same time the fixing adopted should be such that the assembly can be removed through the smokebox door without difficulty.

It might be thought that high superheat temperatures would cause damage to the bores and valves of gunmetal or phos/bronze cylinders, but if lubrication is reliable, such cylinders should be quite satisfactory for steam temperature of up to 550 deg. F. For very high steam temperatures (600 to 700 deg. F) it would be safer to specify cast-iron cylinders with proper rings and also piston valves with rings and water relief valves.

COMPOUNDING

In full-size practice, compound locomotives have never achieved any

Dr. Varga of the Hungarian State Railways with some of his models.

great success in Great Britain, although the well-known Midland 4-4-0 compounds were quite successful. Yet in other countries, notably in France, the compound locomotive has shown excellent economy of both fuel and water, while at the same time giving outstanding performance. The Chapelon 4-6-2 and 4-8-0 compound locomotives were probably the most efficient steam locomotives ever built.

Not many model compound locomotives have been built, but the late C. M. Keiller built a successful 2½ in. gauge Midland compound years ago, and more recently C. R. Amsbury completed a 5 in. gauge Great Western "French" compound 4-4-2 which has also proved very successful.

In models, the three or four cylinder compound system gives the best chance of success; the working pressure should be made fairly high while the cut-off in the high-pressure cylinders should not be made too late.

It has been suggested that an intermediate superheater should be arranged between the high pressure and low pressure cylinders. The drawback to this scheme, however, is that lubricating oil from the high-pressure cylinders would be carried through into the intermediate superheater with possible overheating or even burning of the oil. Perhaps the best solution is to make sure that the primary superheater really does its job.

FLASH STEAM BOILERS

In an attempt to simplify the somewhat complicated locomotive type boiler, a few model engineers have experimented with the flash steam system. The basis of this system is a closely coiled length of tube enclosed in an insulated casing, the tube being heated by either a coal fire or an oil or bottled gas burner. The water supply is carried in the tender and is pumped through this tube by means of one or two axle-driven pumps or by crosshead pumps. On meeting the heated part of the tube, the water is rapidly converted into steam at high temperature and pressure. From the first series of coils, the steam passes to the regulator, then through a secondary series of coils and finally to the cylinders. To start the boiler, it is of course necessary to use some form of hand pump, but once steam is raised, the locomotive's own pumps take over.

While a powerful locomotive can be produced in this way, the flash system cannot be recommended as there is too little control over either the pressure or temperature attained, neither is there any reserve upon which the cylinders may draw when required. There is also difficulty when the locomotive is standing, when some water must be kept in the coils so that they do not become burnt by the heat from the fire.

RECENT DEVELOPMENTS

Recent developments in the design of the model steam locomotive include stainless steel radiant superheaters, thermic syphons and poppet valve cylinders, all of which are proving highly successful.

A few years ago, the author thought that some means should be found for making the reading of the locomotive water gauge easier, and also to make it possible to read the gauge easily at night. Not being well acquainted with electronics, an approach was made to Mr. C. R. Amsbury to see if he could come up with some electronic solution to the problem. What was wanted was a small electric light which would glow green when the water level was appreciably above the top of the firebox crown, but red when the water level fell below this. The principle behind the apparatus which Mr. Amsbury was able to devise is very simple – that electrodes placed above and below water level will have very different resistances. The circuit shown in Fig.5 was used and light-emitting diodes were used.

The indication given by the system is – low water level – red light; water between upper and lower probes – green light, water over the top probe two green lights. An amber light-emitting diode can be substituted for the top green light, but amber l.e.d's are expensive and not very bright. Two sizes of l.e.d's are available and both take about the same maximum current; the system is fail-safe in that one light at least should always be visible.

The electronics are quite compact, about 1¼ in. x 1¼ in. x ¾ in. and clip on the top of a battery of four pen cells in a

FIG. 5

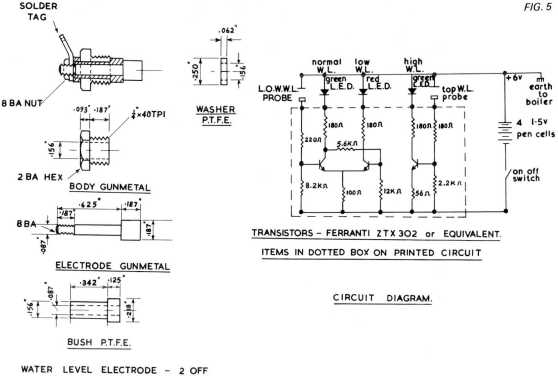

SOLDER TAG

8 BA NUT

WASHER P.T.F.E.

2 BA HEX

BODY GUNMETAL

8 BA

ELECTRODE GUNMETAL

BUSH P.T.F.E.

WATER LEVEL ELECTRODE – 2 OFF

TRANSISTORS – FERRANTI ZTX 302 or EQUIVALENT.

ITEMS IN DOTTED BOX ON PRINTED CIRCUIT

CIRCUIT DIAGRAM.

convenient plastic holder which can be obtained from most radio component shops.

The light-emitting diodes require a suitable mounting to suit the particular locomotive. The large ones are about $3/16$ in. o.d. x $1/4$ in. long, and the smaller ones about $1/8$ in. o.d. x $3/16$ in. long (plus leads). The lamps can be any reasonable distance from the rest of the equipment.

It is important that the l.e.d's are connected the right way round, as even momentary reversed connections can ruin them. The circuit has been arranged to give the minimum number of leads between the electronics and the external elements, i.e. one to each lamp and probe and one common lead to the boiler.

Light-emitting diodes give very good indications in poor light conditions, but are a bit weak in full daylight. They are best when viewed end on and should be positioned so that they are viewed in this way from the normal driving position of the locomotive.

The electrodes in the boiler are simple, being made of gunmetal with p.t.f.e.

insulation. They should be mounted with the centre-line about $1/8$ in. above the desired operating water level in each case, and the internal projections should be at least $1/8$ in. away from any metal in the vicinity, otherwise drops of water may cling between the centre electrode and the offending metal, giving a false reading.

The use of this electronic water gauge depends on the conductivity of the water, so that distilled water would not be suitable, but so far as experiments have been made, any normal water used for steam locomotives should be suitable. Possibly operation of the equipment in an area of very hard water will cause a deposit build-up on the electrodes that would gradually insulate them, in which case an occasional removal for cleaning would be required.

Other applications of this system are possible; for instance it might be possible by replacing lamps with relays to operate an electrically-driven feed pump or turn on an injector. Here is an unexplored area for the ambitious and inventive model engineer!

CHAPTER FIVE

Main frames, stretchers, axleboxes, horns

In building a model steam locomotive, it seems logical to make a start on the main frames, and then follow these with the buffer and drag beams, hornblocks, axleboxes and frame stretchers.

The earliest full-size locomotives did not have separate frames, the bearings for the wheels being attached to the underside of the boiler. Modern British locomotives used plate steel frames 1 in. to 1¼ in. thick, while overseas, cast bar frames were generally preferred. Some later American locomotives actually had frames and cylinders cast in one piece, a remarkable piece of pattern-making!

It is a mistake to make the frames of a model locomotive to scale thickness, as something heavier is required to stand up to hard work; the table below gives suitable thicknesses of frames according to the scale of the model, and also the recommended distance between frames, although these dimensions may of course be modified where the locomotive is of a very small type.

DETAILS OF MAIN FRAMES

Gauge	Thickness of frame	Distance between frames
1¼in.	¹/₁₆in. or 1.6mm.	⁷/₈in. or 23mm.
1¾in.	³/₃₂in. or 2.0mm.	1¼in or 31mm.
2½in	³/₃₂in. or 2.0mm.	1¹⁵/₁₆in or 49.5mm.
3½in.	⅛in or 3.0mm.	2⁷/₈in or 73mm.
5 in.	⅛in. or 4.0mm.	4⅛in or 105mm.
7¼in.	³/₁₆in. or 5.0mm.	6¹/₁₆in. or 154mm.
9½in.	¼in or 6.0mm.	8in. or 204mm.
10¼in	⁵/₁₆in. or 8.0mm.	8⅜in. or 214mm.

Bright mild steel is the most common material used for frames. For one thing, it is the same material as used for the full-size locomotive; it is strong, ductile and reasonably cheap. Black mild steel makes a fair alternative though it is not so nice to work on for marking out and drilling, but has the advantage that it is less likely to distort when cut.

Stainless steel is sometimes used, having the advantage of being non-rusting but it is expensive and much harder to drill, and is often difficult to obtain in the required sizes. Ground gauge plate (tool steel) has been used for locomotive frames. It has some advantages such as accuracy, absence of warp and greater strength than mild steel. However it is expensive and harder to drill and saw.

The frames of the locomotive are held together and at the desired distance apart by stretchers and by the buffer beam at the front of the engine and by a similar beam, the drag beam, at the rear end. On tank locomotives, the rear beam may be indentical to the front, both carrying buffers and couplings and possibly vacuum or Westinghouse brake pipes and steam heating pipes.

Even on model locomotives, the design and positioning of frame stretchers is very important. Very often the smokebox saddle (that is, a casting supporting the smokebox and hence the front end of the boiler) acts as a strong frame stretcher. If the cylinders are inside, they also serve to stiffen the frames a great deal at the front end.

With outside cylinder locomotives, it is important to stiffen the frames between the cylinders and the driving axle, and it is in this position that the stretcher should be the largest and strongest.

Frames for the 3¹/₂in. gauge 2-6-2T William by the author. Photograph by Laurie Lawrence.

As the firebox of the locomotive boiler may extend downwards between the frames (i.e. a narrow-type firebox) no stretchers can be placed in this area, but a stretcher can generally be fitted immediately in front of the firebox and if there is much distance between the rear of the firebox and the drag beam or rear beam, another stretcher may be placed here.

BUFFER BEAMS

Buffer and drag beams are often made from bright steel angle. Suitable sizes are ¾ in. x ¾ in. x ⅛ in. for 2½ in. gauge engines, 1 in. x 1 in. x ⅛ in. for 3½ in. gaugers, and 1½ in. x 1½ in. x ³/₁₆ in. for 5 in. gauge locomotives. The angle buffer beam is strong and has the advantage of a convenient platform on which the running boards may be bolted.

To follow full-size practice more closely, flat steel bar is often used for the buffer beams of larger scale models. For models under ½ in. scale gunmetal

castings are sometimes used in which lugs are provided to receive the ends of the frames, while guard irons may also be cast integral with the beams

Some model engineers braze or weld the frames of the locomotive direct to the buffer beams. This makes a strong assembly, but there are several disadvantages – it is impossible to separate the frames, an operation which might prove necessary at a later stage for a variety of reasons; the frames are liable to distort owing to the high temperature to which they are subjected, while the brazing or welding operations leave the metal in a discoloured and scale-covered condition.

To return now to the frames of the locomotive, it is seldom that steel plate that is really straight can be obtained, but this trouble can often be overcome by arranging the two plates so that the bulge is equal and opposite, so that when the stretchers are fitted, they will pull the frames in to the correct spacing.

Before starting to mark out the frames, which need be done on only one frame

Chassis for Iron Duke locomotive by V. M. Lewitt.

FIG. 6

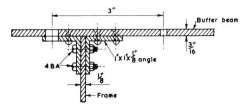

ASSEMBLY OF BUFFER BEAM FOR 5" GAUGE

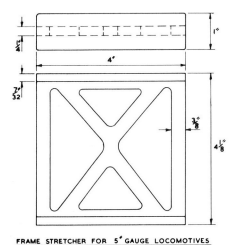

FRAME STRETCHER FOR 5" GAUGE LOCOMOTIVES

The important points to watch in marking out a locomotive frame are to scribe in clearly the vertical and horizontal centre-line of the driving and coupled axles, the centres of the cylinders and the outline of the cylinder block, which will be found most useful when lining up the cylinders on the frames later on. The outline of the main horns should also be scribed and the wheel arches if there are any bogie or trailing wheels to be considered. The ends of the frames, where the buffer and drag beams are to be attached, should also be clearly marked. The positions of as many holes as it is possible to determine at this early stage should also be marked out.

The next thing to do is to bolt or rivet the two frames plates together, ready for drilling and sawing, so three suitable holes can be chosen, one at each end and one near the middle, and these can be drilled through both plates. It is a good plan to use copper rivets, say ⅛ in. dia. for ¾ to 1 in. scale locomotives, and lightly countersink them on both sides, filing flush. The pair of frames can then be held in any position in the bench vice or on the drilling machine table, without any protruding bolt heads or nuts getting in the way. The task of sawing out the frames can be made a great deal easier by choosing a hacksaw blade of high-speed steel, with comparatively coarse teeth, and using plenty of cutting oil. On long cuts, it may become necessary to turn the hacksaw blade through 90 deg. in its frame, so as to avoid the back of the saw from fouling the work; builders should not be tempted to use a chisel on locomotive frames, as this will lead to distortion.

Where a concave curve is required, as for instance at the clearance arches over bogie or trailing wheels, a row of small holes can be drilled, close together and just outside the scribed line. These holes are then carefully opened out, when finally the unwanted piece of metal can be broken out.

After all the sawing has been completed, a start is made on the job of filing down to the scribed lines, and a great deal of hard work will be saved if this filing is tackled in a logical way – starting with a good hefty coarse file, such as a 12 in. square file, where some amount of metal has to be removed. When getting close to the finished surface, the files in use can be changed, first to "second-

plate of course, clean the steel throughly, finishing by rubbing lightly over the surface with fine emery cloth, using a circular motion. It will then be found that lines scribed either vertically or horizontally will show up well. Next, coat the steel with marking-out fluid or a solution of copper sulphate, after which the scribed lines will show up nicely. Before marking out true up one longitudinal edge – the bottom edge is usually the most convenient, though if the steel being used has both edges slightly radiused (through being sheared commercially) it is sensible to choose a wider piece of steel and position the bottom edge of the frame at a suitable distance from the edge of the steel.

Buffer beam for William, a simple freelance design.

Photograph by Laurie Lawrence.

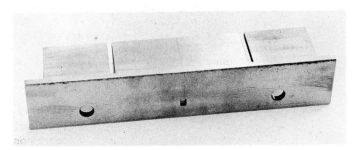

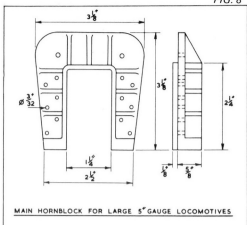

FIG. 8

MAIN HORNBLOCK FOR LARGE 5" GAUGE LOCOMOTIVES

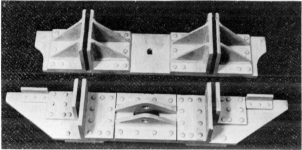

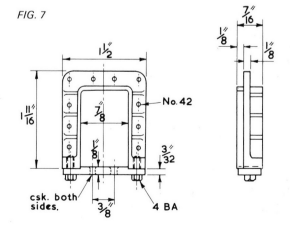

Frame stretchers, buffer beam and drag beam for the 7¼in. gauge 4-6-0. Highlander.

cut" and then to "smooth", finally finishing off with an emery block. (Emery cloth should not be used directly as this will tend to round the edges too much).

After all sawing, filing and drilling operations have been finished, separate the frames and remove all burrs – there will be a lot of these between the frames – and if necessary, run the drills through again.

Before the buffer and drag beams can be fitted to the frames, the horns must be fitted. Hornblocks are essential for all driving and coupled axle-boxes, except in the smallest scales, or where the frames are of the thick, bar type, when the axleboxes may work directly against the edges of the frames. Horns are supplied in gunmetal or cast-iron and are satisfactory in either metal; being castings, it pays to give them a good clean up with old files so that any sand or scale is removed which would otherwise quickly blunt lathe tools or milling cutters. For the smaller scales, "hot-pressed" gunmetal horns are sometimes available, and these save a good deal of work, though they will still have to be machined lightly on their inside working surfaces.

To machine the horns, set them up on a vertical-slide, the slide being arranged facing the lathe headstock. The horns can be held by a short length of steel bar, at least ¼ in. thick and just long enough to span the gap. An end-mill is then used in 3-jaw chuck or collet and this is worked all around the bolting face of the horn, to ensure that this is flat and true. Most of the flange can also be machined up to the clamping bar, the small amount of metal under this being removed afterwards by filing.

The horns are now turned round and a light cut taken around the flange and base to bring the overall thickness of the horn to the required dimension. After machining the horns, they are riveted or bolted to the frames, using iron rivets or steel bolts, the horns being placed on the inside of the frames and the rivets countersunk on the outside. The drilling is done through the horn first, the horn is then clamped against the frame and the drill run right through. If hexagon-head bolts are used to hold horns to frames,

FIG. 7

HORNBLOCK & STAY FOR 3½" GAUGE LOCOMOTIVES

41

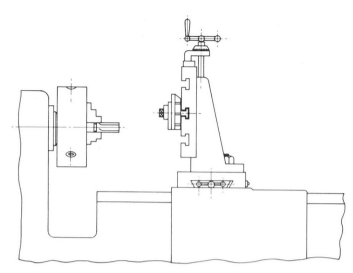

FIG. 9
The set-up
for milling
the hornblocks.

large as can be held on the table of the vertical-slide, is then bolted to the slide, and the pair of frames clamped in this facing the headstock. The frames can be set square by traversing them right across a dial-test indicator, or even by bringing them hard up against the lathe faceplate. An end-mill is now used in the 3-jaw or collet, of sufficient length to reach to the top of the horn. This method is not as rigid as one would like and there is bound to be rather a lot of overhang. If a pair of large toolmaker's clamps are fitted tightly to the frames on each side of the horn being machined, just clear of the chuck when the end-mill is at the end of its cut, some improvement in rigidity is achieved. But in any case, the end-mill should not be expected to take off more than about 8 thou from each face and cuts should be extremely light. It is a job that calls for plenty of patience when done on the average model engineer's lathe!

It is often asked why these horn faces cannot be filed, using the axle-boxes themselves as gauges. The answer is that this can be done, but it calls for considerable skill with the file. Perhaps the best compromise is to file the horn faces to within 6 thou or so of the finished size and then adopt the end-milling operation described above for the finishing cuts.

When both the frames and the horns are too big for any of the operations mentioned above to be used, the answer is to machine the horns completely beforehand and rely on the cutting of the frame slots to achieve the required accuracy. It is in any case much easier to file the frame slots truly than to file the horns in position on the frames. If this procedure is followed, the completely machined horns should be tried in the frame slots from time to time while filing proceeds, as they should be a fairly tight fit. Then erect the frames temporarily, using the buffer beams and stretchers to get everything as true as possible, and lay the assembly on a surface plate, or piece of thick plate glass (or the lathe bed with saddle and tailstock removed) then obtain a true bar of steel somewhat longer than the width over the frames and a close fit inside the working faces of the horns.

It will now be possible to check for squareness, using a large engineer's try-square. If the horns are "out", make use of a feeler gauge to find out how much

the nuts should be put on the outside and may have to be filed down slightly after tightening in case they should foul the wheels, depending on axlebox flange thickness etc. It is also important to prevent them coming loose in service; they could be lightly burred over, but a neater method is to take advantage of one of the new adhesives such as Loctite. A light smear of Loctite on the threads before applying the nut works wonders, but the threads must be clean otherwise the adhesive will not "take".

The next operation on the frames is to bolt them together again, back to back, while the inside, working surface of the horns is machined. This is not an easy operation with the average equipment available to the amateur, as the ideal would be a big vertical milling machine. Anyone who has that unusual but quite inexpensive machine, a filing machine, can do this job quite easily. Others may have to fall back on the lathe.

One method is to use a large side-and-face cutter on an arbor between centres in a large lathe, the pair of frames being clamped under the tool-holder or supported on the cross-slide on suitable true packing blocks, but there are snags here. To reach to the top of the horns, it is necessary to use a cutter of very large diameter, and this will be beyond the capacity of many machines. There is also the problem of long frames fouling either the headstock or the tailstock, or both, so that this method has little to recommend it. A method which the author has used with success is to set up a vertical-slide on the cross-slide facing the lathe headstock. A machine vice, as

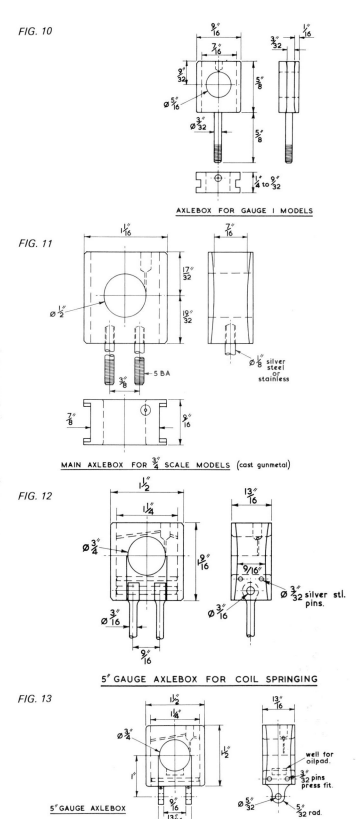

FIG. 10

AXLEBOX FOR GAUGE I MODELS

FIG. 11

MAIN AXLEBOX FOR ¾" SCALE MODELS (cast gunmetal)

FIG. 12

5" GAUGE AXLEBOX FOR COIL SPRINGING

FIG. 13

5" GAUGE AXLEBOX
FOR LAMINATED SPRINGING

one horn is offset from its opposite number. It is not likely to be more that 2 or 3 thou "out". Next, remove one of the horns and file the required amount away from the frame on the edge which will bring the horn in line once again. Cut off a slice of steel shim of the same thickness as the feeler gauge used (every model engineer's workshop should contain a small quantity of steel shim stock, which is quite cheap), clean it thoroughly and also the edge of the frame, with a drop of petrol, and use a light smear of Loctite to hold the strip of shim to the edge of the frame. Replace the horn, which should now be a tight fit, clamp in place and rivet up.

AXLEBOXES

The next items to be considered are the axleboxes. The design of axleboxes will depend on a great deal on the scale of the locomotive. The drawings show some designs of main (driving and coupled) axleboxes suitable for models from Gauge "1" to 7¼ in. gauge. Full-size locomotive axleboxes were made from solid gunmetal at one time, but later designs were steel castings with bronze bushes lined with white metal, the latter metal being useful as it does not damage the axle should the bearing run hot.

For a Gauge "1" locomotive, it is a good plan to adopt fairly thick frames and dispence with horns altogether, the axleboxes bearing directly against the edges of the frames. For 2½ and 3½ in. gauges, the one-piece axlebox machined from a gunmetal casting is the most commonly used. When we come to 5 in. gauge the price of a solid gunmetal casting is so high that some other form of construction is worth considering. A plain cast-iron axlebox gives quite good results and is cheap; if the axle could be hardened, the cast-iron axlebox would be an excellent choice. Another idea is to use a plain steel axlebox with an "oilite" bush. To save having to mill the working faces to produce the usual flanges, such an axlebox may be built up from a thick flat section plus two flat sections of 3/32 to 1/8 in. thickness on each side. The flanges could be held on by four countersunk screws. If an oilite bush is used it must be a fairly tight fit in the axlebox, otherwise it will prove to

FIG. 15

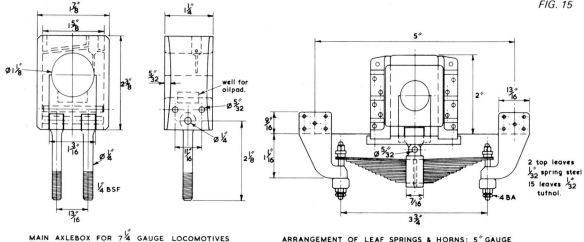

MAIN AXLEBOX FOR 7¼ GAUGE LOCOMOTIVES

ARRANGEMENT OF LEAF SPRINGS & HORNS: 5″ GAUGE

FIG. 14

be sloppy on the axle. Incidentally, oilite bushes should not be bored out or reamed to size as this tends to close the "pores" and destroy their property for providing continuous lubrication. The normal oil hole can be drilled into such an axlebox, but not right through the oilite bush. Oilite bushes can be obtained for inside diameters from 3/16 in to 2½ in (larger to special order) so that they could be used for any scale of model. Suitable sizes for main axleboxes would be ½ in. bore 9/16 in. long for ¾ in. scale engines, ¾ in bore x 13/16 or ⅞ in. long for 1 in. scale, and 1⅛ in bore x 1¼ in. long for 7¼ in gauge locomotives. Nevertheless, for the best results, full-size practice should be followed and a proper split axlebox specified.

MACHINING AXLEBOXES

There are several methods which can be used for machining cast axleboxes.

Trailing frames for a ¾in. scale L.N.E.R. "Pacific" by George Thomas.

Many suppliers provide them in a form of cast sticks, either four or six in the one casting, which is more economical. To the beginner, the problem with axleboxes is to get the two sides parallel and the axle bore truly central. One method is to machine the two sides to the finished width either by milling in a horizontal or vertical miller or by using the lathe and vertical-slide, and then to mark off, drill and ream the bores, measuring from the sides. This is reasonably easy if the builder is the fortunate owner of a height gauge, but even if the marking out and centre-popping is accurate, drills have a tendency to wander. The author prefers to bore axleboxes in the lathe. If the centre-popping is accurate, the axlebox can be set up in a small Vee-angle plate on the faceplate, or using the 4-jaw chuck, but the former is the more accurate.

A better way to tackle axleboxes is to face one side only to start with, then mark out the centre of the bore as accurately as possible by normal methods (odd-leg calipers, scriber and centre-punch), drill, bore and ream to finished size. Next, set up the vertical-slide facing the lathe headstock and bolt to this a small angle-plate. The partly-machined axlebox is now bolted to this using a fitted bolt which is turned previously to an exact fit in the bore. A nut and soft washer are used on top and the axlebox arranged so as to overhang the edge of the angle-plate. To ensure that the axlebox is quite square, use a true bar (such as a piece of square silver-steel) between the back of the axlebox and face of the slide. Take lights cuts only, in case the axlebox should twist round, although this can be prevented by a piece of true packing between the axlebox and the slide. The face and the flanges can now be machined and by turning the axlebox round through 180 deg. the other side can be machined truly and the bore will be equidistant from each side. The top and bottom of the axlebox can also be accurately machined by this method simply by turning the axlebox through 90 deg. rather than 180, and finally another 180 deg. turn to take the second cut.

This leaves only one side of the axlebox unmachined- that on which the nut and washer are bearing. To machine this really accurately, the well-known dodge of a mandrel turned in the lathe can be adopted. All we have to do is to chuck a suitable length of brass rod in the three-jaw, of a diameter slightly greater than the bore of the axlebox, and turn this very carefully with very light cuts until the axlebox won't quite go on, (say ½ thou over the reamer diameter). A very slight taper is now put on, using a dead smooth flat file, until the axlebox can just be got on by hand pressure alone. The final side of the axlebox can then be faced off to size without any difficulty.

There is another method of machining axleboxes that is worth mentioning. In this method, the outside surfaces of the axlebox are first machined to size, using any of the set-ups described previously, but the axle hole is not drilled, although its position is marked out as accurately as possible by the use of the usual square, odd-leg calipers and scriber. The axleboxes should be a good working fit in their respective horn-slots and both these and the axleboxes should be clearly marked with small letter or number punches. The main frames are assembled with buffer beams and stretchers as already described. Toolmakers' "buttons" are now turned up, from silver-steel. A suitable size of button would be ⅝ in. dia. x ½ in. long for a 5 in. gauge axlebox, other scales in proportion. They must all be exactly the same diameter, but slight variations in length will not matter. They are drilled about $7/32$in. diameter, all burrs removed, then the axleboxes are drilled and tapped 4 BA at the centre of the bores. The buttons are now attached to the axleboxes with cheesehead or Allen screws, the axleboxes assembled on the locomotive frames, and the buttons lined up across the engine, using the try-square, this being done by slightly slackening the screws holding the buttons and tapping lightly. The screws are then tightened down and the axleboxes removed with buttons still attached. The axleboxes are now set up on the lathe faceplate (a small Vee-block is useful here) and shifted around until the button is running dead true, checking by dial test indicator. The button is now removed, and the axlebox bored out in the usual way, using a simple plug gauge, or the axle itself, until the correct diameter is reached.

FRAME STRETCHERS

It is most important that the main frames of a locomotive are quite rigid and able to stand up to the severe stresses and strains to which they are subjected. The frame stretchers should therefore be sited with care and designed to absorb these forces. In the case of inside-cylinder locomotives, the motion plate, which carries the outer ends of the slide bars, also acts as a strong frame stiffening. Plain round stretchers are quite satisfactory for models up to 2½ in. gauge, and they have the advantage, if turned, drilled and tapped in the lathe, of ensuring that the frames are erected quite square. For larger models, at least one of the stretchers should be rather more elaborate, either a well-ribbed casting being used, or a strong built-up construction adopted.

Apart from the strength angle, correctly designed frame stretchers enormously improve the appearance of the locomotive chassis.

CHAPTER SIX

Wheels, axles, crankpins

In modern full-size locomotive wheels, two distinct parts are involved, the centre, which is usually a steel casting toughened by annealing, comprising the boss, the spokes and the rim, and the tyres, which are rolled in one piece from good quality open hearth or Bessemer steel. The tyres are turned all over and shrunk on, being additionally secured by studs or retaining rings. On some small goods and shunting engines, the wheel centre may be an iron casting. The balance weights, essential to counter-balance the weight of the crankpins and motion, may be cast in, though modern practice appears to favour the fitting of separate balance weights, which are held to the wheel by rivets and plates on the outside and inside of the spokes.

The wheels of most model steam locomotives up to about 1½ in. scale are made as one piece castings in a good quality grey iron. However, it has been found that steel tyres give better adhesion than cast iron, so some builders have fitted separate steel tyres to cast-iron wheel centres on both 1½ in. and 1 in. scale locomotives.

It is difficult, when casting small wheels, to prevent hard spots, due to "chilling" in cooling in the mould. Such hard spots will quickly spoil the ordinary type of turning tool, though carbide tools will deal with them without difficulty.

Locomotive wheels are of five types:- driving wheels, coupled wheels, bogie, trailing and tender wheels. The two former types are almost identical, the only difference being the size and weight, and arrangement, of the balance weights, although some full-size locomotive driving wheels had thinner flanges. Bogie, trailing and tender wheels are generally of similar type, dif-

A 5in. gauge L.N.E.R. A4 "Pacific" by Alfred Nash.

A superb L.B.S.C.R. "Terrier" by Ron Fenwick. Note spokes painted over balance weights.

fering only in diameter and/or number of spokes.

Driving and coupled wheels generally have number of spokes as follows: shunting engines 8 to 14, goods engines 12 to 14, mixed traffic engines 14 to 18, express engines 20 to 24. Bogie wheels generally have 10 spokes, though one or two designs had only 9, while the older locomotives often had bogie wheels with 12 spokes. Trailing and tender wheels generally had 10 to 12 spokes.

Some modern locomotives had carrying wheels of the disc type; for instance the ex-L.N.E.R. A.4 "Pacifics" had disc tender wheels. Early locomotives sometimes had "Mansell" type bogie and tender wheels, that is wheels having hardwood centres bolted to steel bosses and rims.

Some recent locomotives were fitted with the so-called "Boxpok" driving and coupled wheels. These wheels had box section spokes and rim with lightening holes arranged around the periphery of the wheel, the holes being partly round and partly "egg-shaped". The Boxpok wheel is stronger than the conventional spoked wheel, giving better support to the tyre. On the well-known ex-Southern Railway "Pacifics", a somewhat similar type of driving and coupled wheel was evolved by Mr. Bulleid in conjunction with Firth Brown of Sheffield; these were known as the B.F.B. type.

PATTERNS FOR WHEELS

Patterns for wheels are generally made in Yellow Pine or Honduras Mahogany, or wood of similar quality. The rim and tyre and the front and back of the boss are left a good deal thicker than the finished dimensions required, other parts being made finished size plus the usual shrinkage allowance. In the case of driving and coupled wheels, it is a good plan to first obtain a set of castings in brass, clean these up, add the desired balance weights, and then obtain the final casting in grey iron. In this case, double shrinkage allowance must be made.

The question of whether the treads of model locomotive wheels should be coned is a debatable one. This is certainly done in full-size practice, but then the full-size rail is canted inwards at a similar angle. However, even if coning

FIG. 16

A $\frac{3}{4}$" SCALE DRIVING WHEEL

showing spoke sections.

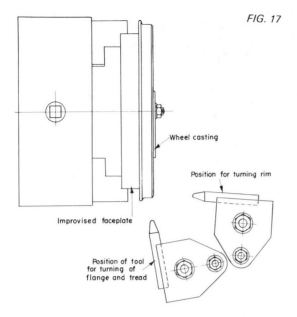

FIG. 17

Wheel casting

Position for turning rim

Improvised faceplate

Position of tool
for turning of
flange and tread

does not assist to ease an engine around curves, as is sometimes asserted, the author's opinion is that it does help to centralise the wheels upon the rails and may reduce friction slightly when the train is in motion; on the other hand, unless the rails are well worn to the same angle as the wheels, the locomotive may be more inclined to slip than if it were fitted with wheels with parallel treads.

Although the spokes of most full-size locomotive wheels are oval or elliptical in section, in the smaller sizes of model wheels, the spokes are usually made flat on the back and evenly tapered towards the front of the wheel, as this section make for easier moulding with small wheels.

TURNING WHEELS

Before attempting to turn cast iron locomotive wheels, the builder would be well advised to acquire a suitable carbide turning tool. The most useful shape for wheel turning is the very common type, with a uniform taper, coming to a point but with a tip radius of about 3/32 in. (or 1/8 in for wheels of 1½ in. scale.)

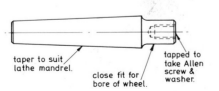

taper to suit
lathe mandrel.

close fit for
bore of wheel.

tapped to
take Allen
screw &
washer.

FIG. 18   LOCATING SPIGOT FOR WHEEL TURNING

Such a tool can now be obtained with a 3/8 in. square shank at most good tool-shops. It should have no top rake, or at least only a very slight one, and the usual front clearance which will probably be less than that usually provided on a high speed tool, as carbide tools tend to be rather brittle.

It is often stated that carbide lathe tools are unsuitable for amateur use on light lathes, as the spindle and slides are not rigid enough to enable them to cut properly. This may be true when talking about general turning, but it is not the case with cast iron wheel turning. High-speed tools are fine until a hard spot is reached (and unfortunately many wheel castings supplied today do have the occasional hard spot) which will in most cases blunt the tool tip and necessitate a visit to the grinding wheel. Sometimes the hard spot can be got rid of by pulling the lathe belt by hand after re-sharpening the tool, but a carbide tool will sail through it with no trouble and the only sign left on the wheel will be a small bright area.

Apart from its ability to cut through hard spots in castings, the carbide tool will last very much longer between re-grinds and the work can be turned at a much higher speed than with high-speed tools. It is true that a special "green-grit" grinding wheel is needed to sharpen carbides, but these are not dear, and once the carbide tip is right for the job in hand, all the wheels for even a large and complex locomotive can be turned without touching the tool again.

Before starting to turn wheel castings, it is always worth while to remove some of the sand and scale, and maybe some of the spokes will need attention in the way of filing. Another point worth looking into is whether it is worth while painting the wheels before starting turning. The author always paints his wheel castings before turning, this being done by dipping them bodily in the paint – a circular tin is ideal for holding the paint. The tin should be filled with the paint to a depth slightly greater than the thickness of the wheel casting and the casting lowered into it by a piece of wire around the spokes. It is then lifted out again almost immediately, given a shake to remove excess paint and then laid on something flat to dry. There is no need to remove the paint from the boss or rim as the lathe tool will see to this.

Facing a Springbok *driving wheel. Note minimum overhang of turning tool.*

Finishing the rim of a driving wheel.

The usual first lathe operation on wheels is to set up the casting in the 3-jaw chuck (or the 4-jaw if the 3-jaw is not large enough) back outwards, to machine the back and bore for the axle, but some castings are not quite true and this method may lead to a wheel centre which is eccentric in relation to the tread. So a better way is to chuck face outwards first and take a light cut across the tread, sufficient to get down to clean metal all around. Then reverse and chuck by the tread. Mount the lathe tool crosswise with as little overhang as possible. The saddle should be clamped to the bed, the tool being advanced by the cross-slide. The spindle speed will of course depend on the diameter of the wheel.

Using carbides, the slowest direct drive can be used, but with high-speed lathe tools, the middle back-gear speed will suit most wheel sizes, the lowest speed only being needed for very large driving or coupled wheels.

Start by taking a good cut right across the back of the wheel, to get under the hard outer skin of the casting, then shift the tool round and take a cut across the flange, going as far as possible without catching the chuck jaws. At this stage, we must decide how much metal has to be removed from the back to allow a reasonable amount to be taken off the front. It too little is taken off the back, the spokes will end up too close to the face of the wheel.

Having finish-machined the back, change over to the highest spindle speed and using a fairly large centre-drill in the tailstock, centre deeply and drill right through the wheel, starting with a drill about $3/16$in. diameter and finishing at $1/64$ in. below final size. A small boring tool should now be used to open out the bore to about 5 thou under final size, after which a reamer can be used. For the reaming operation, run the lathe at the slowest speed and move the tailstock bodily along the lathe bed, the reamer being held in a tailstock drill chuck if a small one, otherwise it should be held hard against the tailstock centre and prevented from rotating by a carrier. Slide the reamer steadily in and out, then a nice uniform bore will be produced and all wheels will finish the same to quite close limits.

The next operation on the wheels is to hold them in the chuck by the partly turned flanges – which will be square at this stage – and face the boss to final thickness. For this, the outside jaws are used and the wheel is pressed hard up against the chuck while the jaws are tightened. There are several ways of gauging the thickness of the wheels at this stage, that is over the boss. Take the wheel out of the chuck just before reaching the final cut and measure the thickness over the boss with a micrometer or vernier caliper. If the wheel is too large to permit this, turn up a short length of steel to the required dimension and lay this and the wheel on a surface plate or the lathe bed and compare the two for thickness, with D.T.I. if available, or by using surface gauge and feelers.

Now calculate how much has to come off the boss, put the wheel back in the chuck and advance the top-slide the required amount with the saddle locked to the bed. Take this reading, then all the

Right, boring a driving wheel, using self-act. Far right, machining a tender wheel clamped to the faceplate.

wheels can be dealt with, with no further measuring.

We now have to turn the tread and flange. My favourite way is to use the faceplate and a special arbor which is made beforehand. This arbor consists of a Morse taper shank to fit the lathe in use, plus a short parallel part of the same diameter as the bore of the wheels to be dealt with, and a short threaded portion beyond this, fitted with a washer and nut, so that the wheels can be mounted on this and screwed up until they are backing hard up against the faceplate. The nut should not be over-tightened as this will result in the Morse taper shank being pulled out of the lathe spindle (a drawbar can be fitted to prevent this

Machining a ³/₄in. scale driving wheel on the faceplate.

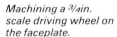

happening if desired, though it should not be necessary). Rely on a small stud in the faceplate, between the spokes of the wheel, to give a positive drive.

The lathe tool is now mounted close to the left-hand side of the top-slide and inclined slightly towards the chuck. The flanges are now finished to size and the treads turned.

On small lathes, it is possible that there will be some chatter as the tool comes up against the side of the flange. If this trouble is encountered, the lathe should be stopped and the belt pulled by hand for the last few revolutions. The thickness of the flange can be determined by the top-slide handwheel reading, and as for the tread diameter, this can be measured by vernier caliper, height gauge or what-have-you, and this can be held for the whole batch of wheels by taking a reading on the cross-slide handwheel. The rim of the wheel is turned in exactly the same way, the tool being slewed round for this.

FINISHING OPERATIONS

To finish the wheels we need to chamfer the front edge of the rims, to mark the "separation" between the rim and the centre (full-size locomotive wheels having normally separate centres and tyres) and to round off or shape the flange.

The chamfering operation is sometimes done with a flat file, but this is not

FIG. 19

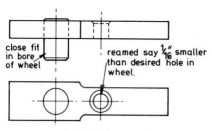

CRANKPIN DRILLING JIG
silver steel or M.S. case hardened

recommended and a better way is to use a lathe tool, with a square cutting edge, put in at 45 deg. to a definite reading, then all the wheels will be exactly the same in this respect. The "separation" operation is done with a knife tool and only involves removing a few thou. The rounding of the flanges is also sometimes done with a file, but again a much better way is to make up a simple form tool. Ordinary silver-steel appropriately hardened and tempered will last long enough to do a set of wheels if the very lowest spindle speed is used. If a file IS used, it is most important to see that it is fitted with a handle, as it is very easy to catch the chuck jaws by mistake, which could be rather nasty!

When turning small diameter driving wheels with long throw bosses, beginners often have trouble facing the balance weight. The difficulty is that before the tool has completely passed across the balance weight, it strikes the tip of the crank, and as this is proud of the balance weight on most types of wheel, machining has to stop. The way to get over this is to stop the lathe and work it by hand, moving the wheel around by pulling on the belt just far enough to prevent the tool hitting the crank. The lathe tool is advanced a few thou at each "pull", and with practice, a reasonable finish can be achieved.

It should not be necessary to use emery cloth or anything of that kind on locomotive wheels; a polish finish would be quite wrong. The finish left by

FIG. 20

toolmakers clamp
drill
packing

table of
drilling machine

CRANKPIN DRILLING JIG IN USE

the turning tool should be adequate. Full-size locomotive wheels are comparatively rough if examined closely!

To revert to the question of coning, full-size railway wheels are coned on the tread, the standard (British) angle used being 1 in 20, with the rail canted inwards to match. The main purpose of this is to minimise "hunting" – that is the rapid side-to-side movement or vibration of the wheels and axle as far as the "play-in-gauge" allows, but its effectiveness is debatable.

The Society of Model & Experimental Engineers/Model Engineer recommendations include the coning of wheel treads, as the table on page 11 shows.

DRILLING FOR CRANKPINS

Care must be taken in drilling driving and coupled wheels for their crankpins, to ensure truth and correct throw. A simple jig should always be made, which can be clamped to the wheel, the drilling bush being hardened if a number of wheels are being dealt with. If the jig is designed so that it can be bolted to the wheel, either the drilling machine or the lathe can be used for the drilling operation, a reamer being used for finishing.

On large scale locomotive wheels (1½ in. scale and upwards) boring should be adopted rather than drilling.

AXLES

Axles for model locomotives are generally made from bright steel (not lead-alloy steels) and where possible, the precision-ground variety should be used. Nothing is gained by using silver-steel.

Small axles can be turned holding them in a collet, or even a self-centring chuck if reasonably true. Larger axles are turned between centres, but in either case, centres are always left in the ends of axles. Hollow axles are often employed, with cross-drilled holes to allow for lubrication to the axleboxes.

The "wheel-seats" of axles may be turned to a press fit for the wheels, in which case they should be made 0.0005 in. larger than the bore of the wheel for each ½ in. of axle diameter (for instance, for ¾ in. dia. axle, the wheel-seat should be 0.00075 in. larger).

Another method of fixing wheels on their axles is by the use of an adhesive such as "Loctite". For this method, the

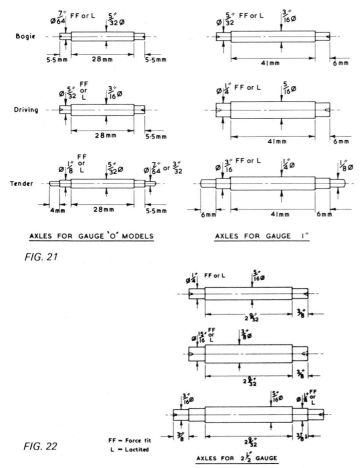

AXLES FOR GAUGE 'O' MODELS   AXLES FOR GAUGE 1"

FIG. 21

FIG. 22

FF = Force fit
L = Loctited

AXLES FOR 2½ GAUGE

put on and twisted round a few times to ensure that the adhesive is evenly spread. The wheel and axle is then left standing upright for at least 6 hours, before the second wheel is applied, this of course only after axleboxes, eccentrics, etc, etc, have been put on the axle. Great care should be taken to prevent the adhesive seeping out and adhering to the axleboxes etc. The use of Loctite for fixing wheels makes the operation of "quartering" easier – more of this later.

Axle wheel-seats should be turned very slightly longer than the thickness of the wheel boss, so that when the wheel is right home, the axle protrudes on the outside by this small amount – it should not be more than 0.005 in. for a one-inch scale locomotive.

CRANKPINS

Crankpins can be turned from silver-steel or mild steel case-hardened. Where the crankpin has a threaded end, a nut should be put on before heating for case-hardening, while the case-hardening compound should be kept well away from the part of the crankpin that is to enter the wheel – a length of steel tube will do this nicely, while at the same time providing a useful "handle" to hold the crankpin by in the flame.

Opinions differ as to whether crankpins should be press-fitted into their wheels, or fitted by adhesive such as Loctite. The author prefers a press fit here, but if Loctite is used, the "high-strength" variety should be chosen. Special attention is needed when fitting crankpins which carry return cranks for Walschaerts and similar valve gears. With these gears it is most important that the crankpin be unable to turn, so that length of the crankpin should be such that it comes out flush with the back of the wheel, and a small silver-steel pin is pressed in at the back, half in the pin and half in the wheel.

As regards the design of the crankpins themselves, on models larger than ½ in scale some positive means should be adopted to ensure that the nuts or retaining collars do not come off in service. For this purpose either a split pin or a taper pin may be used. In full-size practice, a taper pin with an additional nut is generally adopted, the retaining collar having two flats machined on it.

On outside-cylinder locomotives, there is often very little clearance

wheel-seat is turned to at least 0.001 in. smaller than the bore of the wheel (or 1 thou smaller per ½ in. of bore). It is most important to ensure that the parts are clean before applying the adhesive. Having smeared the wheel-seat of the axle with the Loctite, the wheel should be

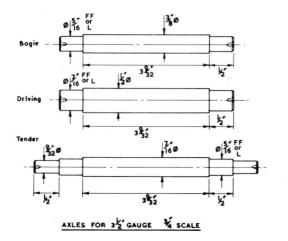

Bogie

Driving

Tender

FIG. 23   AXLES FOR 3½" GAUGE ¾" SCALE

FIG. 24

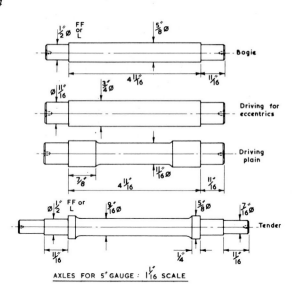

AXLES FOR 5" GAUGE : 1 1/16" SCALE

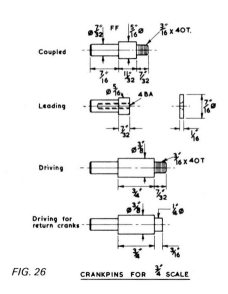

FIG. 26   CRANKPINS FOR 3/4" SCALE

between the leading crankpin and the crosshead or slide bars, so that a special short crankpin is required. The solution here is to use a thin retaining washer, which in the larger scales is usually turned down partly to enter the body of the crankpin, an Allen type countersunk screw being used to hold it firmly in place.

QUARTERING

The usual practice for a two-cylinder locomotive is that the right-hand crank leads and that the right and left-hand cranks are set at 90 deg. to one another.

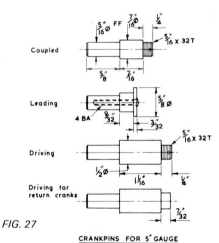

FIG. 27   CRANKPINS FOR 5" GAUGE

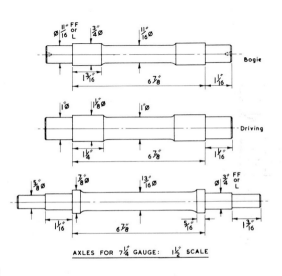

AXLES FOR 7 1/4" GAUGE: 1 1/2" SCALE

FIG. 25

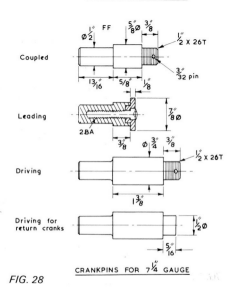

FIG. 28   CRANKPINS FOR 7 1/4" GAUGE

Another view of A. G. Peacock's G.N.R. "Single".

The important thing to remember about "quartering" is that it does not matter a great deal if the wheels are set at, say, 89 deg. or 91 deg. rather than the exact 90 deg., so long as they are all exactly the same. For this reason, the author favours making a simple jig for the operation of "quartering". Even though this takes a little time, the jig can be used again and again and is probably the most accurate of the various methods used, that is of course if the jig itself is carefully made!

A quartering jig for 5 in. gauge locomotives might consist essentially of two plates of bright mild steel 4 in. wide x ³/₈ in. thick. These plates are drilled together in the four corners to take cross stretchers turned from ½ in. dia. silver-steel. The stretchers are turned down a close fit in the holes, which are reamed, and they are tapped at the ends to take Allen socket-head screws and washers, so that the two plates can be bolted up truly and at the required spacing. In the

Some of the wheels for Springbok *(driver, coupled, bogie and tender) ready for their axles.*

centre of the plates, there is another reamed hole into which silver-steel "centres" can be pushed, to register into the centres in the ends of the axles. Additional holes are drilled and reamed to the exact diameter of the crankpins at 0 deg., 90 deg., 180 deg. and 270 deg., the extra pair of holes being very useful to accommodate locomotives having different crank throws. These holes are set out as accurately as possible to the above angles by normal methods (square and scriber etc.) which is sufficiently accurate for the purpose.

If using Loctite adhesive for fixing the wheels on their axles, one driving or coupled wheel is first put on its axle and allowed to set (24 hours may be allowed for this, to be on the safe side) the side plates of the jig are then separated, the second wheel put on the axle (after the axleboxes and any eccentrics of course) the Loctite being applied to this, turned to the desired angle and the pair mounted in the jig, the plates being bolted up with the crankpins passing through the holes in the plates and the two centres being pushed right home, through the centre holes in the plates and into the axle centres.

The pair of wheels on axle is now left to set, still in the jig, for 24 hours, after which the next pair is dealt with in a similar manner.

It will be appreciated that this set-up does not determine whether the cranks are actually at 90 deg. – this depending on the accuracy with which the jig is made – but it does ensure that all pairs of wheels are set at exactly the same angle, to quite close limits.

If using the press-fit method for securing the wheels on their axles, the second wheel should, at first, be pushed on only as far as it will go by hand pressure alone, after which the pair of wheels is inserted in the jig and the second wheel driven on about half-way. The pair can then be put in the bench vice or arbor press to be pressed right home.

Another method of quartering, where the wheels are small enough, is to use the lathe, placing the pair of wheels on axle between lathe centres. The crankpin in the right-hand wheel is rested in a horizontal position against a turned piece of steel of suitable length stood on the lathe bed. Meanwhile the crankpin in the left-hand wheel will be in the upright position and its exact position relative to the crankpin in the other wheel can be determined by a dial-test-indicator, with an extended probe, bearing against the crankpin. After taking a reading, the first pair of wheels is carefully removed without disturbing the D.T.I., and the next pair put in its place, the "loose" wheel being turned until the same D.T.I. reading is obtained.

Quartering of the wheels of three-cylinder engines can be dealt with in the jig described above. Instead of drilling and reaming the holes for the crankpins in the two plates at 90 deg. to one another, they are drilled at 120 deg. to one another. The best way to arrange these holes would be to have the outside crankpins in the lower half of the plates and the inner (the crank-axle) standing up vertically. The position for the inner crankpin can then be set by means of a long bar of steel of width equal to the width of the crank webs. This can be lined up if a central slot is cut in its lower end of width equal to the diameter of the crankpin and length sufficient to reach past the driving axle centre. It is then quite a simple matter to check whether this bar is vertical by measuring from its top corners to some suitable fixed points on the "base", the "base" in this case being a surface plate or sheet of plate glass.

For some Gresley locomotives, the two outside crankpins will be at 120 deg. to one another, but the inside crankpin will be at 126 deg. to the left-hand crankpin and at 114 deg. to the right-hand, due to the centre cylinder being inclined at a steeper angle than the outside cylinders.

There is one further point in connection with the quartering jig. It may be that the driving crankpins on the locomotive being dealt with are larger in diameter than the leading or trailing crankpins. In this case, the holes for the crankpins in the two plates must be drilled and reamed to fit the driving crankpins", which are dealt with first. Bushes are then turned up a good fit in the holes but bored an exact fit for the smaller crankpins. These bushes are then inserted and the other pairs of wheels dealt with.

A fine Welshpool and Llanfair 0-6-0T by the late J. H. Balleny, in 3¹/₂in. gauge.

CHAPTER SEVEN

Crank-axles

Beginners in model locomotive building are often advised to avoid engines with inside cylinders, owing to possible difficulties in making the crank-axle. But so many of the most attractive British locomotives of the late 19th and early 20th century had inside cylinders that it seems rather a pity to pass them over.

Most of the troubles encountered in making crank-axles, especially those of the two-throw type, seem to arise from trying to braze the joints, as it is very difficult to avoid distortion where brazing is used. With the introduction of adhesives such as Loctite, there is no reason why a beginner should not tackle a two-throw crank with every confidence.

There are at least six (possibly more) methods of making crank-axles-

1 Turn the whole crank from the solid, in free-cutting mild steel, complete with eccentrics (if any).

2 Turn the crank axle itself from the solid but fit separate split eccentrics.

3 Adapt a built-up construction, but braze the joints and eccentrics.

4 As no. 3, but with separate split eccentrics.

5 Built-up crank-axle, using press-fits, afterwards fitting pins, the eccentrics being turned separately and secured by grub screws.

6 Built-up crank-axle using Loctite instead of press fits, the eccentrics being secured by grub screws.

Shrinking has been suggested – a process of heating the webs and cooling the axle and crankpins; the author's experiments in this direction have shown that it is extremely difficult to do on a small scale, owing to the rapid cooling of the heated parts. The method may well be successful in the larger scales (2 in. scale and upwards).

To deal with the six principal methods, No. 1 should only be considered by a highly-skilled turner, prepared to make a lot of swarf! There is also the point that no adjustment is possible for the eccentrics, calling for very accurate marking out.

No. 2 is little better, as split eccentrics are not too easy to make.

Nos. 3 and 4 have the disadvantage mentioned previously – that distortion is probable.

No. 5 is a sound method, but again calls for careful turning; it is very easy to end up with a slight wobble.

One method, if press fits are adopted, is to use a normal driving axle to start with, but to turn the axle between centres, making the part of the axle between the webs (on which the eccentrics would be mounted for Stephenson and similar valve gears) very slightly larger in diameter than the normal driving axle.

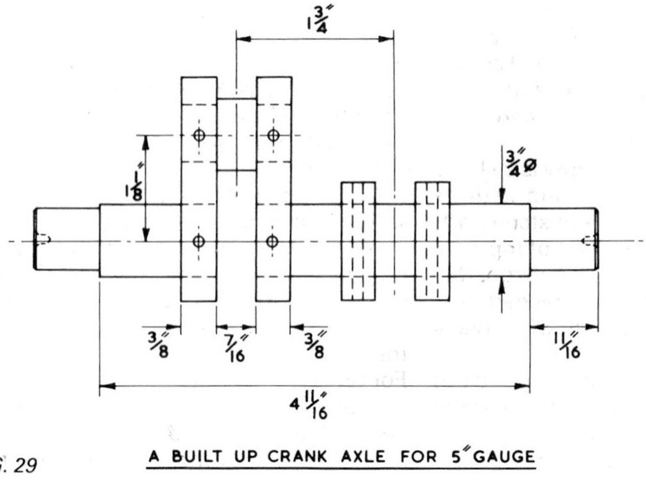

FIG. 29   A BUILT UP CRANK AXLE FOR 5" GAUGE

A two-throw crank-axle with eccentrics, made by the author.

Then the part of the axle on which the inner pair of webs is to be mounted is made, say, 2 thou larger in diameter than the normal axle, and the part of the axle on which the outer pair of webs is to be mounted is made 1 thou larger in diameter than the normal axle.

To make the webs, the four pieces of flat steel bar are first sweated together, marked out, drilled and bored for the crankpins using the lathe faceplate and a small vee-block. After the webs are bored a suitable press fit for the crankpins, the vee-block is shifted on the faceplate and the second hole bored, the two outer ones being bored to suit the outer part of the axle, and the two inner ones to suit the inner part of the axle.

The four webs are now melted apart and all traces of the solder cleaned off, the sharp edges around the holes are removed by a scraper, and if the ends are to be radiused, this can be done at this stage.

Next, the eccentrics, required for such valve gears as Stephenson Gooch or Allan, are taken in hand. They can be made from mild steel or cast-iron. A simple plug gauge is turned up, of diameter equal to the middle part of the axle less ½ thou (0.0005 in.). If the 4-jaw chuck available is in good condition, this can be used for boring. Sufficient bar to make all four eccentrics is chucked, allowing enough for parting off and cleaning up. One end is centred and supported by the tailstock.

The lathe tool required now is a sharp parting tool with its face ground off dead square and its sharp corners stoned off. It should have a fair amount of top rake for mild steel but none for cast-iron. Not much front clearance is needed. On steel, plenty of cutting oil will give a good finish.

The eccentric blank is now shifted out to the required throw – the original centre can be used to measure from, or a dial-test indicator can be pressed into

service. Centre deeply, drill and bore out until the plug gauge can be pushed in without effort. Part off the eccentrics carefully, leaving a little for facing the sides truly – which can now be done individually by either mounting them on a mandrel or by using an improvised parallel mandrel and a grub screw in the eccentric.

The crankpins are made next. These should be a straightforward turning job, but the ends which are to enter the webs should be a bare 1 thou larger (0.001 in.) in diameter than their respective holes. To press the webs on to their crankpins truly without distortion, a special washer or collar will be needed. This should be turned to the exact thickness of the working part of the crankpin, and its bore should be such that it can be put over it. It is then sawn in half so that the two halves can be removed after the webs are right home.

To keep the webs in line during the pressing operation, slip a length of close-fitting round bar through the axle holes in the webs. At this stage the webs can be pinned to the crankpins.

The eccentrics should be a good fit on the centre of the crank-axle, any slackness here is fatal. It should just be possible to twist them on by hand. Beginners sometimes have difficulty in getting this fit. The best way to do it is to take the axle down very slightly by means of a dead smooth (Swiss) flat file. It should not be necessary to remove more than one or two "tenths".

Final assembly is quite straightforward. The eccentrics are put on first, then the first pair of webs is pressed on, not forgetting to insert the special spacing washer mentioned previously, otherwise the webs would be immediately forced together and spoilt. For the pressing operation, we will want a length of round steel bored slightly larger than the axle diameter, and with both ends faced off dead true. Next, the

second pair of webs is started on the axle, set at 90 deg. to the first pair, using surface plate and square, the webs that are arranged horizontally being supported on a suitable bar of steel. The right-hand crank normally leads.

After the second pair of webs have been pressed right home and pinned, the unwanted parts of the axle are sawn away, and to prevent the saw damaging the insides of the webs or the crankpins while sawing, a piece of thin brass sheet should be held between saw blade and web. A flat smooth file can be used to finish.

LOCTITE METHOD

The sixth possible method for making a crank-axle is to use a built-up construction but with Loctite in place of press fits. Loctite high-strength No. 601 (formerly No. 35) should be used. Construction is similar to the previous method, but the holes in the webs are made a bare 1 thou larger than the diameter of the axle or crankpins, as the case may be. (For 1½ in. scale axles, the holes should be about 1¼ thou larger or for small gauges such as "0" and "1", ½ thou should be sufficient.

Assembly is carried out exactly as described for the previous method, but the parts to be treated with Loctite must be scrupulously clean; any trace of oil or grease will prevent the adhesive "taking".

If Loctite is used for the crank-axle, it should also be used for securing the driving wheels on this axle, and therefore the quartering jig previously described is ideal for assembly, the complete assembly of crank-axle and wheels being left in this jig for 24 hours, though the wheels should not be put on before any pinning of the crank is carried out.

Beginners often have trouble getting the pins right home without bending them; one often sees a crank with pins that don't go quite right through the axle! To avoid this trouble, the drill to be used could be tried out beforehand on a scrap of steel similar to that used for the crank. For instance, a No. 31 drill could be tried for a ⅛ in. dia. pin. Unless the drill is cutting considerably oversize, it will be impossible to get the pin right through; it may in fact bulge in the middle! The answer therefore is to thin the pin down slightly and also to put on a very slight taper, this being done with a smooth flat file. To prevent the pin bending while being pressed in, a series of collars can be used. For a ⅛ in. dia. pin, these would be bored No. 30 and lengths in ⅛ in. steps, the longest being about ⅛ in. shorter than the overall length of the pin, and the shortest just ⅛ in. long. The longest collar is slipped on first and the pin pressed in as far as the collar allows. The next collar is then put on, and the pin pressed in a further ⅛ in., and so on, until the pin is right home.

An alternative to a conventional parallel or taper pin is the "roll pin", a hollow spring pin which is very easy to fit.

CHAPTER EIGHT

Bogies, pony trucks, radial trucks

Locomotive bogies are normally of the four-wheel type, and they are attached to the engine in such a way as to support some of the weight of the front of the locomotive and also to help to guide it on the track, especially as the locomotive enters a curve or a turnout. Its central pivot is therefore given side play and the bogie must also have a considerable self-centring action if it is going to fulfil its proper functions.

The main types of locomotive bogie in general use are the Adams type with plate frames, the Adams type with bar frames, the Swing-link type with plate frames and the Swing-link variety with bar frames.

The most commonly used bogie in this country was the first mentioned, the frames usually being held at the desired distance apart by a large central casting and two or more turned frame stays. A centre casting is then arranged in the middle of this, free to slide to either side

under the control of coil or laminated springs. The horns are generally riveted to the outside of the frames, though in some modern designs, these were placed on the inside, so that the frames were further apart. An equalising bar is arranged to span the axleboxes on each side of the bogie, a laminated spring inside this being held to the frames at its centre, its ends linked to the equaliser.

A variation of the Adams type of bogie was adopted by the late Great Western Railway, in which the weight of the front of the locomotive was transmitted by hemi-spherical "pads" on the plates extended outwards from the bogie frames. This design actually originated in France.

The Swing-link bogie differs from the Adams type in that the controlling gear is vertical instead of horizontal. The weight of the engine carried on the bogie is applied by means of a set of links connecting the bogie centre cast-

A ³/₄in. scale locomotive bogie by the author.

FIG. 30

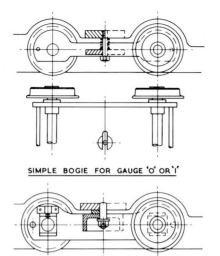

SIMPLE BOGIE FOR GAUGE 'O' OR '1'

FIG. 31

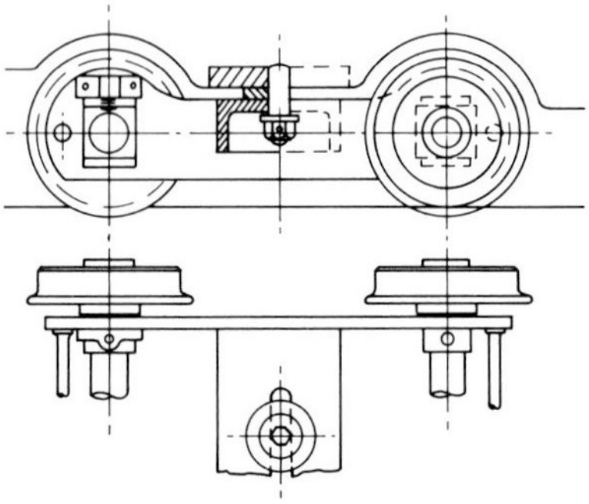

2½" GAUGE BOGIE

FIG. 32

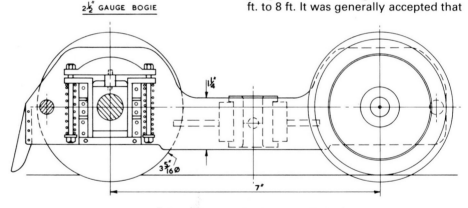

5" GAUGE BOGIE WITH INDIVIDUAL SPRINGING

saddle plate is dished and its curvature is followed by an equivalent concave curvature on the bogie centre casting. On curves, the outer rail tends to lift the engine and this increases the pressure on the outer wheels, and due to the inclination of the links the bogie slides bodily to suit the radius of the track.

The Swing-link bogie was used extensively on the old Great Northern Railway and on the L.N.E.R. Today, it is not thought as reliable as a guiding medium as the Adams type bogie.

A special type of bogie was adopted for the G.W.R. "King" class locomotives. As the inside cylinders were arranged above and behind the leading bogie wheels, the leading bogie axleboxes, horns and springs were placed outside the frames, which were of the plate type and were bent outwards from just forward of the rear bogie wheels, so as to lie outside the front wheels.

The wheelbase of full-size standard gauge locomotive bogies varied from 6 ft. to 8 ft. It was generally accepted that

FIG. 33

THE SWING-LINK BOGIE

ing to the bogie frames. The links are arranged at an inclination to the vertical on each side of the bogie. A central pivot pin is used, but the lower surface of the

the longer the wheelbase the better, within reason, though space and weight limitations often kept this down to 6ft. 6in. The permitted side play varied from 2 to 5in. each way, average for British express locomotives being about 4in.

In some cases, the bogie centre pivot was not located exactly in the centre of the wheelbase of the bogie, but was set up to 6 in. nearer the rear axle. By this means, the possible lateral movement of the leading axle was increased, and some of the weight on the leading axle transferred to the trailing axle. Some locomotive engineers claimed that this offset improved the riding of the engine, but this was not definitely established.

In models of Gauge 1 and below, side-control springing is not often fitted, but

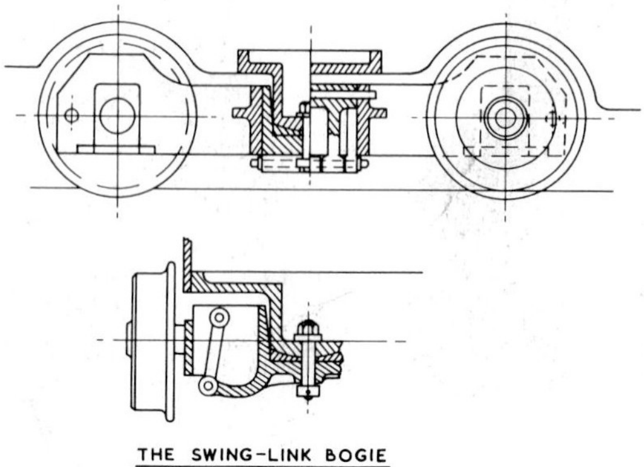

FIG. 34

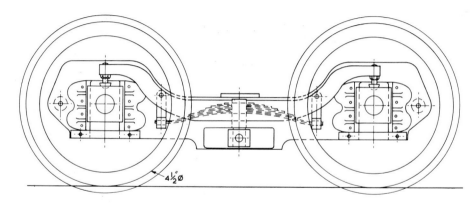

MIDLAND RAILWAY BOGIE: 5″ gauge

FIG. 35

PLAN VIEW OF EQUALISER AND SPRING BUCKLE OF
THE MIDLAND BOGIE

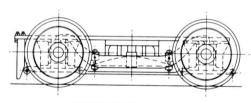

G.W.R. TYPE BAR FRAME BOGIE

on larger models, it is well worth while as it makes for a steadier locomotive at speed. In its simplest form, the Gauge 0 and 1 bogie consists of two frame plates, of similar thickness to the main frames of the locomotive, held at the desired distance apart by a rigid central stretcher having a transverse slot for the pivot pin, and two round stretchers, one at each end of the bogie. A further stretcher is arranged across the main frames of the engine, carrying the pivot pin, and a coil spring and washer are fitted between the two stretchers.

A better method is to dispense with the spring on the pivot pin and use separate axleboxes sliding directly in the frames, with a small coil (compression)

Views from above and below of a bogie for the 5in. gauge Claud Hamilton *by Len Labram.*

61

Top and underside views of a ³/₄in. scale "Britannia" bogie with side-control springs.

spring above each axlebox. In the smaller gauges, the gap in the frames for the axleboxes need not be cut right through, thus doing away for the need of separate keeps.

Bogies for 2½ in. gauge and larger gauges should have proper horns riveted to the frames. Springing should be individual, with one coil spring above each axlebox, or by equalisers, the equalising beams being slung on tension springs or arranged to bear against compression springs.

Bogies for 5 in. gauge models of the Adams type can have equalisers with laminated springs built up from Tufnol strips with two or three spring steel leaves, these being the longest leaves. In most cases, these can be ³/₈ in. wide and about ¹/₃₂ in. thick, and the total number of leaves may be anything between 8 and 14, according to the weight of the locomotive.

The easiest way to arrange for side-control springing is to use a deep bogie centre casting with a double-flanged sliding member, bored for the pivot pin and arranged to slide transversely against coil springs on each side of it. If the centre casting is bored right through, the springs can be allowed to bear directly against the insides of the frames.

In most cases, plate frame bogies will have bright mild steel frames of the same thickness as used for the main frames of the locomotive. Gunmetal castings are generally used for the bogie axleboxes, while the main frame or pivot stretcher casting and the bogie centre casting can be in either gunmetal or cast-iron.

An interesting point that may be observed in the design of most fullsize bogie axleboxes is that these do not entirely surround the axle, but bear only on the upper half of the axle, and in some cases on rather less than half, there being a distinct clearance on each side of the axle.

In model locomotive design, there is sometimes a tendency to limit the weight carried by the bogie, in order to increase the adhesive weight. This should not however be carried too far, since a bogie that is too lightly loaded may prove dangerous in service owing to the possibility of it jumping the track at speed.

PONY TRUCKS

A pony truck consists of a truck with two wheels only, pivoted at some point behind the wheels in the case of a leading truck, or in front of the wheels in the case of a trailing truck.

The wheels of a leading pony truck are generally made small enough to swing clear under the main frames on curves, avoiding the need to narrow the main frames at this point.

One of the first things to be decided in designing a pony truck is the radius of swing, or the distance between its pivot pin and the axle. Two formulae have been in general use for full-size work and these seem to work well on model locomotives. These formulae are the Von Borries rule and the J.D. Baldry rule.

FIG. 37

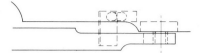

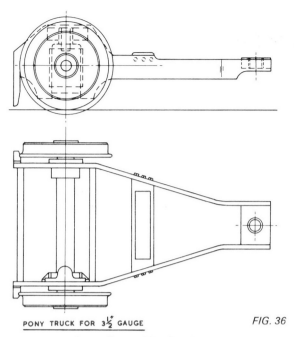

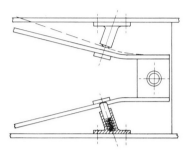

PONY TRUCK FOR 3½ GAUGE   *FIG. 36*

ARRANGEMENT OF SIDE—CONTROL SPRINGING

According to Von Borries:-

$$R = \frac{D^2 - B^2}{2D}$$

where R is the required radius, D is the total wheelbase of the locomotive and B is its rigid wheelbase.

According to Baldry:-

$$R = \frac{1}{2} \left(E - \frac{F^2}{E} \right)$$

where E is the distance from the pony truck axle to the centre of the rigid wheelbase and F is half the rigid wheelbase of the locomotive.

Leading pony truck for a G.W.R. 2-6-2T.

Baldry's rule usually gives a slightly lower figure for the radius of swing.

In full-size practice, many pony trucks were compensated with the leading coupled springs, by means of a long compensating beam pivoted near its centre on a bracket fixed to the engine frame and with its rear end attached to a transverse member fitted to the front main spring hangers on each side of the locomotive. The axleboxes were as usual arranged to work in horns riveted to short plate frames, similar to those on a plate frame bogie, the axlebox springs being generally above the axleboxes.

On Great Western locomotives, bar frames were used for pony trucks as with the bogies, and the compensating gear described above was also fitted.

The fully compensated pony truck is a complicated affair, and unless the builder delights in a great deal of intricate work, is hardly justified on a model locomotive below 1½ in. scale. Side-control, however, is worth while even on 3½in. gauge.

Pony trucks for small gauge models usually consist of quite a simple triangular framework, the axleboxes working between horns riveted to the frames, and either a single coil spring is fitted directly above the axlebox, or two coil springs on each side of the axlebox with the usual spring beam above. The drawings show how the side-control springs can be arranged. The difficulty in models is the great angle of swing that has to be

FIG. 38

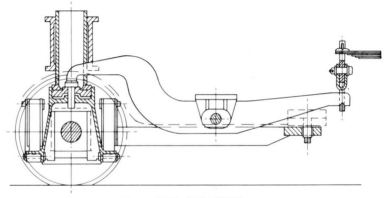

COMPENSATED PONY TRUCK

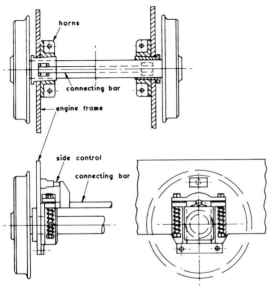

FIG. 39

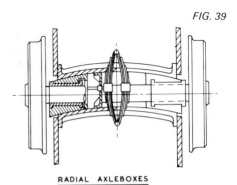

RADIAL AXLEBOXES

FIG. 40   A SIMPLIFIED ARRANGEMENT OF RADIAL AXLEBOXES

Radial axle-boxes with side control springs.

allowed for and particular care must be taken to ensure that when the pony truck has swung to the maximum angle on one side of the engine, the spring and plunger on the other side do not fall right out of their housing.

RADIAL AXLEBOXES

Radial axleboxes are sometimes used instead of pony trucks, especially where rather less flexibility is required, as for instance on 2-4-2 tank locomotives, or on the trailing wheels of 0-4-2, 0-6-2 and 2-6-2 tank engines. The axleboxes are generally mounted inside the frames, are tied together and guided by curved horns, or by horns set at an angle to the normal arrangement. A well-known example of the latter design is the trailing axlebox and horn of the Gresley "Pacifics" and "Green Arrows".

The radial axleboxes with curved guides used on some ex-L.N.W.R. and L.Y.R. locomotives are rather difficult to copy in model form. One solution is to machine the axleboxes and horns at an angle approximately tangential to the required radius, and to join the axleboxes by means of a round bar across the top on which the spring beams can bear. In this case, the axleboxes should not be made too good a fit in their horns, otherwise binding will take place.

CHAPTER NINE

Cylinders

Locomotive cylinders can be classified into five main groups:-

1 Outside cylinders with valves on top — typical of most modern locomotives.
2 Outside cylinders with valves between the frames — well-known examples of these are the G.N.R. and L.B.S.C.R. "Atlantics".
3 Inside cylinders with valves on top.
4 Inside cylinders with valves underneath.
5 Inside cylinders with valves between the bores — typical of many of the older types of locomotive.

Cylinders may then be further classified as slide-valve type, piston-valve or poppet-valve.

Advocates of the inside cylinder arrangement used to claim that the hefty cylinder casting provided an excellent frame stay, while the fact that the motion was being transmitted between the frames made the engine much steadier, there being little of that "shouldering" effect particularly noticeable on some of the long-stroke outside cylinder Great Western engines.

The disadvantages of inside cylinders may be summarised as the difficulty (?) of making a two-throw crank-axle, possibly with four eccentrics, the difficulty of getting in two large enough bores without cramping the steam chests, and the inaccessibility of the motion. (One might also add that the motion cannot be seen and admired from the outside!)

From the foregoing, it is not therefore very difficult to decide that the outside cylinder locomotive is the better bet for the beginner, and preferably one with the valves on top.

Most of the more recent designs of two-cylinder locomotives were fitted with piston valves and Walschaerts valve gear, though poppet valves were used to some extent towards the end of the steam era, particularly in France and the U.S.A.

Whether to use piston or slide valves in model locomotive cylinders has always been a bone of contention wherever model engineers congregate. The machining and fitting of piston valves, especially in the smaller sizes where rings are not normally used, calls for very accurate workmanship if success is to be achieved. Leaking piston valves have been the downfall of more than one class of full-size locomotive. It is of little use to put a piston-valve engine into mid-gear and open the regulator to see if steam emerges from the exhaust. A piston valve may well be steam-tight when at rest, but when moving there may be considerable leakage.

One argument which is sometimes put forward on behalf of slide valves is that these valves tend to "wear themselves in". But this is really only valid if the area of the steam chest on which the valve works is slightly proud of the remaining area, otherwise the valve will tend to wear a slight hollow in the middle of its travel.

The great majority of modern locomotives with outside piston-valve cylinders had outside valve gear, but the Great Western was a notable exception, as nearly all their engines had inside valve gear — the "Kings" "Castles" and "Stars" had Walschaerts, while the "Saints", "Halls", "Granges", "Manors", Counties", "Moguls", 2-8-0's and many tank locomotives had inside Stephenson gear, the motion being transmitted to the outside of the

Parts of a 3½in. gauge slide valve cylinder ready for assembly by the author.

BALANCED SLIDE VALVES

The outside cylinders with steam chests between the frames were generally arranged for use with Stephenson valve gear, with direct drive to the valve spindles, the steam chests passing through large gaps in the main frames. It is a type quite suitable for use in model locomotives, although visual valve setting is not quite so easy as with cylinders having the valves on top. The steam passageways between the ports and the bores are of necessity rather longer than in other types of cylinder, but as against this, balanced slide valves can be adopted, and these can be designed to give a very direct exhaust.

FIG. 42

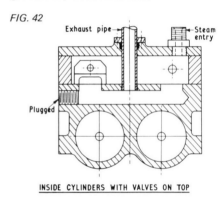

INSIDE CYLINDERS WITH VALVES ON TOP

locomotive by means of a rocking shaft.

The chief reason why the piston valve "drove out" the slide valve in full-size practice was the much lighter load placed on the valve gear, especially with long valve travels.

Experience has shown that as regards performance, there is little to choose between piston and slide valves in model locomotives up to 1½ in. scale.

If slide valves are used for modern piston-valve type cylinders, their presence can be disguised to some extent by providing large cylindrical bosses at each end of the steam chests. If outside Walschaerts or Baker valve gear is to be used, the top joints of the combination lever will have to be reversed, altering the layout of the valve gear as compared with the inside admission piston valve arrangement, unless a very complicated system of double porting is adopted in the cylinders.

STEAM PASSAGES

Another controversial matter in cylinder design is the size of the steam passages between the ports and the bores. In the smaller scales, it has been general practice to use two or three drilled holes, which in most cases had a total cross-sectional area very much less than the area of the steam ports. Where the regulator port, cross-sectional area of superheaters and steam pipes, etc, etc, are on the small side, the drilled hole passages may be quite satisfactory, but if the maximum efficiency is aimed at, rather larger passages than can be obtained from drilled holes may be preferred.

In this connection, it must be remembered that there are two sides to a steam port – the admission and the exhaust, and the exhaust steam needs a much larger cross-sectional area of passage if it is to get away to the blast pipe without too much back-pressure. For this reason the width of the exhaust port should always be made at least twice as great as the width of the steam port.

FIG. 41.
Outside cylinder for Gauge "0".

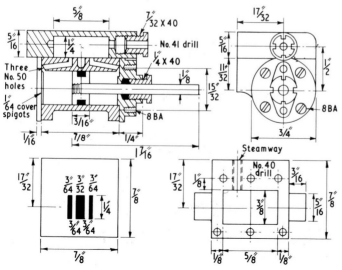

FIG. 43

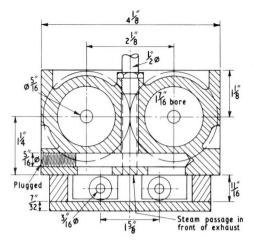

INSIDE CYLINDERS WITH VALVES UNDERNEATH FOR 5"
GAUGE MODEL

FIG. 44

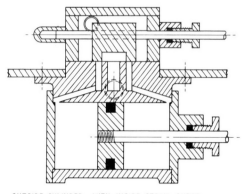

OUTSIDE CYLINDER WITH INSIDE STEAM CHEST

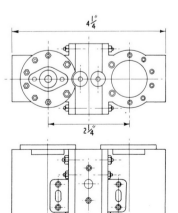

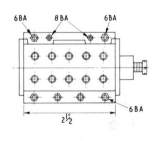

FIG. 45
Cylinders with valve
chest between the
bores, for 5in. gauge.

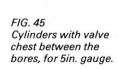

MATERIALS FOR CYLINDERS

If the model locomotive concerned is not likely to be put into steam very often, it is safe to specify the cylinders to be cast in a non-ferrous alloy. A good-quality gunmetal or phosphor-bronze is generally used.

On the other hand, if the engine is to see considerable regular service, there is nothing to beat cast-iron, not only for the cylinder block, but for the pistons, valves, covers, steam chests, etc. Cast-iron cylinders are best fitted with proper rings, which should be made from best quality centrifugally-cast iron. There must be a little spring in the ring if it is to serve its purpose and in diameters over 3/4 in., it should be possible to spring the ring over the piston into its groove without breaking it, assuming that it is of the correct dimensions. Modern practice favours rings in which the length is equal to the thickness, in other words, the ring is of a square section.

If lubrication is reliable, there is no reason why rings should not be used in gunmetal cylinders, rather than the graphited yarn packing generally used; in this case, the rings may be made from a hard phosphor-bronze, or stainless steel may be tried. Another possibility is the use of packing containing PTFE.

Slide valves for gunmetal cylinders can be made from drawn bronze bar or from stainless steel. They are sometimes made in two parts, silver-soldered together, so that the cavity can be completely finished by filing, rather than to have to end-mill the cavity from the solid metal.

Piston and valve rods are generally made from ground stainless steel and care should be taken to ensure that the material chosen is really straight – it is difficult stuff to straighten.

MACHINING CYLINDERS

In machining model locomotive cylinders, it is logical to make a start on the block or body of the cylinder. If the lathe used is large and heavy enough, the block may be clamped on an angle-plate bolted to the faceplate or on one of the special vee-angle-plates, such as the "Keats". As this set-up will probably be considerably out of balance some kind of balance weight will have to be bolted to the faceplate.

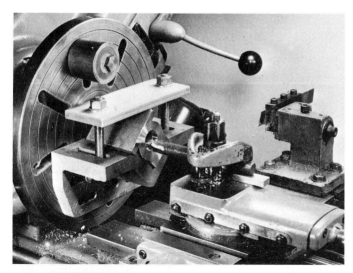

the slots close to the cylinder. This is now tried at low speed, and the speed gradually increased up to the maximum, when any vibration due to the "out of balance" will be obvious. The balance weight is next shifted further out in its slot and the lathe started again. A position will soon be found where the vibration at top speed is at a minimum. On now reducing the spindle speed to about half full speed, all vibration will disappear, when facing and boring the cylinder may proceed.

The cylinder, incidentally, should be set out far enough from the faceplate to enable the boring tool to pass right through without fouling it. As stiff a boring tool as can be accommodated should be used and when finishing cuts are approached, the tool should be removed for re-sharpening. Having reached the final size, the boring tool should be put through again without altering the setting, in case of any "spring" in the tool. The self-act, with the finest feed, is generally worth while for cylinder boring.

Opinions differ as to whether reaming cylinder bores is either necessary or desirable. Generally speaking, the amateur's lathe will not be heavy enough to cope with machine reaming over ⅝ in. diameter, and few model engineers can manage hand reamers in the larger sizes!

Quite a good finish should be obtainable from boring alone, both in gunmetal and cast-iron, but if a better finish is required, one has the choice of lapping, honing or burnishing. The latter two processes are seldom available to the amateur, but lapping may be considered, especially for cast-iron cylinders. The lap must be of a metal softer than that of the cylinders, and for cast-iron the finer grinding paste as used by garages for grinding in motor-car valves may be used.

The lap is held in the 3-jaw chuck, extending to about twice the length of the cylinder, which can be held in the (gloved) hand, so as to allow it to float. Only a few thous should be removed and great care taken to avoid "bell-mouthing". A very smooth bore that is not parallel is much worse than a truly parallel bore that is not quite smooth.

After lapping, care must be taken to remove all traces of the lapping compound used, by washing repeatedly in paraffin.

Boring a cylinder block, top with a Bond's vee angle plate, above in a four-jaw chuck and, below, with a boring bar.

Beginners sometimes have difficulty in obtaining this balance, even though only an approximate balance is required. One method is to choose a short length of round steel, perhaps 1½ in. diameter, drill this through ⅜ in. diameter and bolt to the faceplate using one of

FIG. 46

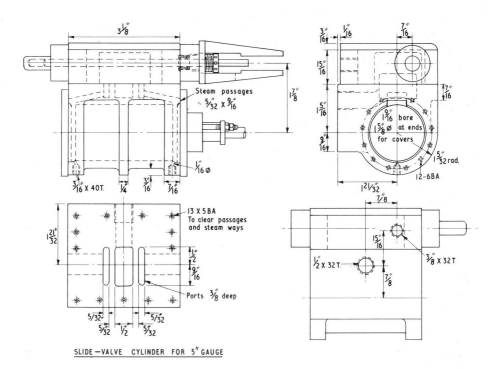

SLIDE—VALVE CYLINDER FOR 5" GAUGE

Although lapping is possible for gun-metal cylinders, the difficulty is to avoid particles of the lapping compound becoming embedded in the walls of the cylinder; the process should in this case be approached with caution, though Crown polishing composition (Tripoli) is worth trying.

When dealing with inside cylinders, if the cylinder block is being dealt with on the faceplate, it may be lined up for the second bore by shifting the angle-plate only; this also applies to boring the piston-valve cylinder for the valve liner. An outside cylinder, after boring and facing, is now removed for facing the other end. In the absence of a proper mandrel, a length of round brass or aluminium-alloy may be turned up to a tight push fit for the bore, the cylinder being pushed on to this for facing. In case the bores of the two cylinders are not exactly the same diameter, care should be taken to turn the mandrel to suit the larger bore first, after which it can be skimmed down to suit the smaller bore (something easily overlooked!)

When cylinders are too large or too heavy to be mounted on the faceplate or held in a chuck, they may be bored by bolting them down on the lathe cross-slide. The cylinder block is packed up so that the centre of the bore is exactly at lathe centre height; a boring head or a between-centres boring bar is then used, and the latter should be as large and heavy as will pass through the un-machined bore. Care must also be taken to see that the clamping bars used to hold the block down do not distort it; to avoid this trouble, these bars are usually arranged over the flanges, where the metal of the casting is considerably thicker than between them

After completing the bores and facing the ends, the port face (of a slide valve cylinder) and the bolting face of the cylinder block may be machined. A large 4-jaw chuck can be used here, but great care will have to be taken to ensure that the block is held square, and pieces of a soft metal (copper or brass) should be put between the chuck jaws and the cylinder — especially if a gunmetal one.

Another method is to bolt the cylinder block on end on an angle-plate attached to a vertical-slide, by means of a large bolt through the bore, the machining being carried out by end-mills. The same set-up can then be used to cut the ports if the cylinder is of the slide-valve type.

Although the steam and exhaust ports of a slide-valve cylinder can be cut by "gang-milling", either in the lathe or on a milling machine, this method leaves the ports in a "quarter-moon" shape, too shallow at the ends, causing difficulty when drilling the passages to the

Above, cutting the ports in a slide valve cylinder block.
Below, a steam chest, showing how the valve is driven.
Bottom, tapping the exhaust hole in a slide valve cylinder.

bores. With the end-milling set-up, either a regulation end-mill can be used, in collet or 3-jaw chuck, or a slot-drill – slot drills can be obtained as small as $1/16$ in. dia., about right for the steam ports of Gauge "0" locomotive cylinders.

Where the lathe in use has graduated dials or handwheels to the cross-slide and vertical-slide, the width and length of the ports can be quickly read off from these, though the outline of the ports should always be marked out beforehand as a precaution and as a check on one's figures. If the lathe lead-screw has a graduated handwheel, by engaging the saddle, the depth of the ports being cut can also be determined with accuracy.

On large scale locomotive cylinders, the steam passages between the ports and the ends of the bores may be cast in, but if not, these will have to be drilled or milled and filed out, a process which should be done with care, Whether a milled or drilled passage is required, a start should be made by filing a good chamfer, at the appropriate angle, on the outside edge, to give the drill or end-mill a fair start, so as to break through fairly low down in the steam port.

For the "drilled" method (for gunmetal cylinders) one may proceed as follows:-
Mark out the shape of the passage and centre pop deeply (at three or five points according to size) at intervals equal to $1\frac{1}{2}$ times the diameter of the drill to be used. Drill right through. Cut off some lengths of brass rod an easy fit in the holes, the full length of the passages; "tin" them with ordinary soft solder, insert in the holes until flush at each end and heat the cylinder gently until the solder just melts.

Next, centre-pop again *between* the original holes, drill again, heat up the cylinder until the solder melts again and shake out the "bits". With a flat coarse-cut needle file, the slot can now be finished to size. Incidentally, the cylinder block should be carefully set up on the drilling machine table and clamped at the required angle, which can be determined by "sighting" the drill against the side of the block before drilling. A depth stop should be used if available.

If it is preferred to mill the passages, the use of a long-series end-mill will be found essential in most cases. Before using this, it is advisable to drill one hole right through to the same diameter as the end-mill to be used, and at one side

Cylinders with balanced slide valves with direct exhaust to blast pipe, by Bill Carter.

sential that the piston rod should run absolutely true while the piston is given its final skim. It should not be necessary to lap pistons.

When fitting piston rings, the ring should be turned very slightly larger than the bore (about 0.0005 in. per 3/4 in. of bore). The slot can then be made from the inside at an angle of 45 deg. by filing through with a knife-edge needle file, or by using a very fine metal fretsaw blade. However, small piston rings (up to 1½ in. dia. or so) may be dealt with by breaking the joint, the rough edges left without cleaning up apart from a very light touch on the outside with a fine stone; in this case, the rings should be turned to the same diameter as the bore, to fine limits. When assembled in the cylinder, the gaps should almost close. The slots in adjacent rings in the piston are arranged opposite to one another; in large models, the rings are arranged so that they cannot turn around in the cylinder, this being achieved by a small pin engaging a hole on the inside of the ring.

Piston rings are best made from a good quality centrifugally-cast iron. Piston rods are normally made of stainless steel and their diameter may be about 1/5 of cylinder bore up to 1 inch scale, or 1/6 of cylinder bore for larger scales.

of the slot-to-be. The end-mill is then brought in a short amount and worked across to cut the desired slot. Needless to say, these small passages must be done with great care, only very light cuts being taken.

PISTONS

Pistons must be turned to a good close fit but without any sign of mechanical tightness. No amount of packing will make up for a piston which has been badly fitted in the first place. There are several methods of fitting pistons to their rods.

The piston blanks should be turned a few thou over the finished size before mounting them on their rods, and the grooves for packing or rings put in with a parting tool. For the final machining, the piston rod may be held in a collet in the lathe. If no collet of suitable size is available, a split bush could be made as it is es-

Referring now to slide-valve cylinders, in most cases the steam chest will be deep enough to enable the valve to be slotted, so that a rectangular nut, threaded to suit the valve spindle, can be used to drive it. Sometimes a plain valve spindle is used, the nut being clamped to it by a hexagon-socket grub screw. This will bite into the valve spindle sufficiently firmly to prevent it slipping in service. However, care must be taken here not to tighten such a grub screw too

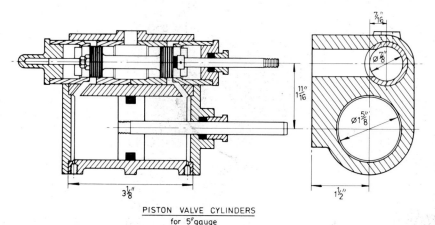

PISTON VALVE CYLINDERS
for 5" gauge

FIG. 47

much before valve setting has been completed, otherwise the slight depression or indentation made by the screw will prevent it locating on either side of the indentation.

Where the steam chest is necessarily shallow, as for instance in cylinders with the valves between the bores, it is usual to employ a "buckle" embracing the valve, one side of this being drilled and tapped to take the valve spindle, the opposite side being likewise drilled and tapped to take an extension of the valve spindle, forward into the front wall of the steam chest and into an extended boss.

One often sees slide valves driven by a valve spindle supported only by the rear part of the steam chest wall. This, though sometimes unavoidable, is not good practice and eventually leads to much slop in the spindle, resulting in inferior valve events.

Steam chests can generally be machined without difficulty in the 4-jaw chuck, the inside surfaces being filed by hand, but care will have to be taken over drilling and reaming for the valve spindle, in order to get the holes through both the rear and front walls of the steam chest in line. It is not possible to drill from one end only, as when the drill emerges from the front wall of the steam chest, it will almost certainly start to run out before it reaches the second wall. One way to avoid this trouble is to mark out both walls as accurately as possible, centre and drill a short distance, using a drill somewhat smaller than the required size for the valve spindle, then drill one end at a time, supporting the steam chest at the other end by a centre in the lathe tailstock. Reverse, complete the drilling, then ream right through.

Screwed glands are often used in cylinder stuffing boxes; although they are not normally used in full-size locomotive cylinders they may sometimes be justified on the grounds of easier adjustment or accessibility. The problem is to get them true. When tapping the stuffing box, use a pilot tap if possible, the pilot pin being a good fit in the previously reamed hole in the cover or steam chest boss. The gland itself is best screw-cut in the lathe, though a circular die may be used to finish off the thread. Finally, the gland is screwed right home and a reamer passed through the lot. The

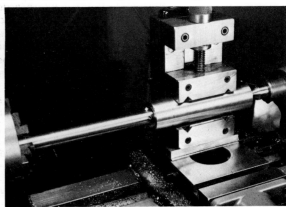

FIG. 48

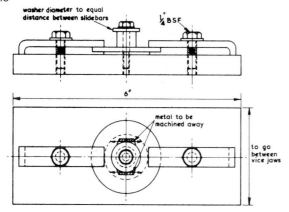

washer diameter to equal
distance between slidebars

¼" BSF

6"

metal to be
machined away

to go
between
vice jaws

JIG FOR MACHINING REAR CYLINDER COVER

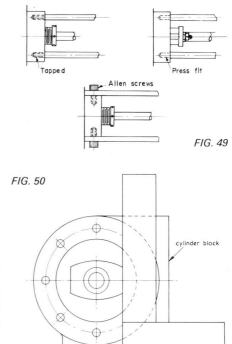

Tapped

Press fit

Allen screws

FIG. 49

FIG. 50

cylinder block

surface plate

LINING UP REAR CYLINDER COVER

threads of screwed glands should always be left on the tight side so that they do not slack back in service; in fact a simple catch is often used to prevent this, as if a screwed gland were to slack back enough to be struck by the crosshead, serious damage might be caused.

A studded gland certainly looks much better than a screwed one. The oval flange of this type of gland is first drilled, and the gland itself used as a drilling jig to drill the rear cover or steam chest boss for the studs. This is then tapped, and if the drilling machine is used to start the tap, this should ensure that the studs stand out square.

Reverting now to piston-valve cylinders, these are best bolted down on the lathe cross-slide for boring both the main bore and the valve liner bore. Most builders of piston-valve cylinders would probably agree that the greatest difficulty is involved in getting the valve liner into the cylinder body successfully.

A one-piece liner is sometimes recommended, to be turned to a press fit in the cylinder, and to be forced home in the bench vice, or drawn in by a large diameter bolt. But this method cannot be recommended. Very often the liner "goes tight" before it is right home and efforts to shift it may cause it to collapse at the point where it is weakest – on the line of the steam ports cut in the liner.

The author favours either a three-piece or a two-piece valve liner, with a slight preference for the latter. The two parts of the two-piece liner are pressed in from each end, to meet in the middle of the cylinder. To avoid any danger of the liners collapsing on the line of the steam ports, the first part of the liner to enter the bore can be taken down to a

very light press fit (little more than a "hand-push" fit) which can be achieved by a dead-smooth Swiss flat file in the lathe. The liner should tend to enter tighter towards its outer end.

Should, by chance, the liner turn out to be too slack a fit, it need not be scrapped, but may be smeared with a suitable adhesive such as Loctite "Hot-strength" before pressing in, care being taken to avoid the adhesive getting into the steam ports. A small grub screw, made of gunmetal or stainless-steel, could also be used, put in at the back. In any case, there is very little tendency for the pressure of the steam to force the liner out, so the main endeavour is to prevent cross-leakage of steam.

Although piston valves machined from good quality cast-iron (Meehanite or similar) may be used without rings, there is no doubt that a ringed valve is superior. For a 5 in. gauge locomotive cylinder, the rings could be of $1/16$ in. x $1/16$ in. section; such rings can be sprung into position if care is taken. Stainless-steel rings have been tried in gunmetal cylinders with apparent success, but lubrication must be reliable.

An alternative to rings on piston valves is to turn a number of fine grooves about $1/32$ in. wide and $1/32$ in. deep,

73

FIG. 51

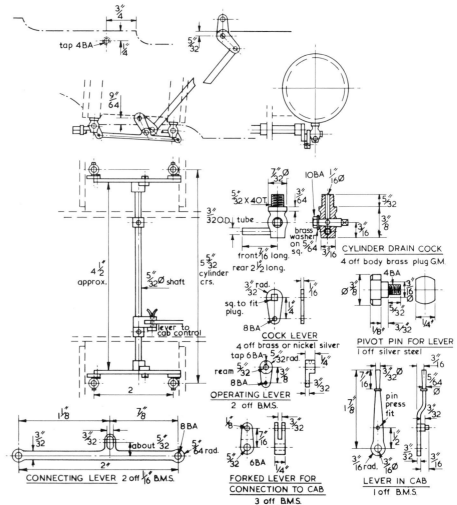

ARRANGEMENT OF CYLINDER DRAIN COCKS FOR $\frac{3}{4}$ SCALE LOCOMOTIVES

which will help to retain the lubricating oil.

The valve spindles of piston-valve cylinders are often fitted without any form of packed glands on the grounds that these are only subjected to the pressure of the exhaust steam, but if glands are used, they should not be tightened up too much as this will only cause unnecessary friction.

DRAIN COCKS & RELIEF VALVES

All model locomotives above ½ inch scale should be provided with cylinder drain cocks, preferably for both ends of the cylinder. These cocks enable the driver to clear condensed water from the cylinder and also to warm up the cylinders quickly at the start of a run. To be really useful, such cocks should be capable of being operated from the cab. Although "Bowden" cables, as used on bicycle brakes etc, are sometimes used, a more positive drive, by rigid rods and cranks, is to be preferred.

Ordinary taper plug cocks are quite satisfactory in cylinders, as they will be kept well lubricated by the cylinder oil, which will prevent them sticking. Ball-type drain cocks are inclined to dribble; sometimes little conical valves are used, which can be ground in, the operating bar using a cam action to raise the valves off their seats. Sometimes steam-operated drain cocks are used, all four (or more) cocks being operated by a steam valve in the locomotive cab.

On large scale models, automatic relief cocks should be fitted to both cylinder covers; these may be simple ball valves, the balls being kept on their seating by springs, adjusted to "blow" at

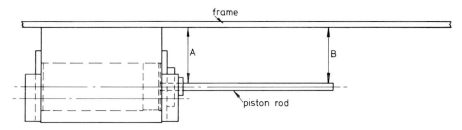

LINING—UP OUTSIDE CYLINDERS

Measure at A and B

FIG.52

slightly above boiler pressure. These will prevent possible damage from trapped water. Large scale piston valves should also be fitted with relief valves above each valve head.

LINING-UP CYLINDERS

Before bolting to the frames, the cylinders must be carefully lined up with the driving axle. The driving axleboxes are first clamped in the correct running position (which is normally shown on the General Arrangement drawing). The cylinder is then lightly clamped to the frame by a large toolmaker's clamp and arranged in the correct "fore and aft" position as given by the drawing. A straight length of silver-steel rod about twice the diameter of the piston rod or a little less is now selected, one end machined to an accurate point while the other end is drilled and reamed to a close fit over the piston rod. This rod should be of such a length as to reach to the driving axle centre when the piston is approximately in the middle of the cylinder.

It will now be quite easy to align the cylinder correctly, with the pointed end of the extension rod aligned with the axle centre. A similar method can be employed for inside cylinders, the crankpin being put into the back dead-centre position, and the pointed end of the extension rod aligned with the centre of the axle.

Cylinders should be held firmly to the frames by hexagon-head bolts of adequate size, or if their appearance is not objected to, by Allen hexagon-socket head screws. Cylinders of 1 inch scale and larger might also be fitted with a couple of dowels, fitting into reamed holes in the frames. Sometimes gaskets made of some kind of heat-insulating material are used between cylinder and frames, to reduce as far as possible heat loss from the cylinders. A sheet steam packing material such as Messrs James Walker's "Walkerite" or "Golden Walkerite" is ideal for this purpose.

The outsides of outside cylinders are generally lagged with some kind of insulating material, this being covered by thin steel sheet.

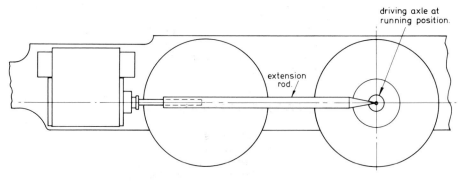

LINING—UP OUTSIDE CYLINDERS

FIG.53

CHAPTER TEN

Crossheads, slide bars, motion plates

Locomotive crossheads are designed for one, two, three or four slide bars. The single-bar crosshead was not used a great deal in full-size practice, although it was common on the old Great Eastern Railway and was used by some other companies such as the L.N.W.R., the Lancashire & Yorkshire and the London & South Western. It is a useful type for model locomotives.

The two-bar crosshead, where the bars are vertically one above the other with the piston rod between, was probably the most popular design, and was used on many Great Western, L.M.S. and Southern Railway locomotives. It makes a neat and nicely balanced crosshead for model work, not too difficult to make.

Many of the ex-L.N.E.R. locomotives were fitted with the "Laird" three-bar crosshead, and this design was also used on some of the British Railways locomotives. It is somewhat more difficult to make for models of the smaller scales.

Crossheads for four slide bars are generally straightforward in themselves, though it is not very easy to fit the four bars so that they are correctly located and aligned.

Crossheads for model locomotives are generally made in mild steel, with the working surfaces case-hardened. If kept well lubricated, such crossheads work quite well with steel slide bars. Sometimes separate "slippers" made of hard phosphor-bronze are employed and these work very well against hardened steel slide bars. Although the yellow colour of such slippers may be objected to, this may not be much of a dis-

Crosshead and slide bars on a G.W.R. 4-6-0 "Manor" by Keith Tucker.

FIG. 54

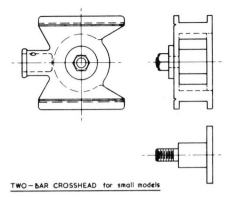

TWO — BAR CROSSHEAD for small models

FIG. 55

Two-bar crosshead for one inch scale models.

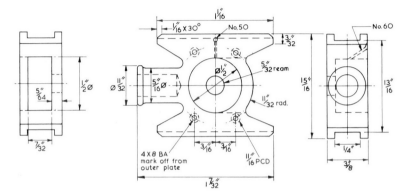

"pin-drilling" or counterboring from the back, the gudgeon pin having a head made a close fit in the recess. The boss or neck of the crosshead can be turned in the lathe using the 4-jaw chuck, this being done after the slide bar grooves have been cut by face or end-milling.

One disadvantage of this design is that the gudgeon pin can only be removed from the back, making it difficult to dismantle the connecting rod; this applies particularly to locomotives having coupled wheels immediately behind the crosshead, as in 2-6-0's, 2-8-0's etc.

advantage as in service crossheads tend to get oily and dirty.

For models of 2½ in. gauge and smaller, crossheads are generally made from the solid, the recess for the little end of the connecting rod being formed by

FIG. 56

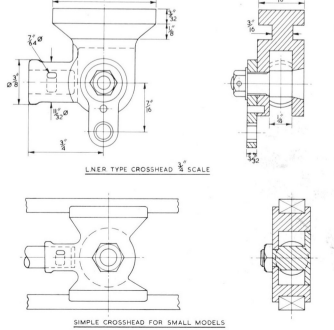

L.N.E.R. TYPE CROSSHEAD ¾" SCALE

SIMPLE CROSSHEAD FOR SMALL MODELS

This disadvantage is overcome in the author's design, where the recess for the little end is cut out on the front of the crosshead; a thin circular washer is then used at the front of the crosshead with a plate, fitting closely over the gudgeon pin, bolted to the body of the crosshead. Thus by removing this plate, the washer and the gudgeon pin can be withdrawn from the front. An additional advantage is that the washer, being a close fit in the recess, prevents the thrust of the piston coming directly on the bolt. If a drop arm is required for Walschaerts or Baker gear, this can be held to the crosshead by the lower bolts holding the plate.

The crosshead gudgeon pin may be turned from silver-steel or maybe mild steel, case-hardened will be specified; an alternative would be a nickel-chrome oil-hardening steel such as EN.23 or EN.39A.

Reverting to the single slide bar crosshead, in the smaller sizes, the slide bar groove can be milled out by a face cutter or a small side-and-face cutter, and the top plate can be brazed or silver-soldered on. Crossheads of this type in 1 inch scale or larger will be found wide enough to enable the top plate to be held down by fitting bolts, as in the full-size crosshead.

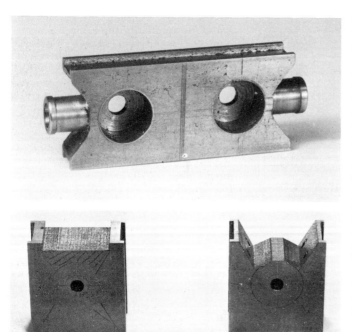

Crossheads (³/₄in. scale) under construction; bottom picture shows separate blanks marked out and partly shaped.

for such castings, iron being on the brittle side while nickel-silver is insufficiently hard-wearing.

The fitting of the piston rod into the crosshead is a job that needs care; although some builders prefer a screwed fitting, as this enables the clearance at each end of the cylinder to be adjusted very easily, others may prefer a plain parallel fitting, or a taper fitting for the larger scales, on the grounds that this is more likely to ensure concentricity. But there must be no slackness at all with a plain fitting, and a silver-steel pin, not smaller than ⅛ in. diameter for a ¾ in. scale locomotive, put in after the piston and rod assembly has been checked for correct length. For 1 inch scale models, two pins should be used, close together and put in at an angle of about 45 deg. to the vertical. It is advisable to drill, ream and fit one pin at a time, to ensure that each pin carries its fair share of the load.

For 1½ in. scale or larger locomotives, a proper flat cotter may be used, through this will entail careful fitting to be effective.

The slide bars are generally made of silver-steel or mild steel and are left unhardened; this is on the grounds that when wear takes place, it is better to allow the slide bar to wear rather than the crosshead.

Slide bars are nearly always carried from the rear cylinder cover and supported at their outer ends by the motion plate. In full-size, there was a notable exception to this in some of the Great Central Railway locomotives, where the outside piston rods were extended to reduce the length of the connecting rod, the slide bars being bolted to a bracket attached to the frames.

The little end recess of crossheads larger than 1 inch scale may be cut out from the rear by end-milling, though it will be found helpful if four small diameter holes are first drilled in the corners.

Castings are sometimes used for crossheads, thus avoiding a considerable amount of machining. Phosphor-bronze is probably the best metal to use

In small gauge models, the ends of the slide bars can be turned circular and made a tight push fit into holes drilled in the rear cylinder covers; alternatively, the ends can be threaded and the bars screwed home. The drawback of both these methods is that it is very difficult to ensure that the slide bars are truly at right angles to the cover and at the right distance from the piston rod centre, and no correction can be made by shims.

A better method, practicable in ½ in. scale and larger models, is to hold the slide bar down on a step milled across the rear cover, using one or more hexagon-head or Allen cap screws, thus any correction for mis-alignment or wear can be made very easily by shims.

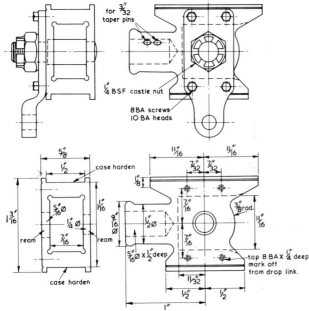

FIG. 57   G.N.R. TYPE CROSSHEAD

Crosshead and motion of ³⁄₄in. scale 2-6-4T by the author.

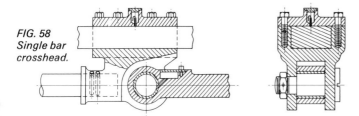

FIG. 58
Single bar
crosshead.

The outer ends of slide bars are usually bolted to lugs cast on the motion plate, or to short lengths of angle, though on small models, the ends may merely be put through slots cut in the motion plate; provided that there is no slackness at this point, the method is generally adequate.

While most locomotive slide bars are of very simple shape, in fact in some cases nothing more than plain rectangular bars, some are more elaborate. A notable example of rather elaborate slide bars would have been found in the ex-

Great Western Railway four-cylinder locomotives, the "Stars", "Castles" and "Kings". Here, the cross-section of the slide bar is in the form of a thick "T", the base of the T forming the working surface against which the crosshead works. At the outer end, the base of the T is bent upwards and outwards (upper bar) and downwards and outwards (lower bar). The extreme ends of these slide bars then straighten out to form a connection with the motion plates.

There are two methods for making these G.W.R. style slide bars. The base of the T could be bent up and a full-length piece to form the upper part of the T silver-soldered to it. Alternately a complete T section could be milled out first, this being suitably cut and bent, the angled part being then silver-soldered to the upper part. The first method is probably the easiest, through some difficulty may be experienced in holding the two parts in correct relation while silver-soldering.

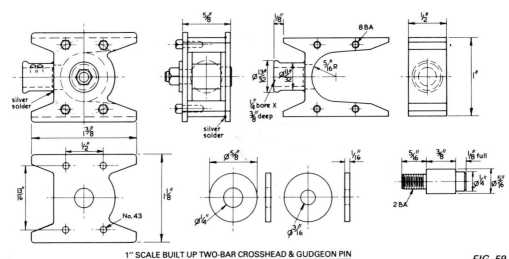

1" SCALE BUILT UP TWO-BAR CROSSHEAD & GUDGEON PIN

FIG. 59

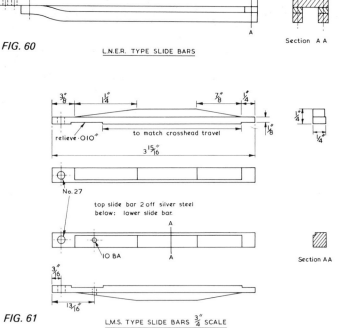

FIG. 60

L.N.E.R. TYPE SLIDE BARS

Section A A

FIG. 61

relieve ·010″

to match crosshead travel

3 15/16″

No. 27

top slide bar 2 off silver steel
below: lower slide bar.

10 BA

L.M.S. TYPE SLIDE BARS 3/4″ SCALE

Section AA

ing solder such as Easyflo. After cleaning up, the joint should be scarcely visible.

The three-bar arrangement of slide bars, as used by the L.N.E.R. and to some extent by British Railways, should not present any problems, though the two lower bars, of square section, to be strictly correct should be bent up to meet the top bar at the cylinder end, which makes construction rather more difficult. It should be noted that in L.N.E.R. (Gresley) designs, the spacer at the outer end of the slide bar is cut away in he middle (between the two lower bars) to give sufficient clearance for the connecting rod when this is at its highest point.

MOTION PLATES

The design of motion plates varies a great deal, depending on whether the cylinders are outside or inside or both, on the type of valve gear in use, and so on. On some L.M.S. and L.N.E.R. locomotives, the motion plates were combined with brackets to carry the expansion links of the Walschaerts valve gear. The Great Western four-cylinder locomotives, too, employed quite an elaborate inside motion plate combined with link supports. When this type of motion plate is employed on model locomotives, it must be designed so that the expansion link, together with the radius rod, can be inserted or removed without difficulty.

The answer is probably to make up a simple jig, using aluminium or some other metal to which the solder will not adhere. The base is arranged to lie flat on the surface of the jig, being located by short pins to act as stops. The upper part is then cut so as to extend a short distance beyond the base at both ends, and is supported by further pins pressed into the base. The silver-soldering is then carried out at the back, using a free-flow-

L.N.E.R. type
crosshead and slide
bars by J. Wills.

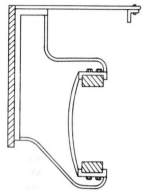

G.W.R. TYPE OUTSIDE MOTION PLATE

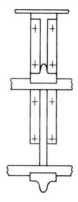

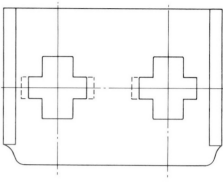

FIG. 63

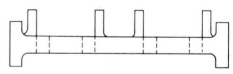

MOTION PLATE FOR INSIDE CYLINDERS

FIG. 62

Top of page – motion on a 3¹/₂in. gauge 0-6-0 tank by L. A. Green.

In many cases, motion plates have a great deal of ribs or beading incorporated in the casting, to give additional strength, and the easiest way to accommodate them is to use a gunmetal casting. The thickness of such castings will however have to be considerably greater than the "scale" thickness, otherwise they are liable to warp.

Inside motion plates are nearly always castings, and will have slots to take the ends of the slide bars and probably lugs for their attachment. In some cases,

further slots and possibly fixing lugs will be provided for a crosshead feed pump.

Machining of cast motion plates is generally a matter of 4-jaw work, the bolting faces being machined at each end, after which the various slots can be end-milled or filed to shape.

Peter Dupen driving his 5in. gauge Midland 4-4-0.

CHAPTER ELEVEN

Coupling rods, connecting rods, eccentrics, straps

Many of the earlier steam locomotives were fitted with coupling rods having individual adjustments at the bearings, using separate brasses and a tapered cotter and push-plate or "glut", the bearing ends of the rods and the intermediate parts of the rod, if the engine was six or eight-coupled, being of rectangular shape.

With the improvement in bearing metals, however, the plain bush gradually superseded the more complicated adjustable bearing. Hard bronze of about $1/2$ in. thickness, plus about $3/16$ in. thickness of white metal, was used in British practice. The bush was generally secured by a rectangular key, though in some cases (the L.N.E.R. "A.4" class for instance) a set screw was used in addition.

Floating bushes were sometimes used in full-size practice, especially on American locomotives, where the bushes were usually in three sections with $1/32$ in. cuts between each segment to allow for expansion.

In some cases, the distance between the coupling rod centres was made slightly greater than that between the centres of the coupled axles, $1/32$ in. being an average amount; this was done to allow for the effects of strains arising in the frames when loaded and also for expansion due to heat radiated from the firebox when this was adjacent to the coupled wheelbase. Allowance for this was made in the diameter of the bushes.

On most modern locomotives, the coupling rods were fluted very deeply on both sides, an extreme case being the L.N.E.R. "A.4" and other classes where the section of the rods was 5 in. x 2½ in., yet the thickness of the web was only ³⁄₈ in. This was made possible by the use of high-grade nickel-chrome steel. Even so, full-size coupling rods were heavy items, the weight of the "A.4" rods being 463 lb. each.

Some railways, especially those which had curves of rather small radius, specified an additional joint in the coupling rods having a vertical pivot. The trailing bearing of the rods of the Great Eastern "1500" 4-6-0's were of this type.

Most model engineers used ordinary bright mild steel for coupling rods, it being considered hardly worth while going to the extra expense of some kind of stainless steel, which is generally considerably harder to drill and machine. Stainless steel does however look rather nice on a model locomotive intended mainly for exhibition. A suitable stainless metal would be K.E.40A, generally called stainless iron.

The most important point when making coupling rods is to ensure that the spacing of the bearings is correct. A good way to tackle the problem is to make up a simple drilling jig. If the wheels and axles have not yet been fitted to the locomotives, but the axleboxes are in place, the procedure is as follows;- a length of steel of section about 1 in. x ¼ in. (according to the scale of the model) and straight and true is drilled at the necessary spacings, using dividers adjusted from the model. A plain reamed hole is used for the driving centre, but the holes for the leading and trailing centres are opened out to an oval shape. Drill bushes are now turned up from silver-steel, one end of which being made a close fit in the axleboxes, while the other end is threaded to a size to pass through the holes in the jig, and

FIG. 64

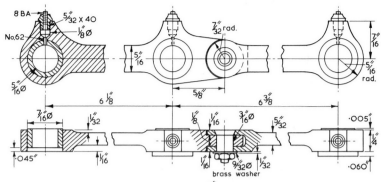

COUPLING RODS FOR A ¾″ SCALE ENGINE

furnished with a nut. The jig, with the bushes in place but with the movable bushes loosely nutted up, is now applied to the locomotive, the bushes being entered into their respective axleboxes (which must of course be strictly in line) when the nuts on the movable bushes are tightened up. The jig is then ready for use.

A complication does of course arise in the case of coupling rods for locomotives having six, eight or more coupled wheels, due to the intermediate joints (which are essential to allow for track which is not dead level). It is therefore a good plan to make up the embryo coupling rods with these joints finished off before drilling the crankpin holes. The intermediate joints may consist of plain case-hardened pins working directly in the rods, or press-fitted bronze bushes may be used.

Referring again to the drilling jig, this should be used to drill the coupling rods to exact fits on the crankpins so that the rods can be "offered up" on the locomotive. If they won't go on at all, it should be evident where they are "out", if they do go on but with a tight spot on rotating the wheels, a bright mark will quickly show up where the rod is tight; the hole can then be drawn over with a round file, then re-drilled and finished off ready for the bushes, which are best made a good press fit. The bushes are finally opened out to produce a fairly easy fit on leading and/or trailing crankpins, but those on driving crankpins should be a good fit.

The bushes in coupling rods may be made from a good quality cast phosphor-bronze, through cast-iron is a sound alternative, if kept well lubricated. On models of 1 inch scale and larger, some of the newer bearing materials may be considered, such as the Glacier Metal Company's DU bearings. These are steel-backed bearings lined with PTFE and lead, and will operate without

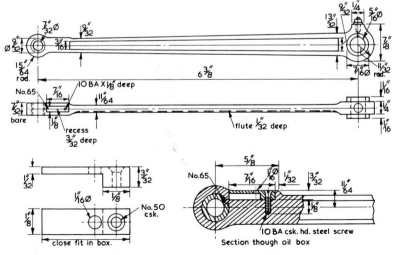

FIG. 65

L.M.S. TYPE OUTSIDE CONNECTING ROD

Milling a flute in a coupling rod.

longer than the longest coupling rod likely to be dealt with, and this is bolted to the vertical-slide which is set up facing the lathe spindle. The angle can be brought up against the lathe faceplate to ensure that it is square across the lathe axis , and to ensure that it is also truly horizontal, it can be traversed across a short rod held in the chuck and feelers used; better still, a D.T.I. could be set up on the lathe bed or attached to the faceplate, and the cross-slide traversed right across, through its full travel.

As much commercial steel angle is not exactly at 90 deg., a very light cut may be required, across the whole of the upper, working face of the angle before commencing operations.

The coupling rod blank is held down on the angle by suitable bolts and washers through its bearing holes, into tapped holes in the angle, and the machining can then be carried out by a small face milling cutter a small side-and-face cutter, or a Woodruff cutter, according to the size of the rod. However, owing to the possibility of the rod distorting or warping during or after machining, it is strongly recommended that the rod blank be annealed before starting maching operations – this can be done by heating it to a bright red colour, then allowing it to cool down very slowly.

If the coupling rods are required to be fluted, it is probably best to cut the flute to the full depth required first, then follow up by milling right across the face of the rod, for its full width, then mill on each side of the flute. In this way, it is easy to see that the flute is left exactly central.

Although much fluting of model rods is done with standard cutters, these will inevitably leave the flute with square corners, which is not strictly correct. If the correct flute with radiused corners is required, the cutter used for the job will have to have its cutting teeth radiused off on both sides, an operation which really calls for a proper tool and cutter grinder, if the essential "backing off" of the cutting teeth is to be achieved.

Some coupling rods for four-coupled locomotives are "fish bellied", i.e. wider in the middle than at the ends. In this case, it is probably best to machine them to the width across the middle and finish the job by filing. The shaping of the radiused ends and the oil boxes of coupling rods sometimes presents dif-

FIG. 66

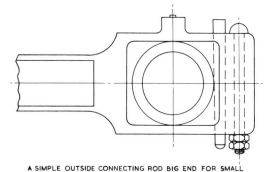

A SIMPLE OUTSIDE CONNECTING ROD BIG END FOR SMALL LOCOMOTIVES

FIG. 67

MARINE TYPE CONNECTING ROD BIG END

Opposite, using a side and face cutter in a horizontal milling machine to mill a connecting rod.

lubrication, though lubrication is still desirable.

For shaping the outside surfaces of coupling rods, a horizontal milling machine is ideal for removing the quite considerable amount of metal involved, though if a substantial vertical-slide is available, nearly all the machining can be done on the average model engineer's lathe. A length of stout steel angle, about 2 in. x 2 in. x ¼ in. section should be obtained, several inches

ficulties. In the absence of a vertical milling machine, one method is to drill a series of holes about 3/32 in. dia. all round the ends just outside the scribed lines. If the holes are carefully spaced, not quite touching one another and not too close to the scribed lines, a drill a lit-

tle larger can be used until all the holes break into one another, when the unwanted metal can be broken away. The job is then taken a stage further by filing, leaving the final cut to be done by an operation in the lathe.

A length of brass rod, from 3/8 in. to 3/4 in. square according to the size of the coupling rod, is set up in the 4-jaw chuck and one end turned down to a good fit in the holes in the coupling rod, for a length somewhat greater than the thickness of the rod. This is then clamped firmly under the lathe toolholder and set exactly parallel to the longitudinal axis of the lathe. A small end-mill is now used in chuck or collet and the coupling rod swung by hand against the rotation of the end-mill, using a medium spindle speed and very careful feed. Great care must be taken not to swing the rod "with" the rotation of the end-mill otherwise it will "catch up" and spoil the job. The rod should be held very firmly using an old glove for preference, and if it is a short one, a toolmaker's clamp can be used to hold it by, which will give better control.

No-one need feel ashamed to use emery cloth to finish coupling and similar rods, in any case no sharp edges should be left – sharp edges as left by the machine are never on full-size coupling rods and they should not be on our model rods. On the other hand, motion rods should not be plated or polished.

At this point, here is a useful tip for beginners using end-mills in the lathe. End-mills have a nasty habit of working out of the 3-jaw chuck, or even out of a collet. To avoid this, Messrs Clarksons make a special "Auto-lock" chuck, into which a threaded type of end-mill can be screwed, preventing this trouble. An alternative is to use the 4-jaw chuck. True, this needs a D.T.I. and a good deal of patience to get the end-mill running true, but the extra jaw ensures that the chuck grips the end-mill much more firmly than the 3-jaw S.C. chuck.

Another problem which arises with six and eight-coupled locomotives with outside cylinders is how to deal with the leading crankpin and its retaining collar, as in most designs there is very little clearance at this point for the connecting rod or crosshead. The usual solution is to recess the end of the coupling rod and fit a thick washer, flush with the rod, the crankpin being drilled and tapped for almost its full depth, and a long counter-

FIG. 68

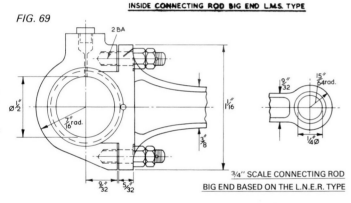

INSIDE CONNECTING ROD BIG END L.M.S. TYPE

FIG. 69

3/4" SCALE CONNECTING ROD
BIG END BASED ON THE L.N.E.R. TYPE

85

An attractive River class 5in. gauge S.R. tank locomotive by John P. Mercer.

sunk screw used to hold the washer. A hexagon-socket type countersunk screw looks better and is stronger than the ordinary slotted screw.

It has been suggested that on the right-hand side of the locomotive, the thread of this screw should be left-hand, so that the friction of the coupling rod working around it does not tend to slacken it, but this should not be necessary if the screw is made a really good fit. Loctite or similar adhesive should not be used, as this might prevent the screw from being taken out, if the coupling rod had to be dismantled for rebushing or for some other reason!

CONNECTING RODS

In full-size practice, connecting rods were usually made from special alloy steels owing to the great stresses and strains which had to be allowed for, though some shunting and goods engines used ordinary mild steel. Mild steel, however, is generally quite suitable for the connecting rods of model locomotives, while for very small models, nickel-silver or bronze can be considered.

The design of connecting rods for outside and inside cylinders varies a great deal, though modern locomotives adopted quite a simple design for outside rods, the boss, of large diameter, being cut from the solid with its oil-box,

and the bush a plain cylindrical affair in bronze with white-metal linings. The rod itself was generally of "H" section, deeply fluted on both sides. This type of connecting rod is generally used on model locomotives.

On older types of locomotive rectangular big-ends having brasses adjustable by means of a taper cotter and glut were generally used. Towards the end of the steam "era", the use of roller bearings in connecting rod big-ends became quite common and some enterprising model engineers have followed this arrangement by using small needle roller bearings, in which the rollers bear directly on the locomotive crankpin which must therefore be properly hardened. However, it is now possible to obtain small needle roller bearings with inside races, so that unhardened crankpins can be used. This type of bearing gives very long wear with the minimum of friction; its only objection may be its appearance being rather large when applied to models below 1½ in. scale.

INSIDE CONNECTING RODS

Inside connecting rods are generally more complicated than the outside type owing to the fact that their big-ends must be made readily detachable from the crank-axle. At one time, the Marine type was used to some extent in full-size practice, the big-end being compara-

FIG. 70

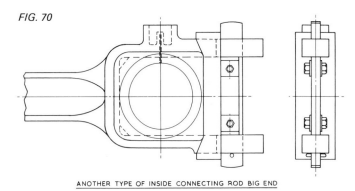

ANOTHER TYPE OF INSIDE CONNECTING ROD BIG END

tively simple in design and quite robust, while the rod itself was generally of round section, but with the steadily increasing power of steam locomotives, the "H" section rod came into general use.

On the L.M.S. Railway, a big-end was adopted having the jaws machined out of the solid, the brasses being put in up against the leading end of the jaws, followed by a "clip" embracing the whole of the jaws, and a large taper cotter of 1 in 16 taper driven in against the lot. A small safety split cotter was then driven in through the bottom of the main cotter, while two bolts with square washers on each side were put through the main cotter with locking plates each side of the latter. The former L.N.E. Railway used a rather unusual type of big end on their inside connecting rods. The strap, which was of high carbon steel, was bent into a "U" shape and the two bolts machined integral with the strap, thus preserving the grain. The circular split brasses were held between the rod and the strap and were prevented from turning by a steel key. The bolts were fitted with locknuts and cotters. Felt pads were provided, held in position by wires, to retain the lubricant, while the oil was fed through a pin trimming from an oil-box integral with the strap. The connecting rod itself was made from nickel-chrome steel of deeply fluted section, measuring overall 5½ in. x 2½ in. close to the big-end, and 4 in. x 2½ in. at the small-end.

The L.N.E.R. type of big-end is not easy to reproduce in model form owing to the difficulty of bending the strap accurately enough after threading the main bolts. One solution would be to bend up the strap without the bolts and to tap the ends of the strap for studs after the bending had been satisfactorily completed.

The type of big-end bearing which originated in France and was adopted by the Great Western Railway, and later by Stanier on the L.M.S., is a very good one and not difficult to copy in model form.

The making of connecting rods is very similar to coupling rods, though where these are fluted, the flute is nearly always tapered, which involves rather more work than the parallel taper of coupling rod flutes. A taper flute can be produced as follows:- the vertical-slide and heavy angle set-up is used as before. The connecting rod is held down on the angle but a fitting bolt is used only at the small-end. At the big-end, a bolt considerably smaller in diameter than the hole in the big-end is used. A light longitudinal centre-line is scribed right along the rod and the rod lined up square to the lathe axis for the first cut, which can be made a few thou short of the final depth required. The cutter is then returned to the small-end of the connecting rod, the bolt in the big-end slackened and the rod slewed slightly to one side (by half the extra width required at the larger end of the rod) with the cutter still in the flute (the movement of the rod at the small-end is so slight that no damage will be done to the cutter). The bolt at the big-end is then tightened.

The cutter is now run along the full length of the flute and then returned to the small-end. The bolt at the big-end is then slackened again and the rod slewed a similar amount to the other side; the amount of "slew" can be gauged by scriber marks on each side of the rod. On again running the cutter right along the flute, the tapered shape will emerge. The same procedure can of course be used for milling the side of the rod.

Referring again to the Marine type connecting rod big-end, it is usual to machine a small groove in the upper bolt immediately below the oil-box, to allow the oil to get to the crankpin. This will not materially reduce the strength of the bolt as the threaded part of it will be the weakest part. The bolts should always be fitted with locknuts and split pins or some kind of anti-vibration nut used to ensure that they cannot slacken off in service.

The lubrication of coupling and connecting rods should not be neglected. Full-size practice cannot really be followed here, as due to the generally higher r.p.m. of model locomotives (especially those with small wheels) the oil tends to be thrown about more. A fairly heavy lubricating oil, or even a light grease, such as that specified for motor-car axle gears, may be advisable. The oil-box can be filled and some kind of plug inserted (or screwed in), the ideal plug being a tiny piece of cane, as this will allow just enough air in to get the oil to flow into the journal, while preventing the entry of foreign matter.

ECCENTRICS & STRAPS

An eccentric is a crank in which the diameter of the crankpin is sufficiently large to enclose the shaft. It will not transform reciprocating into rotary motion, but only rotary into reciprocating.

Eccentrics are mainly used in valve gears, generally inside the frames, but are also used in model locomotives for driving feed water pumps and sometimes for driving mechanical lubricators.

Eccentric sheaves are usually made from mild steel, though in some ways cast-iron is a better material, while the straps may be gunmetal, phosphor-

FIG. 71

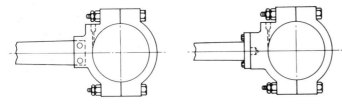

METHODS OF FITTING ECCENTRIC STRAPS TO RODS

bronze or cast-iron. (Cast-iron straps work well on cast-iron sheaves, but gunmetal straps are generally to be preferred for steel sheaves).

The sheaves are often grooved with a rib machined on the strap to match the groove, in order to keep the strap on the sheave. Another method is to machine the rib on the sheave and to recess the strap to match, while a third and easiest method is to dispense with the rib altogether and machine the sheave with a thin flange on each side of it.

Where two sheaves lie side by side, as for instance in Stephenson valve gear, the sheaves may be flanged only on their outsides, which saves space – par-

ticularly useful on inside-cylinder locomotives. Double-flanged sheaves, however, run with rather less friction.

Valve gear eccentric sheaves may be held securely on their axles by hexagon-socket grub screws, which should be of as large a diameter as possible, and put through the larger diameter of the sheave. The end of such a grub screw should not be pointed, but left "as supplied". Being harder than a mild steel axle, it will bite into the axle and will not slip, but this does mean that it must not be finally tightened down until the position of the sheave on the axle has been finally determined.

When machining eccentric sheaves, the flanges may be formed by using a stout parting tool ground off quite square on the cutting edge, the stock set in the chuck with as little overhang as possible, and in most cases, tailstock support given. The lathe should not be run too fast and plenty of cutting oil used. (This applies only to steel eccentrics, cast-iron being turned dry.) They may be drilled and/or bored and reamed in the lathe by holding them in a 4-jaw chuck; to avoid crushing the thin flanges, a brass split ring may be turned up and sprung over the working part of the eccentric.

Before machining the eccentric straps, they should be partly cleaned up with an old file to remove sand, and scale, the holes for the securing bolts drilled right through tapping size, opened out half-way with the exact outside-diameter size of drill for the bolts to be used, and the remainder tapped. The two halves are then sawn apart, and the jointing faces machined or filed flat, removing as little metal as possible. They are then bolted together temporarily and set up to run as truly as possible in the 4-jaw chuck for boring.

It is a good plan to previously turn up a short piece of steel bar to exactly the same diameter as the sheave and use this as a plug gauge for the straps. This piece of bar can then be used again to hold the straps while the two sides are machined. The bolts are slackened off and a strip of paper put between the straps and the bar; on re-tightening, the straps will be firm enough to enable light cuts to be taken on each side.

CHAPTER TWELVE

Valve gears – single & slip eccentric gears

The simplest form of valve gear is the single eccentric motion. This valve gear is not reversible and is thus unsuitable for locomotives. However, the movement of the valve given by this gear enables us better to understand the more complicated valves gears such as Stephenson's.

The setting of a single eccentric driving a valve without lap is always exactly 90 deg. in advance of its crankpin. When

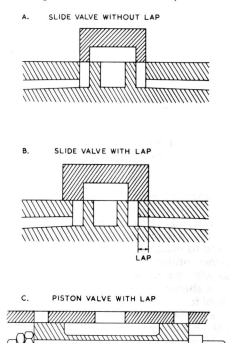

A. SLIDE VALVE WITHOUT LAP

B. SLIDE VALVE WITH LAP

LAP

C. PISTON VALVE WITH LAP

LAP

FIG. 72

the valve is provided with lap, or with lap and lead, the eccentric must be further advanced by that amount. It is important to note that the angle of advance of an eccentric is the angle it is moved *ahead* of the normal 90 deg.

SLIP ECCENTRIC VALVE GEAR

The only really simple reversing valve gear is probably the slip eccentric gear. This gear gives a good steam distribution, if the eccentric rod is long, though no adjustment of cut-off is possible, nor can the engine so fitted be reversed from the cab without much complication (such as a gear and ratchet mechanism operating on the crankshaft). However, as much lap and lead as is desired can be applied and a cut-off suitable for continuous running chosen.

The slip eccentric gear has been used in full-size practice on occasion, a notable example being the Webb 3-cylinder compound locomotives of the old L.N.W.R., in which the gear was adopted to operate the valve of the low-pressure cylinder.

The eccentric is arranged loose on the driving axle and is driven by a stud or pin mounted in a collar which is secured to the axle alongside the eccentric. Alternatively, the pin is attached to the eccentric and is driven by a suitably shaped collar.

The slip eccentric valve gear is ideal for simple steam locomotives of 1¼ in. and 1¾ in. gauges, which are generally run on scenic model railways and not used for passenger hauling. The valve travel should be made rather less than what would be used on a passenger-hauling locomotive. A good all-round

FIG. 73

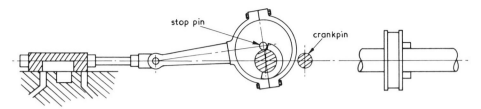

SLIP—ECCENTRIC VALVE GEAR

TABLE 3

figure would be three-quarters the amount of valve travel normally allowed in full gear.

For instance, for a locomotive having $3/32$ in. wide steam ports and a lap of $3/32$ in, the valve travel would be made:-

$$\tfrac{3}{4} \times 2\,(\tfrac{3}{32} \text{ plus } \tfrac{3}{32})\text{ in.}$$
$$= \tfrac{9}{32}\text{ in.}$$

Thus the throw of the eccentric in this example would amount to $9/64$ in.

Recommended valve travels and eccentric throws for slip eccentric valve gear. (dimensions in inches

	Steam ports	Lap	Valve travel	Eccentric throw
Gauge 0	$1/16 \times 3/16$	.050	.171	.086
Gauge 1	$1/16 \times 5/16$	.063	.187	.094
2½″ gauge	$3/32 \times 5/8$	0.94	$9/32$	$9/64$
3½″ gauge	$1/8 \times 7/8$	.125	$3/8$	$3/16$

The Stuart Double Ten engine in the Sentinel locomotive illustrated earlier, showing arrangement of valve gear and drive to the lubricator.

CHAPTER THIRTEEN

The link valve gears

The principal link motions are the Stephenson, the Gooch and the Allan straight-link.

The Stephenson valve gear takes its name from the famous firm of Robert Stephenson & Company. It was not actually invented by Robert Stephenson himself, but was evolved by the Company about 1843. Who first thought of the idea is not known with certainty; probably William Williams, an apprentice draughtsman at Newcastle upon Tyne, first had the idea, but William Howe, one of the pattern makers employed by the Company, worked out the practical details. At all events, the gear proved a great improvement on the clumsy "Gab" gear previously used and with various detailed improvements the Stephenson gear has been used in all types of steam engine ever since.

The Stephenson link valve gear was at one time the most widely used locomotive valve gear in Great Britain, though it was very largely superseded by the Walschaerts gear during the twentieth century. It is still however a very efficient valve gear if properly designed.

The Stephenson gear uses two eccentrics per cylinder, one for each direction of working, the eccentrics being generally mounted on the driving axle. The eccentric rods are connected to each end of a curved slotted expansion link, arranged so as to lie with its concave side towards the driving axle. In the "locomotive type" link, the eccentric rods are connected on the curved centre-line of the link, above and below the link slot, thus the total travel of the eccentrics is made considerably more than the valve travel required in full gear.

The locomotive type link is generally suspended at its centre point by means of a bracket attached to it, carrying a pin upon which works a lifting link which is connected by an arm to the weighshaft. The valve rod usually works in a guide attached to the motion plate, or it may be operated by a link attached to a swinging

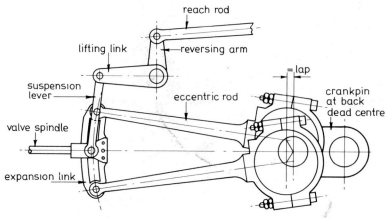

FIG. 74 STEPHENSON VALVE GEAR WITH LOCOMOTIVE-TYPE LINK

FIG. 75

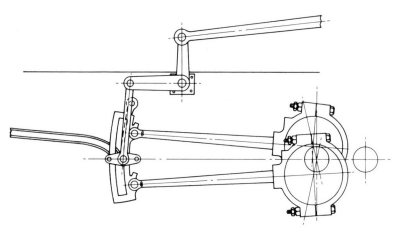

STEPHENSON'S VALVE GEAR WITH LAUNCH TYPE LINK

lever, pivoted to some convenient point on the engine frames. The valve rod obtains its motion from a die-block, upon which the curved slot of the expansion link can slide up and down as controlled by the reversing lever through the weighshaft, lifting arm and lifting link.

On six and eight-coupled locomotives, the eccentric rods are sometimes made very long and set over in order to clear the axle ahead of the driving axle.

Although a direct drive, parallel with the horizontal centre-line of the motion, is desirable with Stephenson gear, if the valves are on top of the cylinders, or below, direct drive inclined to the cylinders is equally satisfactory, although in the case of slide valve cylinders, the port face of the cylinder block has to be machined off at a suitable angle. In the case of piston valve cylinders, careful setting up is necessary, to ensure boring the block at the correct angle for the valve.

Sometimes an indirect drive is used with Stephenson gear, a rocking shaft being adopted, working in bearings at- tached to the frames. While this is quite satisfactory, care must be taken in fitting the various pins, otherwise lost motion will spoil the efficiency of the gear.

An interesting and very useful feature of the Stephenson valve gear is that with "open" eccentric rods, the lead increases towards mid-gear. This is due to the angularity of the rods and effect is greater the shorter the eccentric rods. If "crossed" eccentric rods are used, the lead would decrease towards mid-gear, an undesirable feature in a railway locomotive.

Another type of Stephenson gear is that where the expansion link used is the "Launch-type" link. The true launch link has the point of suspension on the curved centre-line of the link slot but beyond one end of the slot, but in the Launch-type link, the suspension is arranged on the horizontal centre-line of the motion.

Alexander Allan of the L.N.W.R. was probably the first engineer to realise the possibilites of the Launch-type link with Stephenson valve gear, but it was G.J. Churchward of the old Great Western Railway who developed this type of gear to its present high efficiency, by adapting it for use with large laps and long valve travels.

About the year 1904, Churchward adopted long valve travels and large steam laps for his express locomotives; he soon realised however that if he was to use the usual locomotive-type link, the length of link required, and the large size of eccentric sheaves and straps needed, would make the arrangement quite impracticable in the space available. He therefore adopted the Launch-type link with comparatively short ec-

FIG. 76

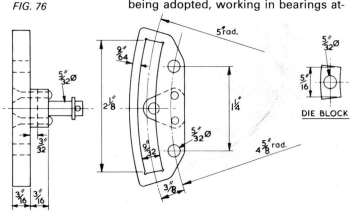

DIE BLOCK

LAUNCH TYPE LINK FOR 5" GAUGE MODEL

FIG. 77

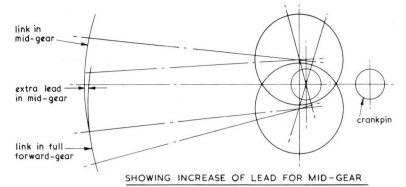

link in
mid-gear

extra lead
in mid-gear

crankpin

link in full
forward-gear

SHOWING INCREASE OF LEAD FOR MID-GEAR

centric rods and as the latter gave a large increase of lead towards mid-gear, he arranged for the valves to be set with negative lead in full-gear, i.e. the valves did not open the ports to steam until after the piston has passed dead centre.

This negative lead would appear to have confused many model engineers, but it should be understood that the negative lead in itself was not necessarily desired, but with the short eccentric rods used, if the valves had been set "line-for-line", there would have been excessive lead when the engine was notched up for fast running.

In fact, it was found that on the Great Western, this negative full-gear lead did not adversely affect starting or acceleration. Such engines as the 4-6-0 "Saints" and "Halls" fitted with this type of valve gear were excellent starters. In any case, as soon as the driver had his train well under way, he would start to notch up his reversing gear, and the negative lead would soon change to a positive one.

Len Labram's 5in. gauge G.W.R. 2-6-2T Firefly, class 45XX, a winner of the International Model Locomotive Efficiency Competition.

STEPHENSON VALVE GEAR OUTSIDE THE FRAMES

Although Stephenson valve gear is nearly always arranged inside the frames of the locomotive, there is no reason why it should not be placed outside the frames, to operate the valves of the typical outside type of cylinder with valves on top.

One of the Stanier 4-6-0 class fives, No. 4767, was fitted with a type of Stephenson valve gear resembling the Churchward arrangement outside the frames. The launch-type link was centre suspended, and the valve rod was carried at the rear end by a long suspension lever just ahead of the link, and at the front end by similar though shorter lever. Instead of the eccentrics used in the more conventional type of Stephenson gear, two cranks were used, attached to the main crankpin. The whole assembly was neat and unobtrusive, yet all parts were extremely accessible for

FIG. 78

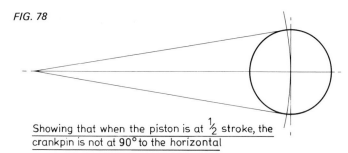

Showing that when the piston is at ½ stroke, the crankpin is not at 90° to the horizontal

maintenance purposes. This type of gear could be used on models with success provided that the main crankpin was made stout enough to carry the extra load, especially if slide valves were contemplated.

DESIGNING STEPHENSON VALVE GEAR FOR MODELS

Before the proportions of the various parts of the valve gear itself can be considered, the full-gear cut-off should be decided. In full-size locomotive work, the point of cut-off in full gear is usually decided by the class of work the engine is required to perform. A two-cylinder Contractor's type of shunting locomotive would probably be given a full-gear cut-off of at least 85% of the stroke, a shunting or goods engine 80 to 85% while an express passenger locomotives would be given about 75% if a two-cylinder machine, possibly less if a three-cylinder with cranks at 120 deg. The express engine would not of course be required to start and stop nearly so frequently as the shunting or goods engine, nor would the maximum load to be hauled be so great in relation to the theoretical tractive effort of the locomotive, thus an earlier cut-off could be used.

In the case of the model locomotive, which may be used equally on a fast continuous track or on a short up-and-down

line, it is advisable to make the full-gear cut-off fairly late. It is of course true that at late cut-offs the angle of the connecting rod in relation to the main crank is very small; even so, it may be taken that anything up to 85% cut-off is useful in starting a two-cylinder locomotive.

In any case, providing that the mechanical layout allows for it, and that there is sufficient clearance for the various parts, there are no disadvantages attending the use of a late cut-off in full-gear. There are, however, two distinct advantages: one is that a late cut-off gives full steam port opening early in the stroke, the other is that a locomotive so arranged has a more even turning movement at slow speeds, so that the tendency to slip at starting is reduced.

To obtain a full-gear cut-off of 80% of the stroke, the full-gear valve travel should be made 4½ times the lap of the valve; for 85%, the full-gear travel should be 5 times the lap. This ignores any lead that might be given to the valve, but with launch-type expansion links and comparatively short eccentric rods, the valves should have no lead at all in full-gear, but should be set "line-for-line" with the edges of the ports, with the cranks on dead centre. With locomotive type links and long eccentric rods, a small amount of full-gear lead may be allowed for and this would make the cut-off earlier.

PROPORTIONS OF STEPHENSON VALVE GEAR

If success is to be achieved, the various parts of Stephenson valve gear must be carefully proportioned and the following dimensions, evolved from successful working models, may be relied upon:-

1 Throw of eccentrics (for launch-type links) — ½ full-gear valve travel.
2 Thickness of eccentric straps – between 1/5 and 1/6 of piston diameter to the nearest round figure.
3 Motion pins – approximately 1/8 of piston diameter.
4 Boss diameters on links, eccentric rods and valve rods – twice motion pin diameter
5 Width of curved slot of expansion link – pin diameter x 1¾.
6 Thickness of expansion link – between 1/5 and 1/7 of piston diameter according to space available.

FIG. 79

Finding the correct length of eccentric rod. To make x equal to y the length of eccentric rod must be increased slightly.
L is the position of the die–block when the valve is central.

7 Distance between eccentric rod pins — full-gear valve travel x 2 for short eccentric rods, or x 2·125 for long rods (by short rods is meant rods of a scale equivalent of less than 4 ft. 6 in.)

8 Length of curved slot of link — eccentric rod pin centre x 1.6

9 Length of die-block in link — motion pin diameter x 2.125 to the nearest round figure.

POINT OF SUSPENSION OF EXPANSION LINK

The point of suspension of the expansion link in Stephenson gear makes a great deal of difference to the valve events obtained. On some models, the lifting link is attached to one of the eccentric rod pins. This however is not good practice, and is probably done to avoid the extra work involved in arranging a proper central suspension; it can only lead to unequal valve events.

In locomotive work, it is very important that the eccentric sheaves and eccentric rods should be fitted up so that the engine has "open" eccentric rods, so that the lead given to the valves increases towards mid-gear. To ensure that this is so, the right-hand motion of the model should be drawn out, to as large a scale as possible, with the right-hand crankpin on the back dead centre (for slide valves) or on front dead centre (for piston valves). The engine should be drawn with the front end to the left of the drawing board. When this is done, the outside eccentric rod nearest to the right-hand frame plate is the "forward" rod, and is connected to the top pin of the expansion link. The inside eccentric rod is the "backward" rod, and is connected to the bottom pin of the link. In this position, the forward eccectric will be up and the backward eccentric down, and the expansion link will stand exactly vertical to the horizontal centre-line of the motion.

If the engine has outside admission slide valves which are operated through the medium of a rocking shaft, the eccentric rods are connected exactly as described above, but the crankpin will be at front dead centre. If the crankpin is now moved to the back dead centre, the eccentric rods will appear to be crossed.

It should be noted that in the first case, and considering slide valves, when the crankpin is at back dead centre, the die-block and therefore the valve and valve rod have been moved forward by an amount equal to the lap of the valve; thus the lifting link or links will not be quite at 90 deg. to the horizontal centre-line of the motion, but will be inclined forward.

It is important that the expansion link should be suspended on its horizontal centre-line. This gives us several advantages. Firstly, the suspension point is never very far away from the die-block in any position of the gear, so that the lifting links always have good leverage to hold the link with minimum of link-slip. Secondly, the steam distribution improves and link-up decreases as the valve gear is "notched up" towards mid-gear, as this brings the suspension centre still closer to the die-block. Also, as the suspension centre is midway along the link, the steam distribution will be equally good in both forward and backward gear.

Another advantage of suspending the expansion link on its horizontal centre-line is that the swing of the lifting link is very small; this of course reduces wear, but more important, it means that there is very little swinging effect transmitted from the lifting links to the expansion link, which would otherwise tend to move the link vertically up and down on the die-block.

It is now necessary to decide upon what point on this horizontal centre-line to locate the pins for the lifting links. It is probably best to ignore the bad effects of link-slip and to concentrate on achieving equal or nearly equal cut-offs at each end of the cylinder at some predetermined point of cut-off. As most model locomotives are generally driven at between 40 and 60% cut-off (once properly under way) it is very convenient to choose 50% cut-off for this purpose, as the piston is then at the middle of its stroke.

As we know the length of the connecting rod, we can establish the upper and lower positions of the crankpin, and the valve will be at the point of cutting off steam.

There seems to be much misunderstanding about the correct radius of the expansion link in Stephenson gear, and also about the correct length of the eccentric rods. The correct radius of the link should be the distance from driving axle centre to the centre of the die-block when the valve is central over the ports. The length of the eccentric rods is then equal to this radius, if the link is of the

FIG. 80

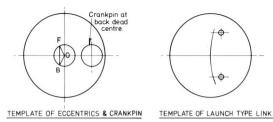

TEMPLATE OF ECCENTRICS & CRANKPIN   TEMPLATE OF LAUNCH TYPE LINK

locomotive-type, or this radius minus the distance between the centre-line of the curved slot of the link and the eccentric rod pinholes in the case of launch-type links. However, if the length of the eccentric rods is taken in this way, no allowance would have been made for the angularity of the eccentric rods, and to achieve equal leads for each end of the cylinder, a small increase in length in the eccentric rods must be made. This increase can be found on the drawing board as shown in Fig.79

To equalise the cut-off for each direction of piston travel, two transparent templates can be used. These can be made from tracing paper. One template should be of the expansion link and the other of the crankpin in relation to the eccentrics. Knowing the length of the connecting rods, the crank positions can be determined when the piston is at half stroke. The eccentric template is pinned through the axle centre and rotated until the crank is at each half-stroke position in turn. The corresponding eccentric centres are then pricked through and labelled.

Arcs are now scribed from each of the four points with a radius equal to the correct eccentric rod length. In the diagram, Fig.79 the point L represents the centre of the die-block in its mid-position (i.e. when the valve is central over the ports). The amount of the valve lap is now marked on each side of the point L, on

the longitudinal centre-line of the motion. When the die-block is at either of these positions the valve must be just closing to inlet steam.

The link template can now be used to find the position of the link when it pushes the die-block to these two positions. By pricking through the link pin centres at each of the two positions, the link's positions can be drawn in when the template is removed. All we need to do now is to find a point on an imaginary line parallel to the longitudinal centre-line of the motion such that the distance from this point to the centre of the curved centre-line of the link is equal or nearly equal for each link position. The point x is then the corrected point of suspension of the link to give equal cut-offs at 50%.

It should be emphasised that the correct point of suspension of the link will vary considerably according to whether the valves are slide or piston type (external or internal admission). It will also vary according to whether the expansion link is the locomotive-type or the launch-type. For locomotive-type links, the suspension will generally be very slightly ahead of the curved centre-line of the link; for launch-type links the suspension point will be behind the centre-line – further behind for slide valves than for piston valves.

When space permits, two lifting links may be used, one on each side of the expansion link, and suitable brackets should be riveted to the link to carry them, with the necessary clearance for the valve rod fork to embrace the die-block.

It is important in Stephenson valve gear, and in fact in other link valve gears, that all the eccentric rods are made exactly the same length, otherwise serious errors in the steam distribution may be caused. To avoid this, some form of jig should be made up. A suitable jig might consist of a length of flat steel bar of convenient dimensions on which is set out the overall length of the eccentric rods as accurately as possible; a silver-steel peg in then pressed in at one end, this being made a good fit in the eccentric rod forks; at the other end, a circular disc, turned to exactly the same diameter as the eccentric sheaves in use, is fitted, the disc being shouldered down and pressed into the jig. When each complete eccentric rod and strap will fit on such a jig, they will be re-

FIG. 81

DECIDING POSITION OF LINK SUSPENSION

latively the same length to quite fine limits.

It is also important that the lifting links are made exactly the same length, though this can be accomplished very easily by drilling the two components together. The lifting arms, which are attached to the weighshaft, must be arranged exactly parallel to each other and in the mid-gear position should be parallel to the longitudinal centre-line of the motion. The reversing arm, which is connected to the cab reversing gear by the reach rod, is generally, but not necessarily, arranged at right angles to the lifting arms.

Quartering driving wheels in the lathe, using a D.T.I.

the matter. With long lap valves and comparatively short eccentric rods, the valve should be set with no lead at all in full gear. It might be thought that this arrangement would give an engine lacking in accelerative powers, but if the engine is driven in the proper manner, starting in full gear with the regulator just open, followed by a reduction in cut-off and an increase in regulator opening as the train gathers speed, the best results will be obtained.

If long eccentric rods are used, the increase of lead towards mid gear will be less, and therefore a small amount of lead may be given in full gear, especially in the smaller scales. There are many variable factors which have a bearing on the amount of lead to allow, but if the lead is made between $1/10$ th. and $1/12$ th. of the lap, this will give satisfactory results in practice.

CONSTRUCTION OF STEPHENSON VALVE GEAR

The expansion links are probably the most important items in the valve gear, and care in their manufacture is well rewarded. The best material to use is "gauge plate" (ground water or oil-hardening carbon steel) which can be hardened just before final assembly. But oridinary bright mild steel, case-hardened, makes a good subsitute and is easier to machine.

The curved slot should be carefully marked out, cut and finished to size and the eccentric rod pin-holes drilled and reamed before the outside of the link is cut to shape. Although the curved slot can be cut by hand, by drilling and filing, this is not easy, especially in the larger sizes, and some kind of milling operation is to be preferred. If a vertical milling machine is available, the set-up for cutting this slot is quite a simple one. For those who must use the lathe, a specially made milling attachment is recommended. The author uses the attachment photographed. It is clamped in a large and heavy toolholder which bolts down directly on the lathe cross-slide, so that the whole affair is very rigid. The piece of steel which is to be used for the curved slots is first bolted to the radial arm of the attachment, the "lifting link" is attached, and the cross-slide moved into such a position that the centre-line of the "slot-to-be" is in line with the lathe

FULL GEAR LEAD

When setting the valves of a Stephenson valve gear, the problem always arises of how much lead to allow the valve in full gear. As mentioned earlier, with the normal arrangements of "open" eccentric rods, the lead increases towards mid gear. The amount of this increase may be calculated as follows:-

$$\text{Increase in lead} = \frac{c \times t \cos A}{1}$$

Where c = half the distance between eccentric rod pins.

1 = length of eccentric rods.
t = throw of eccentrics.
A = angle of advance.

It will thus be seen that the length of the eccentric rods as well as the lap of the valve has an important bearing on

Milling attachment for valve gear curved links, by the author.

should be taken to ensure that they are exactly in line and level with each other.

The making of the eccentric rods should present no particular difficulties, mild steel with case-hardened or bronze-bushed eyes being generally used. The holes for the eccentric rod pins should be drilled first and the slot for the link cut by means of a small face cutter mounted between centres or on a stout arbor in the chuck or collet. The eccentric straps, which are generally gunmetal or phos-bronze castings, are machined to suit the eccentric sheaves before attaching to the eccentric rods. It is generally advisable to drill and tap for the securing bolts before sawing the two halves apart, after which the jointing faces can be finished and the halves bolted together again temporarily and set up in the four-jaw chuck for boring the inside. The method of using a turned steel bar for gauging and, with paper packing, for machining the sides, described on page 88 is recommended.

Before fitting the eccentric straps to their rods, an assembly jig should be made up, as described previously. There are two generally accepted methods of fitting the rods to the straps. One is by slotting the strap, inserting the end of the rod and riveting through the two; the other, used in larger models, is to form a

centre. If the width of the slot is to be, say, 1/4 in, a 5/32 in. H.S.S. slot drill is used first, cutting the full length of the slot. This is followed by a 7/32 in. end-mill, which again cuts full length. Finally, the cross-slide is advanced 0.016 in. and then brought back 32 thou, to bring the slot to the full width of 1/4 in. A medium speed is used on this size of end-mill and plenty of cutting oil, enough to prevent the cutter becoming too hot.

If the radius of the curved slot is not too great, another method of cutting the slot is to clamp the material to the lathe faceplate at the required distance out from centre, and use a milling spindle. The bar used for the link can be made considerably longer than would otherwise be required so as to give a strong hand grip, the bar being swung against the rotation of the end-mill.

After the expansion links have been finished and hardened, they should be carefully checked for distortion. Although milling can also be used for cutting the die-blocks, in the smaller scales, the work of setting up for such a short cut may not be worth while, and careful filing should prove satisfactory. In the larger scales, the die-blocks can be end-milled as described for the link slots. Die-blocks may be hardened right out with advantage.

The link brackets are usually made from mild steel, case-hardened, and riveted to the link in such a manner as to allow working clearance for the intermediate valve spindle or valve rod jaw, and the die-block pin which passes through this. Where link brackets are fitted to both sides of the link, great care

Boring an eccentric strap.

head on the eccentric rod and fit studs to the strap for bolting the two together.

The weighshaft, which should be of stout construction, may be carried in gunmetal bushes into, or bolted to, the frames, and the lifting arms and reversing arm can be held to the weighshaft by means of taper pins through their bosses.

Generally, the valve spindles should be made adjustable for length, unless adjustment can be carried out between the valve and the valve spindle. The valve spindles should work through a regular packed gland, and a tail guide on the front end of the steam chests helps to prevent the valve spindles from sagging and keeps the valves square with the ports.

In full-size practice, it is usual to fit balance weights or springs to the weighshaft of Stephenson valve gear, to lighten the load on the reversing gear, but this is not necessary on models below about 3 in. scale.

THE GOOCH VALVE GEAR

The Gooch or stationary link motion bears some resemblance to the Stephenson gear, as two eccentrics mounted on the driving axle are used, but the expansion link is hung from its centre point and is not raised or lowered by means of the reversing lever; the link is also arranged with its concave side towards the cylinder end of the motion.

The valve or radius rod is raised and lowered by a lifting link attached to the weighshaft, thus reversing the engine or altering the cut-off in the usual way.

The expansion link itself is usually of the box type, consisting of two curved facing channels of radius equal to the length of the radius rod placed facing

one another, distance pieces being inserted at each end.

The expansion link is hung from fairly long suspension links, so that the rise of the link at each end of its swing shall cause the least interference with its proper movement. As the radius of the expansion link is equal to the length of the radius rod, when the crank is at dead centre and the port open to lead steam, reversing the motion simply lifts or lowers the radius rod and does not move the valve; thus the lead is constant for all positions of the reversing lever and open or crossed eccentric rods can be employed without affecting its peculiarities.

To minimise the slip of the die-block in the link, from which this valve gear is liable to suffer if allowed to get slack and worn, it is usual to modify the method of setting so as to make the distribution of steam more nearly correct in forward gear, at the expense to some extent of backward gear, and in practice this is done by suspending the expansion link with its centre just below the centre-line of the motion, the back gear eccentric rod being lengthened and the angle of advance of the back gear eccentric reduced to suit. Die-slip cannot be entirely eliminated as the radius rod has not the power to hold the die-block with the same vertical rigidity as the valve spindle guides often employed with Stephenson valve gear.

In the Gooch gear, the throw of the eccentrics is usually made equal to half the full gear valve travel required, or slightly more. The Gooch valve gear is easier to reverse than the Stephenson as only the radius rod requires to be moved, whereas in the Stephenson, gear, the expansion link and eccentric rods have to be raised and lowered, and the friction of the eccentric straps overcome.

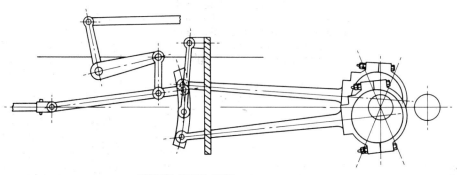

FIG. 82   GOOCH VALVE GEAR

A 3½in gauge Rob
Roy *0-6-0T by the late
L. A. Green.*

THE ALLAN "STRAIGHT-LINK" VALVE GEAR

In the Allan valve gear, both the expansion link and the radius rod are moved, when reversing, but in opposite directions, and as the action is direct, die-slip does not amount to very much. This motion uses two eccentrics on the driving axle similar to the Stephenson and Gooch gears, the eccentric rods being coupled direct to the top and bottom of the expansion link. The radius rod carries a die-block working in the link slot, the weighshaft having two arms, one on each side, coupled to the radius rod and the link respectively. The weighshaft is often placed below the motion, the arm coupled to the expansion link being attached to the top pin of the link.

The respective lengths of the radius rod and eccentric rods are proportioned so that the arcs described by the radius rod and link are always tangential to each other. Thus the die-block will move in a straight line when the engine is reversed.

Either a box-type or an open-type expansion link may be employed, the top eccentric rod pin being extended on each side so that the lifting links may clear both the link and the end of the radius rod. The radius rod should be made as long as possible if an accurate steam distribution is desired.

From the model engineer's point of view, the Allan valve gear is well worth consideration, the machining of the expansion link being somewhat easier than where a curved link is employed; but where space is limited and the radius rods and/or eccentric rods have to be on the short side, better results will be obtained by using the Stephenson gear with launch-type links and central suspension.

The Allan valve gear was used quite extensively in this country towards the end of the nineteenth century, a notable example being the famous Webb 2-4-0 "Jumbos" of the old London & North Western Railway.

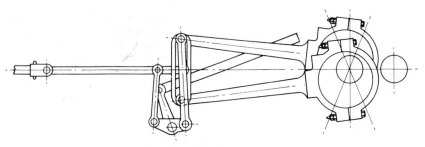

ALLAN VALVE GEAR

FIG. 83

CHAPTER FOURTEEN

Walschaerts & Joy valve gears

WALSCHAERTS VALVE GEAR

The Walschaerts valve gear, invented by M. Egide Walschaerts of the Belgian State Railway in 1844, was the most widely used locomotive valve gear from about 1920 onwards. It is one of the most attractive gears and also one of the most efficient if properly designed. It can be used either inside or outside the frames.

In this valve gear, the travel of the valve is controlled by two quite separate movements, one being that of the cross-head and the other that of an eccentric fixed on the driving axle, or in the case of an outside-cylinder locomotive, a return crank fixed on the end of the driving crankpin.

Walschaerts valve gear may differ a great deal in its mechanical details, especially in the design of the expansion link, its suspension, and the weighshaft arrangements.

Where slide valves are used, with outside admission, the combination lever is arranged so that the valve spindle is attached to it above the radius rod connection, while with the normal position of the die-block – in the bottom of the expansion link for forward gear – the return crank is arranged nominally 90 deg. in advance of the main crank.

With inside admission piston valves, the connections at the top end of the combination lever are reversed, the radius rod connection link being above the valve spindle, while the normal arrangement of expansion link means that the return crank is nominally 90 deg. in retard of the main crank.

Walschaerts valve gear is most convenient when the valves are above the cylinders, and the valve spindles are offset to the outside of the engine. In the case of inside cylinders, the offset of the valve spindles is usually towards the centre of the locomotive. Average valve spindle offsets are as follows:-

Gauge 1	$5/32$ to $3/16''$.
2½ in. gauge	$1/4''$
3½ in. gauge	$5/16''$
5 in. gauge	$7/16''$
7¼ in. gauge	$5/8''$

DESIGNING WALSCHAERTS VALVE GEAR FOR MODELS

As with all valve gears, the first things to decide are the proportions of the valves and ports and the full-gear valve travel required.

If the valve is required to open the ports fully in full gear, the full gear valve travel will be equal to the amount of the lap plus the port width multiplied by 2. But some designers prefer that even in full gear, the valve does not open the ports fully, on the grounds that the full width of the port is necessary to give a free exhaust, while for admission of the live steam, only ¾ or so of the port width is sufficient.

It is most important, in Walschaerts gear, that the swing of the expansion link is not made too great, otherwise it will be very difficult to reverse the engine, particularly if it is at rest at the time. This point applies particularly to the slide type of reversing. Generally speaking, the angle of swing should not be made more than 50 deg. – that is the total swing.

The combination lever is operated by the main crank, its attachment being usually made to the crosshead by a short

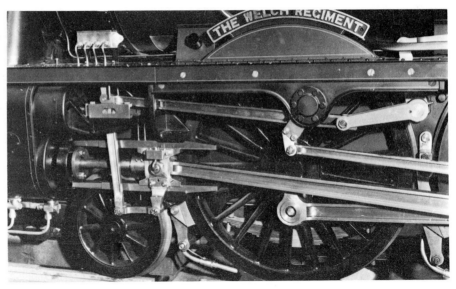

Walschaerts valve gear on a 10¹/₄in. gauge "Rebuilt Scot" by the late Louis Raper.

link known as the anchor or union link. In most British locomotives, owing to the length of the combination lever in relation to the other components, it is usual to employ an additional vertical link, fixed rigidly to the crosshead, in order to lower the rear end of the anchor link and this is generally called the drop link.

The movement of the combination lever is 90 deg. out of phase with the movement obtained from the expansion link. Independently of the position of the reversing lever, the valve is moved by the combination lever to an amount equal to twice the lap plus lead. In Walschaerts gear therefore, the first thing to do, after having decided the proportions of the valve, ports, lap and lead etc, is to decide on the dimensions of the combination lever, as shown in the drawing. Fig.86

For slide valves (external admission)

$$\frac{A}{B} = \frac{2 \text{ (Lap plus Lead)}}{\text{Stroke}}$$

For piston valves (internal admission)

$$\frac{C}{D} = \frac{2 \text{ (Lap plus Lead)}}{\text{Stroke}}$$

If piston valves with outside admission are used, the formula given for slide valves is used. The actual length of the combination lever is largely a matter of convenience, for if it is made too short, trouble may be experienced in arranging the top pins clear of one another.

We now have to settle the pitch circle of the return crankpin to obtain the required movement from the return crank. This of course depends on the movement we require from the die-block in the expansion link and this can be calculated from the following simple formulae:-

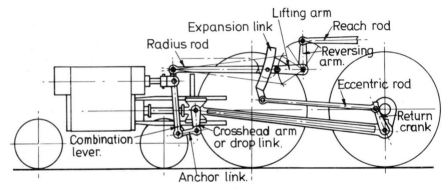

WALSCHAERTS' VALVE GEAR FOR PISTON VALVE CYLINDERS.

FIG. 84

102

FIG. 85

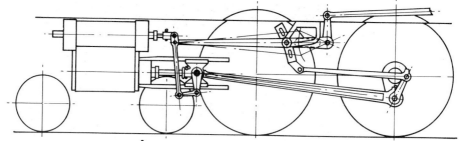

WALSCHAERTS' VALVE GEAR FOR SLIDE VALVE CYLINDER

For internal-admission cylinders.
Movement required from expansion link in full gear

$$= 2\left(\frac{R\sqrt{v^2 - 1^2}}{R - 1}\right)$$

For external-admission cylinders

$$= 2\left(\frac{R\sqrt{v^2 - 1^2}}{R + 1}\right)$$

Where R = radius of main crank (half stroke of engine)
v = half the full gear valve travel
l = lap plus lead

Having obtained the above figure, we can now obtain the pitch circle of the return crankpin. This depends solely on the proportions of the expansion link. In practice it will be found that a good proportion is that the distance the die-block centre is out from the centre of the expansion link when in the full gear position should be exactly half the distance from the link centre to the centre of the link tailpin (to which the eccentric rod is attached). In this case all we need to do is to double the above figure to give us the desired return crankpin pitch circle.

When modelling prototype locomotives having piston valves with inside admission, if it is desired to use slide valves trouble may be experienced owing to the reversed connections at the top of the combination lever. If the radius rod was to be connected to the lower pin, and at the same time, the radius rod was to be arranged so as to lie parallel with the horizontal centre-line of the motion when in the mid-gear position, it is almost certain that the expansion link and/or the lifting links would foul the connecting rod, and perhaps even the coupling rod. There are at least three reasonable solutions to this problem: the valve crosshead may be offset vertically, so as to raise the combination lever and its connections. If this is done, the provision of some kind of valve spindle guides might be considered. A second method is to arrange for the radius rod to be inclined downwards towards the combination lever, while leaving the expansion link etc. in the original position. This method is acceptable providing that the radius rod is a fairly long one. A third solution is to use a separate guide; a die-block which works in this guide is attached by a lug to the valve crosshead, while a pin through the middle of the die-block carries the front end bearing of the radius rod. While this method is thoroughly sound mechanically, its appearance may offend many model engineers!

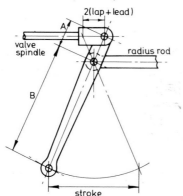

FOR SLIDE VALVES (external admission)

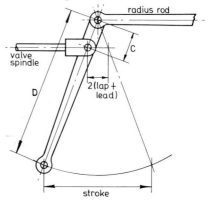

FOR PISTON VALVES (internal admission)

FIG. 86

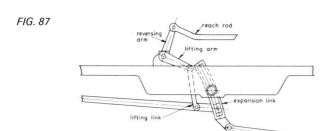

FIG. 87

S.R. TYPE EXPANSION AND LIFTING LINKS

reach rod

reversing arm

lifting arm

expansion link

lifting link

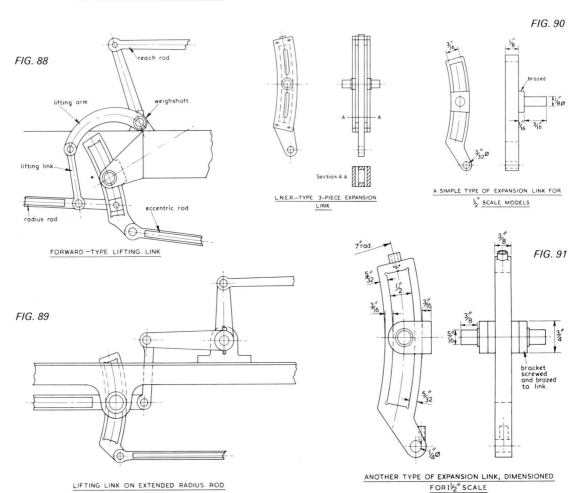

FIG. 88

reach rod

lifting arm

weighshaft

lifting link

radius rod

eccentric rod

FORWARD—TYPE LIFTING LINK

FIG. 89

LIFTING LINK ON EXTENDED RADIUS ROD

Section A A

L.N.E.R.—TYPE 3-PIECE EXPANSION LINK

FIG. 90

brazed

A SIMPLE TYPE OF EXPANSION LINK FOR
$\frac{1}{2}$" SCALE MODELS

FIG. 91

bracket screwed and brazed to link.

ANOTHER TYPE OF EXPANSION LINK, DIMENSIONED
FOR 1½" SCALE

ence to the setting out of the valve gear; the whole drawing may in fact be tilted to the required angle of the cylinders to simplify matters.

The horizontal position of the expansion link may now be decided upon and this should if possible be arranged half-way between the driving axle and the valve spindle crosshead. This arrangement ensures that both the radius rod and the eccentric rod are of reasonable length.

The design of the casting or framework which supports the link varies in almost every class of locomotive. The L.N.E.R. used a steel casting which projected from the frames between the driving and coupled wheels and then forward again to a convenient point for the link bearings. The design of such a bracket should be gone into carefully as with many types of expansion link it is necessary to be able to assemble the link

SUSPENSION OF THE EXPANSION LINK

Wherever possible, Walschaerts valve gear should be laid out so that all parts operate on centre lines which are either parallel to the horizontal centre-line of the motion or exactly at right angles to it.

The cylinders may be inclined for various reasons and this may have a slightly adverse effect on the valve movements due to excessive up an down movement of the driving axle, but it makes no differ-

FIG. 92

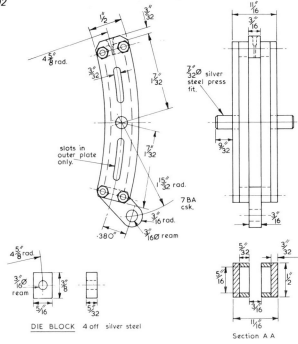

slots in
outer plate
only.

$\frac{7}{32}\emptyset$ silver
steel press
fit.

7 BA
csk.

·380"

$\frac{3}{16}\emptyset$ ream

DIE BLOCK   4 off   silver steel

5" GAUGE L.M.S. TYPE EXPANSION LINK

Section A A

lower part of the expansion link and the connecting rod, and also between the weighshaft and the coupling rod, when this is at its highest point.

It will also be found convenient to draw the whole valve gear in the front dead centre position, as it will then be seen whether there is sufficient clearance between the combination lever and the rear cover and stuffing box, with its gland studs.

BACKSET OF THE EXPANSION LINK

We now come to the design of the expansion link itself and the determination of the correct amount of backset for the eccentric rod pin in relation to the curved centre-line of the link slot. In most designs, it is a requirement that the expansion link should swing an equal amount on each side of its central position. It is sometimes argued that there is no such thing as link backset, the argument being that it is the length of the eccentric rod that determines whether the link swing is equal. However, as the usual practice is to make and erect the expansion link before determining the exact length of the eccentric rod, the backset is a most useful dimension. It may be defined as the distance between the centre of the link tail-pin and the (vertical) tangent to the curved centre-line of the link slot. While both the backset and the length of the eccentric rod can be calculated to a high degree of accuracy, the calculation is somewhat involved, and in any case there is not much to be gained by obtaining these dimensions to a very high degree of accuracy if the components themselves are then to be marked out using dividers and a steel rule!!

The normal graphical method, used by the author for many years, is to draw out the whole valve gear to as large a scale as possible – at least twice full size – and then draw the expansion link in its central position and also draw the arc described by the link tail-pin as the link swings. The return crank is also drawn, the length of this being given by the pitch-diameter-circle of the return crankpin (calculated as described earlier). The required length of the eccentric rod, and hence the amount of backset, is then determined by a process of trial and error, using a large pair of dividers or beam compasses, according to the size and scale of the drawing.

in situ, the outer support being placed into position after the expansion link itself.

Separate girder frames were often employed on the L.M.S., the frames spanning the space occupied by the driving and coupled wheels.

Walschaerts valve gear is best drawn out in both side elevation and in plan to ensure that the necessary clearances are provided, particularly between the

FIG. 93

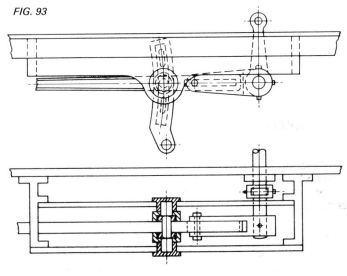

LINK SUSPENSION IN GIRDER FRAME

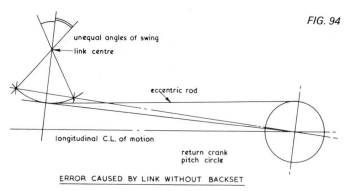

FIG. 94

unequal angles of swing

link centre

eccentric rod

longitudinal C.L. of motion

return crank
pitch circle

ERROR CAUSED BY LINK WITHOUT BACKSET

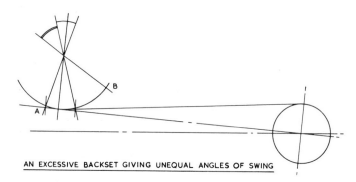

B

A

AN EXCESSIVE BACKSET GIVING UNEQUAL ANGLES OF SWING

In some arrangements of Walschaerts gear, notably in American locomotives, the "tail" of the expansion link is made longer, so that the eccentric rod pin falls on the horizontal centre-line of the motion, giving an "all-square" layout. With this arrangement, the backset appears greater than with the inclined connection more common to British locomotives.

In some models, the expansion link is cut from plain mild steel plate of suitable thickness, and riveted or brazed to its trunnion pin, this pin being on one side of the link only, the radius rod with a single die-block lying on the other side. This scheme is quite satisfactory in small models provided the trunnion pin is of adequate length. An improvement would be to use "gauge plate" instead of mild steel.

A better method for models over ½ inch scale is to arrange for a double bracket to be fitted to the link, each arm of the bracket carrying a trunnion pin; the radius rod is then forked to embrace the link itself. This method was used on many Southern Railway locomotives and is shown in Fig.87. If this design is adopted, the reach rod will be in the opposite position to that normally used, unless the upper quadrant of the link is used for forward gear — which was actually done on some locomotives.

Many railways had a preference for an arrangement whereby the radius rod is raised and lowered by means of a lifting arm behind the expansion link, and for this scheme, the link must be so designed that the radius rod can pass right through it. With this arrangement, there is little die-slip in forward gear, but this increases towards full backward gear. It does however, like the S.R. arrangement mentioned previously, mean that the weighshaft has to be sited rather high up, possibly above the level of the top edge of the frames.

Among students of valve gear design, one hears a great deal about "die-slip" (or link-slip). In Walschaerts gear, especially if the radius rod is raised and lowered by a swinging lifting link, die-slip is considerably worse in reverse gear, but as most model locomotives spend most of their time in forward gear, the matter can be ignored. As far as forward gear is concerned, a small amount of die-slip is always present where the slide type of reversing is employed (as in all Gresley locomotives and in some Stanier and B.R. types), and there is a small amount with the swinging lifting link gear, especially if the lifting link is unusually long. But the small additional wear due to die-slip can be ignored in models under 1 inch scale.

The sliding type of lifting gear, used mainly by the L.N.E.R. and L.M.S., is a good scheme, and has the advantage that the weighshaft position lies well within the frames, being in line with the radius rod when that rod is in the mid-gear position. The L.N.E.R. type of link consisted mainly of a single central member, slotted for the die-block, and two outer plates, to which the trunnion pins were attached, the radius rod being doubled where it passed through the link. Provided that the trunnion pins are

FIG. 95

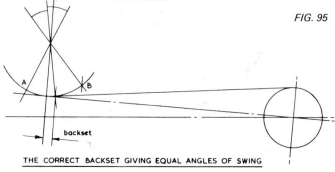

A

B

backset

THE CORRECT BACKSET GIVING EQUAL ANGLES OF SWING

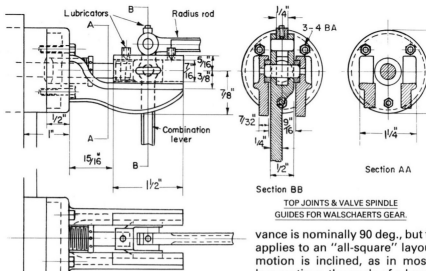

TOP JOINTS & VALVE SPINDLE
GUIDES FOR WALSCHAERTS GEAR.   FIG. 96

arranged exactly in line, this type of link is very satisfactory and not too difficult to make; it must however be designed so that it can be assembled in situ, as not only the outer link bracket member has to be attached after assembly, but the die-block must be put into position in the link slot, and the central member of the link slid into position between the two arms of the radius rod, before the link as a whole can be bolted up.

THE RETURN CRANK

The return crank is fixed to the outer end of the main crankpin and, with the die-block in the lower end of the expansion link for forward gear, is in advance of the crankpin for slide valve, external admission cylinders. The angle of ad-

vance is nominally 90 deg., but this only applies to an "all-square" layout; if the motion is inclined, as in most British locomotives, the angle of advance or retard will be more or less than 90 deg. by an amount corresponding to the inclination of the eccentric rod. It should be noted that there is a different length of return crank for a different return crankpin pitch circle, thus it is not possible to increase the valve travel of the valve gear concerned merely by setting it further out to describe a larger pitch circle; a new return crank of the correct length would have to be made.

The fixing of the return crank is an important point in model locomotives, as there must be no possibility whatever of the crank shifting in service. A good scheme for models of ½ in. scale and above is to split the lower end of the return crank, a clamping bolt being put through this just clear of the crankpin. After the return crank has been correctly set, a standard taper pin of suitable size is put through the middle of both crankpin and crank. This method ensure that, should the return crank have to be removed at any time, it can be replaced in its correct position without difficulty.

In full-size practice, the end of the main crankpin is sometimes squared, the return crank being clamped to this by a bolt immediately below the square; another method is to mill a slot across the face of the crankpin, the crank having a tongue to fit this for driving purposes, the securing being made by means of four set screws or studs. Neither of these methods can be recommended for model work, owing to the difficulty of obtaining the correct setting before machining either the end of the crankpin or the crank.

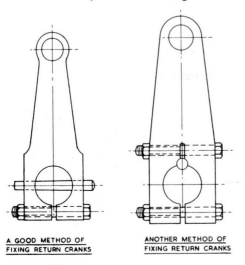

FIG. 97   A GOOD METHOD OF FIXING RETURN CRANKS   ANOTHER METHOD OF FIXING RETURN CRANKS

107

FIG. 98

A.   For all square layout

B.   For inclined layout

RETURN CRANK SETTING

The setting of the return crank in its correct position on the crankpin can be done as follows:-

The axleboxes are first jacked up to the designed running position – this is generally done by inserting strips of metal of the required thickness between the bottom of each axlebox and the hornstays. The expansion link is now clamped firmly in its mid position – that is such that the die-block can be run from top to bottom of the link without imparting any movement to the combination lever or valve spindle. The main crank is now set exactly on front dead centre, while the return crank is set as near as possible by eye in order that the return crankpin describes a circle of the diameter required by the design of the valve gear. With a pair of dividers (or beam compasses) measure the distance from the centre of the hole in the tail of the ex-

Machining the channel for Walschaerts valve gear links.

pansion link to the centre of the return crankpin.

Now shift the main crank around to the back dead centre position, and offer up the dividers again, without shifting them. If they tally in this position, the return crank is correctly set, and can be bolted up and pinned; if the dividers do not tally the return crank should be shifted by half the amount of the difference. The same process should then be repeated, and it should be noted that when the dividers do tally in the two positions, they give the exact length required for the eccentric rod, which can then be made and fitted.

Both sides of the locomotive should receive separate treatment as described above, owing to the possibility of slight differences in dimensions.

In recent years, miniature ball bearings and needle roller bearings have been used with success for the eccentric rod return crankpin bearings of larger models. If ball bearings are used, these may be of the self-aligning type with advantage. Needle roller bearings make a neat eccentric rod big-end, but for this type of bearing both the pin and the eccentric rod itself must be hardened. For models of 1½ inch scale and above, twin-row ball races or proper roller bearings may be considered. Such bearings generally have a much longer life than the more usual gunmetal bushes, especially if fitted with proper dust-excluding caps as in full-size practice.

The making of valve gear parts such as eccentric rods, radius rods, combination levers, etc, may sometimes seem rather laborious, especially in the larger scales, owing to the large amount of metal which has to be removed between the bearings. In large components, much time can be saved, in the absence of a regular milling machine, by first filing out a gap wide enough to allow a hacksaw blade to be inserted. After sawing, the component is finished by milling, the rod being clamped in a machine vice mounted on the vertical-slide in the lathe. Short levers may be dealt with in a similar way, the bearing holes being drilled and reamed first, when the lever can be held down on a stout steel bar, the bar being bolted to the vertical-slide, and an end-mill used in a collet or chuck.

The circular boss so often required at the ends of valve gear components can often be finished quite neatly by swinging them bodily on a pin against a small

FIG. 99

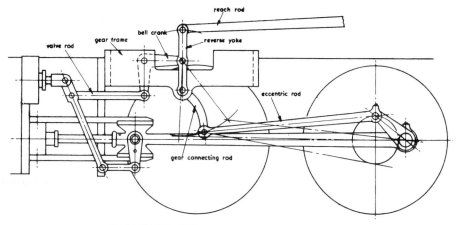

THE BAKER VALVE GEAR

end-mill revolving in the lathe. The pin required can be turned on the end of a piece of square brass bar, which is then clamped under the lathe toolholder parallel to the lathe spindle. When using this method, great care should be taken to swing the job in the opposite direction to the rotation of the end-mill, otherwise the end-mill may "catch up" and spoil the work. A similar method has been used where a suitable grinding wheel replaces the end-mill, though great care must be taken and only very light cuts used.

The pin-holes of as many valve gear components as possible should be bushed with a good quality bearing metal such as cast phosphor-bronze, but if this is not possible owing to the small size of the bearing, the eye of the component can be case-hardened and polished.

THE BAKER VALVE GEAR

The Baker valve gear, invented by Abner D. Baker of Ohio, U.S.A. in 1903, is a modified form of the Walschaerts motion wherein the expansion link is replaced by a system of cranks and levers. For a time it was popular in America and in some other countries, but was never employed on British railways, probably due to clearance problems.

The return crank is arranged to give considerably more throw than is usual in Walschaerts gear, and it drives an eccentric rod which is connected to a lever known as the gear connecting rod. This lever is in turn connected at its top end to a bell crank which drives the valve rod. The gear connecting rod is pivoted to

another lever known as the radius bar, which is itself pivoted to the reversing yoke.

As can be seen in the end section, Fig. 100, the reverse yoke is generally doubled and pivots at its lower end on the gear frame, which is bolted to the main frame of the locomotive. The fulcrum point of the gear connecting rod can thus be moved from its neutral position – in line with the radius bar – to a position either side of it, giving an angular movement to the bell crank and thus a longitudinal movement to the valve rod.

The Baker valve gear has always enjoyed a certain popularity with the model engineer, chiefly owing to the fact

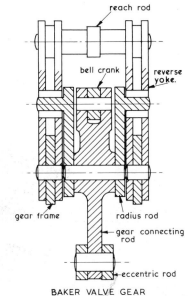

BAKER VALVE GEAR

FIG. 100   (section through gear frame)

109

that no expansion link, with its curved guides and die-blocks, is required. It is also comparatively easy to fit up, the necessary levers being attached to the gear frame which can be bolted to the main frame of the locomotive in a suitable position by angles. In the larger scales, all the pins in Baker gear can work in bronze bushes, so that these can be removed quickly and replaced when wear takes place. It is however important that all pins in this gear are carefully fitted, otherwise there will be considerable lost motion with a corresponding bad effect on the valve timing.

In comparing Baker gear with Walschaerts gear, it must be remembered that although there is no expansion link or die-block, and therefore no dieslip, on the other hand there are a large number of pins, upon which wear takes place, and, expecially when the eccentric rod is short, the return crank carries a considerable load. In Baker gear, the eccentric rod should whenever possible be made at least three times the return crank pitch circle. In locomotive designs where a short eccentric rod cannot be avoided, a smoother working will be obtained by the use of Walschaerts valve gear.

DESIGNING BAKER GEAR FOR MODELS

The author has been unable to find, in any of the model engineering manuals, textbooks or journals, any reference to designing Baker gear for any particular model locomotive, and as a result, the model engineer has had to resort very largely to the unwise practice of trying to adapt an existing design to his own particular case, relying on adjustments to the return crank to increase or decrease the full gear valve travel. In view of this, the following hints on laying out Baker valve gear may be found useful.

The full gear valve travel should of course be settled in advance, as previously described, as should the lap and lead, the latter being dealt with by the combination lever in exactly the same way as for Walschaerts gear.

The horizontal centre-line of the motion, the cylinders, the centre-line of the valve spindle, and the shape of the main frames, also the bottom line of the boiler, should now be drawn out, to as large a scale as possible. The centres of the driving and coupled wheels and their outside diameters should then be added, clearance being allowed for the rise and fall of the wheels in the horns.

Coming now to the reverse yoke, radius bar and bell crank, the horizontal position of these items should be such that the eccentric rod can be of reasonable length, at the expense even of the valve rod. The valve rod in Baker gear does not need to be so long, relatively, as the radius rod in Walschaerts valve gear.

The distances between the pins in the reverse yoke and radius bar are to a large extent settled by the proportions of the model itself, as already drawn — i.e., the vertical distance between the horizontal centre-line of the motion and the valve spindle, the distance from the former to the top line of the main frames, and the distance between there and the underside of the boiler. In the case of American prototypes, there is usually

FIG. 101

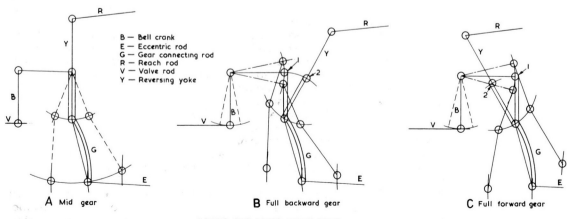

B — Bell crank
E — Eccentric rod
G — Gear connecting rod
R — Reach rod
V — Valve rod
Y — Reversing yoke

A Mid gear

B Full backward gear

C Full forward gear

LAYING OUT BAKER VALVE GEAR

ample room to allow these components being made of reasonable proportions.

A further examination of the gear will now show that the full gear valve travel obtained depends mainly on the following four factors:- the proportions of the bell crank, the angular swing of the reverse yoke, the pitch circle described by the return crankpin, and the distance between the bottom pin of the gear connecting rod and its central pin (relative of course to its effective overall length).

The swing of the reverse yoke should not be made more than about 25 deg. either side of the vertical, i.e. a total swing of 50 deg.

As regards the bell crank, although this is generally made with equal arms, there is no objection to the vertical arm being made longer than the horizontal arm, up to a ratio of about 5 to 4. In this way, the full gear valve travel can be increased quite considerably without the introduction of appreciable errors. A further point to note is that with internal admission cylinders, the lower pinhole of the bell crank may lie considerably lower than the corresponding front pinhole of the valve rod (i.e. where the valve rod is connected to the combination lever); even with slide valves, there is no objection to this within reason. This will be found to assist design, as it allows of more clearance between the front end of the gear frame and the valve rod itself, without any likelihood of the bell crank fouling any other part of the motion.

Coming to the length of the gear connecting rod, the bottom pinhole of this rod should not fall below the horizontal centre-line of the motion, in fact it may lie some distance above it, as is the case in Walschaerts gear on most British locomotives.

Having determined suitable proportions for the bell crank, reverse yoke and gear connecting rod, and their situation on the frames in relation to cylinders and driving axle, etc, the final work to be done is to decide upon the return crank pitch circle to give the desired full gear valve travel. Fig.101 shows a suitable graphic method. The upper and lower positions of the horizontal arm of the bell crank form the key to the situation. Having drawn in the position of the reverse yoke for full forward gear and full backward gear respectively, it will be seen that the middle pin of the gear connecting rod can only move on the arc described with "2" (Fig.101) as centre. As the longitudinal amplitude of the bottom pinhole of the gear connecting rod is at this stage still an unknown quantity, it will be seen that there are two ways of determining the extreme forward and extreme backward positions of this rod. The amplitude can for the moment be assumed, and trial positions drawn in until the pinholes coincide as required, or a simple model of the rod may be made up and applied to the drawing board. If the latter method is adopted (though this may not appeal to the skilled draughtsman!) a suitable model rod can be cut out very quickly from thin tinplate or even cardboard, and the three pinholes accurately drilled or pricked through. The top pinhole is then located on the pinhole in the horizontal arm of the bell crank, and the middle hole located on the arc previously mentioned; thus the three positions as seen in Fig.101 for the eccentric rod connection may be obtained, and the return crank pitch circle decided upon.

THE JONES' VALVE GEAR

The Jones' valve gear is a modified form of Walschaerts gear, having the feature of variable lead. An additional link having a curved slot is connected to the reversing arm and slides between fixed guides. The sliding die-block is restrained from horizontal movement by a guide link pivoted to the main frames of the locomotive, and is connected to the top of the combination lever by a link whose centre is fixed to the radius rod. When the reversing gear is moved, the die-block in the normal expansion link and the additional link are both moved at the same time, resulting in a variable lead which increases to a maximum in mid gear.

The extra complications of the Jones' valve gear does not seem to be justified, although better starting is possible, especially with two cylinder locomotives.

THE BEAMES' VALVE GEAR

The Beames' valve gear is a modification of Walschaerts gear in which the valves of inside cylinders are operated by an outside motion. This valve gear was introduced to avoid troubles that were experienced on certain locomotives fitted with Joy valve gear, mainly

FIG. 102

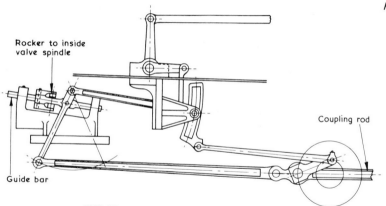

Rocker to inside
valve spindle

Coupling rod

Guide bar

THE BEAMES VALVE GEAR

failures of connecting rods carrying an intermediate bearing for operating the valve gear.

The lower end of the combination lever is oscillated by a rod connected to a forward extension of the coupling rod. The combination lever is suspended from a guide bar supported in a bracket fitted to the outside of the main frames of the locomotive. This bracket also carries a pivoted lever working through a slot in the frames. The outer end of this pivoted lever is connected to the guide bar and its inner end to the valve spindle of the inside cylinder. The return crank, expansion link and reversing arrangements are arranged as in a normal Walschaerts valve gear.

As troubles with the connecting rods are hardly likely in model locomotives, there does not seem much value in Beames' gear for model engineers.

GREENLY'S CORRECTED MOTION

Greenly's corrected motion, which can be used for both inside and outside cylinders, is based on the Joy gear, but uses a slide-shaft with straight slides. It was devised by the late Henry Greenly and has been used on a number of model locomotives with success.

The straight slides of the slide-shaft are easier to machine than the curved slides in the Joy gear; they can be milled from the solid by means of a face cutter, or they could be end-milled. In the larger scales, they could be built up from steel sections without any machining being done at all. This valve gear allows the use of pins of adequate size and is suitable for engines where the pitch of the boiler is not too low, owing to the space required for the slide-shaft. As far as prototype British locomotives with outside cylinders are concerned, this motion may be ruled out on the score of appearance, but it is well worth consideration for inside-cylinder locomotives.

The function of the correcting link is not only to carry the front end of the swinging link, but to lift it at each dead centre to the exact amount required to

FIG. 103

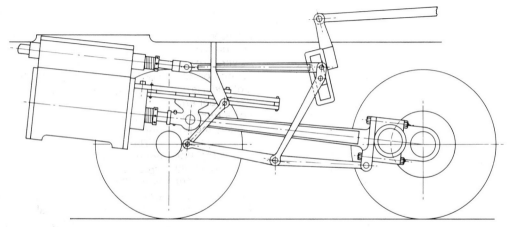

GREENLY "CORRECTED" VALVE GEAR FOR INSIDE CYLINDERS

neutralise the loss in height of the vibrating lever due to the angularity of the latter in these two positions.

The setting out of this valve gear should be done to as large a scale as possible, so that the necessary clearance for the various links may be allowed. The pivot point on the connecting rod should be decided upon first, then a point on the swinging link should be chosen that will lift the die-block sufficiently to open the valve fully to steam when the the slide-shaft is inclined to not more than 25 deg. from the normal vertical position. With the big-end on dead centre, and the vibrating lever swung to its furthest extent, a line should be drawn in representing the swinging link, and further along this link a point should be chosen for the attachment of the correcting link. The length and pivot point of this is chosen so that in swinging the lower end shall lift to coincide with the vertical movement of the bottom pin of the vibrating lever.

With a long valve rod, the steam distribution of this valve gear compares favourably with the standard Joy gear.

THE BAGULEY VALVE GEAR

The Baguley valve gear is an interesting and unusual gear which was used on some narrow-gauge and industrial locomotives. It is unusual in that it takes its drive from the main crankpin, no eccentric or return crank being needed. It combines features of both Gooch gear and Walschaerts gear in using an expansion link concave to the valve rod, and of the Kitson gear in supplying motion for the main port opening via an arm extened horizontally rearwards from the centre of the expansion link, while a method for providing the lap and lead motion is probably unique. A long lever, lying in an approximately horizontal position when at crank dead-centre positions, is mounted at its rear end on the main crankpin, and at its front end it is pivoted to a correcting link; the upper end of this link takes the form of a trunnion on which is pivoted eccentrically the pin on which the expansion link swings. The swinging motion of the correcting link thus provides a to-and-fro motion bodily to the expansion link which provides for the lap and lead functions of the valve.

From a point intermediate between the two ends of the long lever, a link connects it with the rear end of the horizon-

tal arm of the expansion link, which is thus caused to rock about its own centre, and thus provides the main port opening movement to the valve. Reversal or variation of cut-off is arranged in exactly the same manner as for a Gooch or Walschaerts valve gear, by raising or lowering the valve rod in the link.

The Baguley valve gear could be applied to either outside or inside cylinder locomotives and gives an excellent steam distribution.

THE JOY VALVE GEAR

The Joy valve gear was introduced by David Joy in 1879 for locomotive, stationary and marine work. It is not at all certain that Joy was actually the inventor of the valve gear that bears his name as a Mr. A. Verey, a marine engineer of Dover, was using a similar valve gear at least ten years before 1879.

The Joy gear was extensively used in this country at one time, especially by the London & North Western Railway and the Lancashire & Yorkshire Railway. It was mainly adopted for inside-cylinder locomotives, but was occasionally used with outside cylinders. The narrow gauge engines of the old Lynton & Barnstaple Railway used outside Joy gear.

The motion in Joy gear for inside cylinders is taken from the connecting rod through a system of levers, and no eccentrics are used. The connecting rod is constructed with an enlarged boss formed in it at a suitable point about one third of the length of the rod from the small end. This boss is bored out and fitted with a bush through which a pin passes, projecting on either side to carry the forked end of a lever known as the correcting link. The latter is coupled at its outer end to an anchor link which in turn is allowed to vibrate about a fixed point below the motion. This fixed point is generally a bracket attached to the motion plate; it may however be a frame stay or a shaft fixed across the frames, as is found most suitable for the particular engine.

The correcting link has a bearing in its central part to which is connected the valve lever, usually named the vibrating lever. This is further provided with two other bearings, one at the top end for the attachment of the valve rod, and the other close to it for a pin upon which work die-blocks which are able to slide

FIG. 104

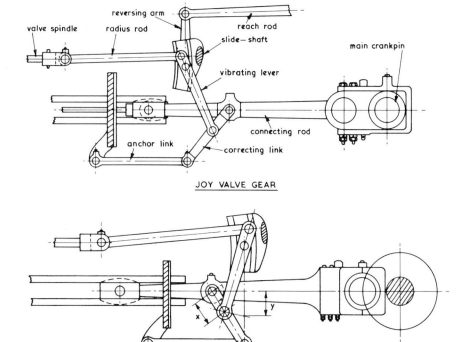

JOY VALVE GEAR

LAYING OUT JOY VALVE GEAR

up and down curved guides attached to the weighshaft, these guides and weighshaft being collectively termed the slide-shaft.

It will be seen that the vibration of the connecting rod when the locomotive is in motion moves the die-blocks up and down in the slide-shaft causing the valve rod to take a course depending upon the position of the guides. Thus when the slide-shaft is in a vertical position, the valve will have the least movement horizontally and the gear will be in mid-gear. On movement of the weighshaft, the guides are tilted, the top end towards the cylinders for forward gear, and away from the cylinders for backward gear.

In full-size practice, the Joy valve gear gave quite a good steam distribution where the valve travel was short, and the gear can be considered simple in construction and maintenance. The drilling of the connecting rod is perhaps a weak point in its design and this was in fact a source of trouble on some full-size engines, the connecting rods fracturing at this point. Another drawback to the Joy gear is the fact that it is affected by the up and down movement of the axleboxes in the horns. This latter drawback applies even more to model locomotives as

miniature tracks are relatively rougher and axlebox rise and fall relatively greater.

As no eccentrics are required with Joy gear, it appeals to the model engineer even though the slide-shaft with its curved guides is not an easy component to make. Where inside-cylinder locomotives for 2½ in. gauge and below are concerned, it will be found that there is very little width between the frames in which to accommodate the main cranks and the four eccentrics of Stephenson or Gooch gear, due to the out-of-scale width of axleboxes, crankpins, crank webs etc; thus Joy gear is often preferred.

DESIGNING JOY VALVE GEAR

When designing Joy valve gear for model locomotives, the first thing to be decided is the full gear valve travel required and the dimensions of the valves and ports. The next point to be settled is the exact position on the connecting rod to locate the bush and pin for the correcting link. As mentioned previously, this position is generally about one third the length of the connecting rod measured from the small end.

FIG. 105

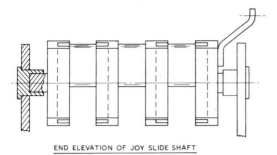

END ELEVATION OF JOY SLIDE SHAFT

The usual method of deciding the exact position is as follows:- the motion is drawn out to at least twice full size, according to the scale of the model, the horizontal centre-line of the motion and the centre of the driving axle being drawn in. The connecting rod and crankpin are now drawn in four positions – the front and back dead-centre positions and the positions where the connecting rod is at its highest and lowest position relative to the horizontal centre-line of the motion. It is now only necessary to locate the pinhole in the connecting rod such that its maximum movement in a vertical direction (vertical amplitude) is twice the full gear valve travel required, or very slightly more.

A vertical line should now be drawn at this position and this locates the correct horizontal position for the weighshaft.

The length of the correcting link can now be decided. Its lower end, which is attached to the anchor link, must be sufficiently far away to allow of the angle between its two extreme positions being less than 90 deg.

The anchor link should be made as long as conveniently possible, so as to allow the end of the correcting link to rise and fall as nearly as possible in a vertical line. It is generally more convenient to fix the anchor link to a point forward of the connecting link.

To locate the correct position for the weighshaft in the vertical plane, the following procedure can be recommended. On the centre-line of the valve spindle, mark out vertical lines on either side of the vertical line previously drawn (when deciding the position for the pin in the connecting rod) at a distance from it equal to the required lap plus lead.

To take an example – if the required lap is 1/8 in. and the lead 0.025 in. then these lines will be 0.150 in. on either side

of the original line, or 0.30 in. from each other.

Now assuming the crank to be upon its front dead-centre, and the correcting link coupled to the anchor link, choose a point in the correcting link, which has for the moment to be assumed, rather nearer its upper pin than its lower pin. Draw a line representing the vibrating lever from this assumed point to the intersection of the rear vertical "lap and lead" line with the horizontal centre-line of the valve spindle; where this line crosses the central vertical line is the position for the weighshaft.

In practice, the weighshaft is often placed a little higher than this, in order to give more clearance between the radius rod and the motion plate, and between the weighshaft and the central boss of the connecting rod. It should, where possible, be a little below the horizontal centre-line of the valve spindle.

The distance between the two upper pins in the vibrating lever is now also determined, as the upper pin is of course the point where the line representing the vibrating lever intersected the horizontal centre-line of the valve spindle.

The exact length of the vibrating lever is determined by the position of the central pin in the correcting link. This position must be such that when an arc the length of the vibrating lever is swung to the vertical centre-line (See Fig.104) then $x = y$. In other words, the length of the vibrating lever is best determined by a simple process of trial and error on the drawing board.

It will be seen that the centre of oscillation of the die-blocks and the centre of the weighshaft trunnions exactly coincide with one another when the piston is at either end of its stroke. Thus it is possible to reverse the motion from full forward to full backward gear without giving any movement to the valve rod. Thus the lead is constant in all gears.

The radius rod in Joy gear should not be made too short, while the radius of the curved guides in the slide-shaft must of course be made equal to the length of the radius rod.

In full-size practice, as has been mentioned before, some locomotives fitted with Joy gear experienced failure through the connecting rods bending or breaking; this is not likely to occur in models provided that adequate metal is allowed around the boss in the middle of the rod.

CONSTRUCTION OF JOY SLIDE-SHAFTS

The only item of Joy gear which might cause trouble in manufacture to the average model engineer is probably the slide-shaft. One method of making the curved guides is to clamp a suitable bar of steel to the lathe faceplate, its centre being arranged at a distance from the lathe centre equal to the radius required. A parting tool, ground with top rake and plenty of side clearance on both sides, is then set up crosswise in the lathe toolholder, at a distance out equal to the radius of the curved guides. Cutting should be carried out at the lowest speed available, a small depth of cut used and plenty of cutting oil provided.

Another method, which generally produces a better finish, is to use an end-

the four sections held to it by a small screw to each one. The sections are carefully lined up with one another and brazed to the weighshaft.

The reversing arm, which is attached to the driver's reach rod, is then fitted to one end, this usually being cranked outwards to bring the reach rod outside the frames, and the two trunnion pins, which work in bushes in the frames, are pressed home at either end. It is a good plan to make the overall length of the complete slide-shaft, measured over the trunnion pins, the same as the width between the frames, the trunnion bushes being put in from the outside and screwed to the frames. In this way, it is possible to slip the slide-shaft out from the frames without having to disturb the frames themselves or any components except vibrating links and radius rods.

FIG. 106

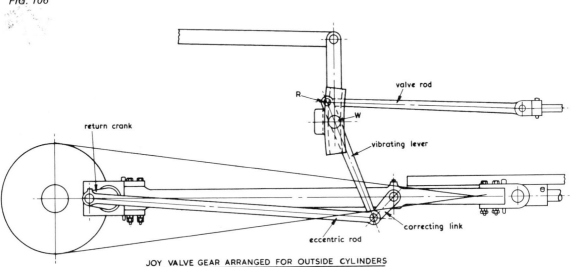

JOY VALVE GEAR ARRANGED FOR OUTSIDE CYLINDERS

mill or slot-drill held in a milling spindle attached to the lathe top-slide or cross-slide, the back gear being engaged and the faceplate slowly rotated against the cutter. Alternatively, the end-mill could be held in the 3-jaw chuck or in a collet, and the blank for the curved guides held on a stout plate attached to the vertical-slide, arranged facing the head-stock. The blank is then rotated on a pin at the required radius.

When sufficient "channel" has been machined in this way to make the four sections of curved guides, these are cut off and cleaned up to size externally; they should also be polished on their working surfaces. The weighshaft is then cut from rectangular steel bar and

JOY VALVE GEAR FOR OUTSIDE CYLINDERS

The Joy valve gear has also been used for outside cylinders, though this application was never so common as the inside arrangement in full-size practice. As it is not generally convenient to use an anchor link, attached to some fixed point on the frames, this link is dispensed with and a short return crank is fitted to the main crankpin. This return crank is made approximately one third the length of the main crank and is arranged 180 deg. out of phase with it. Thus the return crankpin describes a circle of radius approximately two-thirds that of the main crankpin.

To this return crankpin is attached an eccentric rod, and the front end of the eccentric rod is connected to another short link which works upon the pin in the connecting rod, as in the inside cylinder arrangement of Joy gear. The normal vibrating lever and slide-shaft are used, the bottom end of the vibrating lever being connected to the front end of the eccentric rod, and to the link mentioned.

The Joy valve gear is generally regarded as inferior to the Walschaerts when used outside the locomotive, as the number of components and pins used is approximately the same as in the latter type of valve gear, while the Walschaerts gear has the advantage that the lap and lead movement is quite separate from the eccentric or return crank drive to the radius rod, enabling a

FIG. 107

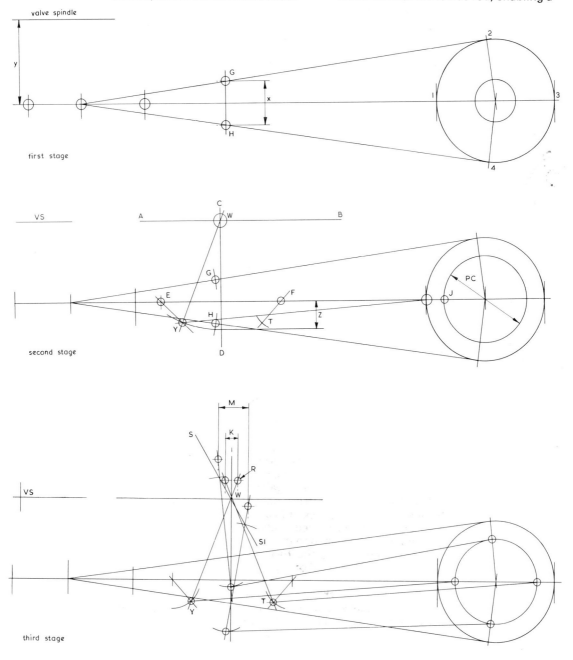

THREE STAGES IN DESIGNING OUTSIDE JOY GEAR

Baker valve gear on the Caribou 0-8-0 design.

The position of this correcting link pin is next marked for the four positions of the connecting rod described previously, i.e. points E.F.G.H. in stage two.

To determine the position of the weighshaft, a vertical line CD is drawn at 90 deg. to the horizontal centre-line of the motion and equi-distant from points E and F. The height of the weighshaft above the horizontal centre-line is generally determined by practical considerations, such as clearance for the connecting rod, proximity of the underside of the boiler, etc, but it may be placed a little below the horizontal centre-line of the valve spindle. (Point W in stage two).

Lines are now drawn from points E and F at 45 deg. to the horizontal.

To determine the length of the correcting link EY and at the same time the length of the vibrating lever WY, a trial position of the point Y should be chosen, such that when the vibrating lever is swung to the vertical (on W as centre) it cuts the latter at such a position that the distance Z equals the length of the correcting link EY.

Having determined EY, the correcting link is now marked off for the back dead centre position of the connecting rod, that is FT in stage two. The distance YT now gives us the required pitch circle of the return crank, that is, YT equals PC. The point J represents the position of the return crankpin when the connecting rod is at the front dead centre position, thus JY gives the length of the eccentric rod.

The next stage is to determine the lap and lead functions. To do this, the vibrating lever is drawn in the two dead centre positions, that is WY and WT, and this lever is then extended far enough above the weighshaft for the point R (to which the valve rod is attached) to move through a horizontal distance equal to twice (lap plus lead), i.e. K in stage three.

The final problem is to determine to what angle, each side of the vertical, the slide-shaft must be rocked in order to produce the required full gear valve travel (M). This angle should be decided upon by a simple process of trial and error, by drawing in a line representing the slide-shaft (S-SI) and seeing to what position R is moved when the connecting rod is at its highest and lowest position respectively.

An important point to note is that the total angle of swing of the slide-shaft

more accurate steam distribution to be obtained for both forward and backward gears. On the other hand, the Joy gear may have an advantage on certain narrow-gauge type locomotives, where the driving wheels are very small and the motion very low and near to track level.

Designing Joy valve gear for outside cylinders is not quite as straightforward as the conventional inside gear. Fig.107 shows, in three stages, how the design of the gear can be tackled. After drawing in the longitudinal centre-line of the motion and the line of the valve spindle, the connecting rod is drawn in four positions: at front dead centre, at back dead centre, and at the highest and lowest positions. The positions of the main crankpin and of the small end pin in the main crosshead are also drawn in, for these four positions of the rod.

A point on the connecting rod, for the attachment of the correcting link, is now chosen such that its vertical amplitude is equal to 1¾ times the full gear valve travel desired, or a shade more (distance x in stage one).

FIG. 108

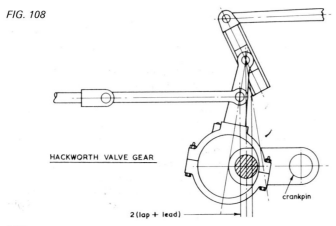

HACKWORTH VALVE GEAR

crankpin

2 (lap + lead)

should never be more than 50 deg. (i.e. 25 deg. either side of the vertical) otherwise there will be excessive friction in the slides. In the drawing (third stage) the angle of S-SI has been exaggerated to make the movements clearer.

If it should be found that even a total swing of 50 deg. does not give the desired full gear valve travel, then the only solution is to start at the beginning once again, and place the point of attachment of the correcting link on the connecting rod nearer to the big-end, i.e. increase the distance x in stage one. It must be remembered however that Joy gear is not an ideal valve gear for long valve travels.

While the drawings given apply to cylinders with outside-admission slide valves, the instructions for determining the proportions of the valve gear apply equally well when piston valves are used, except that the relative position of the main crankpin and valve crosshead are reversed by 180 deg., and the connections at the top of the vibrating lever are also reversed.

HACKWORTH VALVE GEAR

The Hackworth valve gear was invented by John Wesley Hackworth in 1859. It is one in which the valve motion is taken from one eccentric, which is fixed on the driving axle exactly opposite the crankpin, and has its eccentric rod working vertically, the end of the eccentric rod being attached to a die-block which slides in a pair of straight guides. These guides are pivoted, so that they

can be turned to an angle to the vertical by means of the reversing rod. At a suitable point in the eccentric rod, a pin is fitted for connecting the valve rod, the extreme end of which is attached to the valve spindle in the usual way.

When the guides are exactly vertical, i.e. the mid-gear position, the valve rod connection is moved through an oval path, the horizontal amplitude of which is made equal to twice the lap plus lead. In full forward and backward gear, the guides are rotated sufficiently to increase this horizontal amplitude to the required full gear valve travel. With this gear, the lead is of course constant for all positions of the reversing lever.

The Hackworth valve gear is a comparatively easy one to make and has few parts, but it cannot be recommended for model locomotives as unless the eccentric rod is made very short, trouble may be experienced in obtaining sufficient clearance for the guides underneath the boiler. At the same time, if the eccentric rod is made short, the valve events suffer. Another disadvantage of this gear is that the vertical movement of the axleboxes in the horns upsets the valve timing to some extent.

MARSHALL VALVE GEAR.

The Marshall valve gear is a modified form of Hackworth gear which was patented in 1879. A single eccentric is used, mounted on the driving axle, arranged in line with and on the same side of the axle as the crankpin. The eccentric rod has one pin at its end for connecting to the valve rod, and another between its extremities to which is connected a vibrating link. The opposite end of the vibrating link is attached to a pivoted lever which is moved by the reversing gear. Although the straight guides used in the Hackworth valve gear have been replaced in this gear by swinging links, the valve rod connection moves through an oval path similar to that produced by the Hackworth gear, and constant lead for all cut-offs is obtained because the fulcrum of the vibrating link and the point of attachment of the valve rod connection to the eccentric rod coincide in both dead centre positions. The drawing, Fig.109 shows Marshall gear for operating outside-admission valves; for inside admission, the eccentric centre must be moved in relation to the main crankpin through 180 deg.

FIG. 109

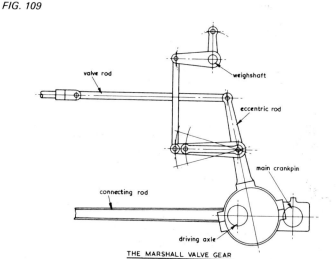

valve rod

weighshaft

eccentric rod

main crankpin

connecting rod

driving axle

THE MARSHALL VALVE GEAR

CHAPTER FIFTEEN

Valve gears for 3 & 4 cylinder locomotives

Many four cylinder locomotives used only two sets of valve gear to operate all four valve spindles. Where the two outside cranks are set at 90 deg. to one another and adjacent outside/inside cylinders at 180 deg. to one another, two sets of valve gear may be used with no more complication than a simple rocking lever having a fixed pivot approximately at its centre.

The valve gears may be outside the frames, as in the ex-L.M.S. "Pacific" locomotives, or inside the frames as in the ex-G.W.R. "Stars", "Castles" and "Kings". In the latter classes of engine, inside Walschaerts valve gear was used, the radius rods being forked to clear the inside valve spindles and their guides, while a bent lever connected the inside valve spindles to the outside via a differential screw.

There has been much discussion as to the reason for the offset in this lever in the four-cylinder G.W.R. locomotives. In fact the offset was introduced so that the

FIG. 110

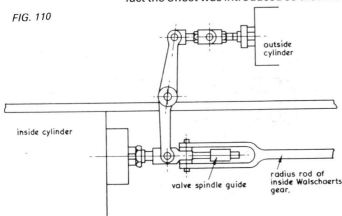

outside
cylinder

inside cylinder

valve spindle guide

radius rod of
inside Walschaerts
gear.

FOUR—CYLINDER ENGINE: INSIDE TO OUTSIDE GEAR

movement of the outside valve would NOT copy exactly that of the inside valve. The angularity of the connecting rod is responsible for the piston being an appreciable distance beyond its mid position when the crank is at half-stroke. In the case of the G.W.R. locomotives this distance is slightly over one inch. As the pistons of the inside and outside cylinders will be moving in opposite directions, one of them will be this distance before the mid-position and the other the same amount after, a difference of about 7½%. As Walschaerts valve gear at short cut-offs derives most of its valve movement from the crosshead rather than from the eccentric or return crank, the directly driven valve will be mainly in phase with its piston, but if the indirectly driven valve copied the movements of the other exactly, then when one valve was cutting off at say 45% of the piston travel, the other would be cutting off at about 52%. The G.W.R. arrangement of the offset rocking lever corrects this, but only approximately.

An interesting type of valve gear was at first fitted to the pioneer 4-cylinder express locomotive of the old G.W.R., No. 40, "North Star", designed by the great G. J. Churchward. In this engine, the valve gear was fitted between the frames, yet no eccentrics were used. The combination levers, as in the normal Walschaerts arrangement, were driven by the main crossheads. The levers to operate the expansion links, however, were derived from the opposite inside crossheads by means of a reducing linkage. This was possible because the main cranks of the leading coupled axle were at 90 deg. to one another; the gear

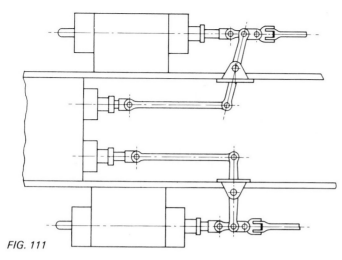

FIG. 111

FOUR-CYLINDER ENGINE: OUTSIDE TO INSIDE GEAR

became known as the Scissors valve gear.

Although this unusual valve gear proved quite satisfactory in service, the Scissors gear was dropped in favour of the normal Walschaerts arrangement in the later "Star" class engines. It is said that this was because of a protest received by the Great Western from the Midland Railway. Apparently Swindon was accused of making use of the Deeley valve gear without acknowledgement. Mr. R.M. Deeley of the Midland Railway designed a valve gear very similar to that fitted to No. 40, and in 1905 fitted it to the famous No. 990, a 4-4-0 type express engine. However, neither Deeley nor Churchward were really first in the field as regards this type of valve gear, for the valve gears originated earlier by

Stevart in Belgium and by Lewis and Young in the U.S.A. were examples of cross-connected valve gears with their movement derived from the main cranks at 90 deg. to one another.

For four-cylinder locomotives with the cranks set at 135 deg. (giving eight impulses per revolution of the driving wheels) the late H. Holcroft showed how the two inside valve spindles can be operated by a conjugated motion derived from the movement of the two outside valve spindles. Three levers were used, one being fully floating and the other two pivoted to the frames of the locomotive. In the diagram, Fig.113 the outside right-hand crank is set 90 deg. from the outside left, the inside left-hand crank is set 45 deg. from the outside right, and inside right-hand crank is set 90 deg. from the inside left and the outside left 135 deg. from the inside right. In the circle shown, a line is drawn connecting the O/L to the I/R. Another line is drawn from the O/R through the centre of the circle to cut the line O/L – I/R at F, and another line is drawn from the I/L through the centre to cut the line O/L – I/R at E. The valve motion consists of a rocking lever AOF attached to the outside right-hand spindle at A, pivoted to the frame at O and attached to the floating lever BEFC at F. The floating lever is attached to the outside left-hand valve spindle at B and to the inside left spindle at C. The other rocking lever DOE is attached to the inside left spindle at D, pivots on the frame at O and connects to the floating lever at E.

While the Holcroft conjugated gear is a very clever solution, it is not likely to

FIG. 112

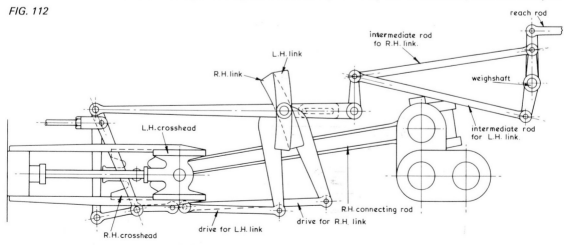

CHURCHWARD'S "SCISSORS" VALVE GEAR

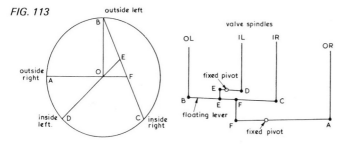

FIG. 113

DIAGRAM OF HOLCROFT ARRANGEMENT FOR 4 CYLINDER ENGINE,
CRANKS AT 135°

levers connected to the two outside valve gears of a three-cylinder locomotive were devised by the late Sir Nigel Gresley and by the late H. Holcroft. The well-known Gresley gear utilises a long lever having a fixed pivot and a short floating lever. The former is made with its pinholes spaced in the proportion 2 : 1, while the floating lever is made 1 : 1. The cranks of the engine must be set at 120 deg., although if the inside cylinder

FIG. 114

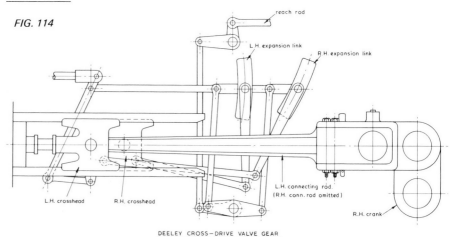

DEELEY CROSS—DRIVE VALVE GEAR

appeal to many model engineers owing to its complication, while its weakness seems to be the very large number of pins required.

CONJUGATED MOTIONS FOR THREE-CYLINDER LOCOMOTIVES

Conjugated motions for operating the valves of the inside cylinder by means of

is inclined at a different angle to the outside cylinders, allowance for this difference must be made when adjusting the driving wheels on the crank axle.

The Gresley gear was used on a very large number of L.N.E.R. locomotives with great success, although when the standard of engine maintenance fell during the 1939-45 War, the conjugation was not quite so effective owing to wear in the various pins and possible weaknesses in the outside gears.

On most of the L.N.E.R. locomotives, the valve spindles of the outside cylinders were extended beyond the front of the cylinders so that a connection could be made to the two-to-one levers. With this arrangement, the expansion of the outside cylinder valve spindles had to be allowed for, but on the 4-4-0 "Shire" and "Hunt" classes and on the 4-6-0 "Sandringham" class, the connections were made at the rear of the cylinders, so this problem did not arise.

While the Gresley gear is quite satisfactory in model locomotives, it is important that the cranks be accurately set and that there be no appreciable lost motion in the various pins, otherwise the events on the inside valve will suffer.

FIG. 115

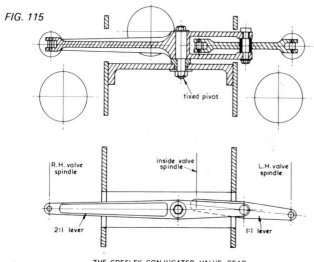

THE GRESLEY CONJUGATED VALVE GEAR

CHAPTER SIXTEEN

Cab reversing gears, valve setting, the indicator

The cab reversing gear of most full-size locomotives was generally of the screw type, though some goods and shunting engines used a long lever attached directly to the bridle or reach rod. As operating the reversing gear on many locomotives proved an arduous task for the driver, coming on top of all his other duties, some railway companies provided power reversing, either by the use of steam from the boiler or by using compressed air from the Westinghouse brake system.

In model locomotives, the screw type is easier and quicker to make and gives a finer adjustment of cut-off. However, where the engine may be required to work mainly on a short up-and-down line, the hand lever is to be preferred.

The screw type can be made reasonably quick to operate if a two-start coarse thread is adopted.

The whole reversing gear should be made quite rigid, the stand being of stout material bolted direct to the engine frames wherever possible. The stand is sometimes riveted to the frames, but this cannot be recommended as it may prove necessary, at a later stage of the building of the locomotive, or during a major overhaul, to remove it altogether. In most types of locomotive, it is usually essential to offset the longitudinal centre-line of the reversing gear away from the frame, so as to bring the lever or screw nearer to the adjacent cab side and clear of the backhead fittings. This can be accomplished by putting a "set" in the stand, or by using a thick spacing piece between frame and stand.

Where a screw reverse is used, the nut itself must be a good fit on the thread and may be made of gunmetal or phosphor-bronze, the screw being cut from a good-quality steel, a left-hand thread being preferable. The nut can be arranged to slide in guides to prevent any rocking motion being imparted to it.

The choice of left or right-hand drive is usually influenced by the arrangement on the full-size locomotive, but if the hand lever type of reversing gear is selected, it will be found easier to operate, at least in the smaller scales, if it is put on the left.

The reach rod, if made to scale dimensions, will probably whip quite considerably; it should therefore be made of fairly heavy section and can be of greater depth towards the middle. On large locomotives of one inch scale and bigger, an intermediate guide or support

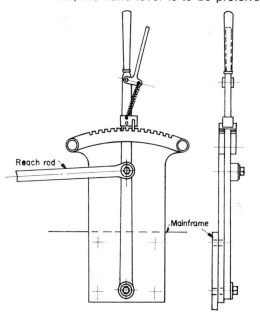

FIG. 116

Reach rod

Mainframe

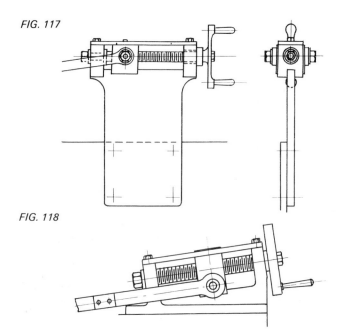

FIG. 117

FIG. 118

may be fitted with advantage, about halfway along its length, allowance being made for the slight radial movement of the reversing arm and lever.

The location of the notches in the lever type of reverse gear may be done by moving the reversing lever forward very slowly, while turning the wheels in a forward direction. When the position of the lever is such that the valves are receiving their designed full gear travel, the lever is clamped and the position of the full forward gear notch marked out. At the same time, it is very important to check that in this position, the die-block of the valve gear does not foul the end of the slot in the expansion link, or in the case of a Joy gear, that the die-block does not run out beyond the end of its curved guides.

The operation is now repeated for backward gear, and the position for full backward gear marked out. For the mid gear position, the lever is moved to such a position that no longitudinal movement is given to the radius rod by the expansion link (in the case of Walschaerts and similar gears). Where Stephenson gear is used, the lever is moved to such a position that the movement of the valve rod or intermediate valve rod, or for that matter the valve spindle itself, is at a minimum. The location of the intermediate notches on the sector plate can then be marked out between the full and mid gear notches as convenient.

VALVE SETTING

Some mention was made of valve setting when dealing with the Stephenson valve gear. The purpose of valve setting is to get the valve events as close to the theoretical movements as possible and to equalise as nearly as possible the steam distribution for the front and back ports. In this connection, it is worth remembering that on tender locomotives, which normally work only in forward gear, it is common practice to adjust the valve gear to give the best possible steam distribution in forward gear, but mainly at a point of cut-off normally used when the locomotive is running fast, even though this may be at the expense, to some extent, of the steam distribution in backward gear.

While careful valve setting is most important, it should be realised that however accurately it is done, it cannot correct errors that may be inherent in the design of the valve gear itself; in other words, if the parts (for instance in Walschaerts gear) such as the combination lever, expansion link, return crank or eccentric rod, etc. etc. are not properly designed and dimensioned, no amount of juggling with the position of the valve on its spindle will correct matters.

In model locomotive work, it is usual to set the valves to equal leads at each end of the cylinder, this being probably the easiest method. But a better steam distribution is usually obtained by setting the valves to give equal cut-offs at each end of the cylinder, at a point of cut-off which might be used for steady running with a load – for instance about 50%. In the case of slide valve cylinders, it is usually possible to observe the movement of the valve in relation to the ports once the top cylinder cover has been removed. Where the engine is of the inside cylinder type with the steam chests between the bores, it is advisable to provide valve setting holes in the steam chest wall, these being made as large as possible and closed, after valve setting has been completed, by plugs screwed to a fine thread. In piston valve cylinders, similar valve setting holes can be provided on the outside of the cylinder wall, the centres of such holes being made to coincide with the edge of the steam ports, so that it can be seen from the outside when the ports are "cracking".

A model of Natal II, *one of the first locomotives in South Africa, by Basil Palmer.*

CYLINDER INDICATORS

The indicator provides a graphic record of what is accomplished by the steam in the cylinder. It is connected by specially drilled holes to the clearance spaces at each end of the cylinder. The pressure in the cylinder at any given moment is allowed to act upon a small piston, which forms part of the indicator and transmits its movements through a system of levers to a recording pencil and drum.

Each indicator diagram shows the distribution of the steam at one end of the cylinder during one revolution.

Fig. 119 shows an ideal steam distribution diagram for a piston moving in the direction of the arrow. The straight line at the bottom is the atmospheric line which is drawn before the steam enters the cylinder. Directly the steam is admitted at A, the pencil goes up to B, which is the highest pressure reached in the cylinder. The valve now closes again, at C, at which point the steam is cut off. From B to C therefore represents the period of admission.

After the steam has been cut off, there is a gradual pressure drop, and this is the period of expansion which ends at D, the point of release, when the exhaust is

FIG. 119

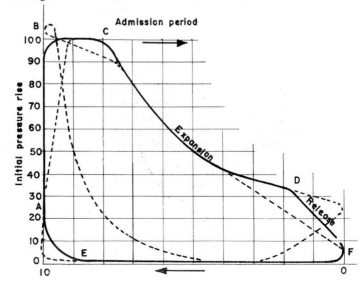

opened. At this point, the pressure drops rapidly and then remains close to the atmospheric line until the piston reaches E. The exhaust then closes, compression begins and pressure rises until the valve once again opens to steam at A.

The indicator diagram shows clearly the economy effected by working at early cut-offs. The diagram will also expose inefficient steam distribution or a faulty valve setting. Such defects are shown in Fig. 119 by a dotted line. A sloping admission line from A to B shows a delay in the opening of the valve, as the piston would have moved a short distance before the full pressure had become effective. If the valve had opened too early, the same line would slope in the other direction.

A line falling from B to C would indicate a throttling of the steam during the admission period. If release takes place too early in the stroke, the line would fall away just before the point D, while if release is too late in the stroke the expansion line would be continued too far towards the end of the stroke and the correct amount of back pressure would not be attained until the piston had moved some way on its return journey.

A too early closing of the exhaust causes excessive compression which could in some cases exceed steam-chest pressure, causing a loop in the diagram at B. If the exhaust valve closes too late, a sharp bend will appear in the line between E and A, compression being insufficient.

The indicator diagram is also used to compute the amount of work done in the cylinders. The indicated horse-power is obtained by multiplying the mean effective pressure (obtained from the diagram) in pounds per square inch, by the area of the piston in square inches, by the speed of the piston in feet per minute, and dividing the product by 33,000.

The big problem in applying the indicator diagram to model locomotive cylinders is the great amount of steam that would be required to operate even the lightest form of indicator. However, an article in the "Model Engineer" (March 6th. 1970) described a novel method of obtaining indicator diagrams. The pressure in the cylinder was measured by a miniature silicon pressure transducer, pressure being converted into an electric voltage. This voltage was applied to the vertical input on a high gain D.C. cathode ray oscilloscope, whilst the output of a crosshead potentiometer, which gave out a D.C. voltage proportional to the piston stroke, was applied to the horizontal input on the same cathode ray oscilloscope.

In order to record the indicator diagram displayed on the oscilloscope, a special Polaroid camera was attached, the advantage of this being that the photographic results could be examined very quickly.

Close-up of the Caprotti valve gear on D. L. Evans' 7¹/₄ in. gauge Duke of Gloucester. *Note fully working universal joints, cam box and cannon axles*

CHAPTER SEVENTEEN

Boilers

Many highly skilled model engineers who would think little of designing and building a four-cylinder locomotive chassis seem to fight shy of tackling the boiler. Perhaps this is because the type of work required in boiler-making is very different from machine work; even the tools required, though actually very simple, are quite different. Again, it may be that there are few formulae available that would assist the would-be model boiler designer. The design of the model locomotive boiler, although based on that fitted to the full-size engine, needs considerable modification and care in design if it is to be efficient as a steam raiser and safe and reliable in service. Nevertheless, a careful study of both successful full-size and model boilers helps one a great deal to grasp the essentials of good design and points out the pitfalls to be avoided.

Simple boilers for Gauges "0" and "1".

The majority of model locomotives built for the smaller gauges – "0" and "1" – are fitted with simple water-tube boilers. The plain "pot" boiler without any water tubes is generally used only in the "semi-toy" type of model and need not concern us here. As far as water-tube boilers are concerned, the following points may help to achieve success:-

1. The barrel should be of seamless copper tube, as thin as possible consistent with safety.

2. The water tubes should be of thin gauge seamless copper.

3. The water tubes should be of reasonable diameter and not spaced too closely

4. The water tubes should be fitted so that they slant downwards from the front of the barrel and be silver-soldered directly to it. They should not be bent up close to the barrel as this prevents the heat from the burners reaching the whole of the underside of the barrel.

5. No soft solder must be used in construction.

6. The ends of the barrel, except for

A splendid ¾in. scale "Britannia" boiler by B. Palmer.

diameters under 2 inch, must be stayed, and they should be of thicker material than the barrel.

7. The barrel should not be too small in relation to the outer casing.

8. The outer casing may with advantage be of steel and lined with asbestos to minimise heat losses.

9. Bushes made of gunmetal may be silver-soldered into the boiler for any fitting required.

10. Where possible, a dome should be fitted, near to the middle of the barrel, to ensure dry steam.

11. The main steam pipe may be passed through the flames to provide some degree of superheating.

For the guidance of the beginner, the following may be taken as suitable dimensions for small water-tube boilers working at 60 to 80 pounds per square inch:-

Outer casing	1¾" dia.	2" dia.	2¼" dia.	3" dia.
Barrel	1¼ x 20 swg	1½ x 20 swg	1¾ x 20 swg	2¼ x 18 swg
End plates	18 swg	18 swg	16 swg	16 swg
Centre stay	nil	1 x ⅛"	1 x 5/32	1 x 3/16
Water tubes	2 x 5/32	3 x 5/32	3 x 3/16	4 x ¼

The ends of the barrel should, for preference, be flanged inwards, which will be found convenient for silver-soldering. In order to fit the tubes at the front end of the barrel, a hole should be drilled and then elongated by inserting a piece of steel rod of the same diameter as the tube and forcing it over to the angle required. This operation will be found

This 5in. gauge Springbok is the work of Alan Fay.

much easier if the barrel is annealed first by heating it to a dull red and allowing to cool.

To give more space for the attachment of fittings the water space at the rear end of the boiler may be continued below the barrel by means of a throatplate and a deeper backhead, the lower ends of the water tubes being silver-soldered into the throatplate.

LOCOMOTIVE TYPE BOILERS.

Although the simple water-tube boiler gives quite good results for Gauge "0" and "1" models, there is no doubt that for models of ½ in. scale and above, the extra work and expense involved in building the proper locomotive type boiler is fully justified, and the final result much more satisfying.

The normal locomotive type boiler consists of a barrel fitted to an internal firebox located at the rear of the engine, the furnace being fitted with firegrate and ashpan below. The products of combustion pass through the barrel to the smokebox via a number of small diameter tubes. Thus the inner firebox, containing the source of heat, is completely surrounded by the water. The so-called "dry-back" type of locomotive boiler should be avoided as too much valuable heating surface is lost, and difficulty is met in finding room for the various fittings, water-gauge, blower valve etc.

There are two main types of locomotive boilers;- those having a long and deep firebox narrow enough to go between the frames and those with a shorter but very wide firebox coming generally behind the driving and coupled wheels and supported by extensions

Roy Amsbury's prize-winning 5in G.W.R. 2-6-2 tank locomotive

from the main frames and by bogies or pony trucks. The barrel of the locomotive type boiler may be parallel or tapered. Several advantages are claimed for the taper barrel: the greatest cross-sectional area is obtained next to the firebox where the heat value is at its greatest. As the products of combustion are drawn through the tubes and flues, their temperature is dropping and it is therefore only natural that one should arrange for the volume of the water to be heated to fall in unison. Another advantage of the taper barrel is that the end-to-end surge of the water in the boiler due to rapid acceleration or braking is less than in the parallel barrel, while the opportunity can be taken to increase the height of the chimney which helps to clear the exhaust from the locomotive, so preserving a clear lookout for the driver. (This last advantage does not of course apply to our small gauge models!).

Another variation in boiler design should be noted: the top of the firebox may be round, or it may be flat, or nearly so, the sides also being flattened; the latter type, known as the Belpaire, gives greater water and steam volume over the top of the furnace, thus it is basically more efficient as a steam raiser, though slightly more difficult to build.

MATERIALS FOR MODEL LOCOMOTIVE BOILERS

In the author's opinion, the ideal metal to use in model boiler construction is copper, at least up to and including models of 1½ in. scale. With the present high cost of copper, steel is sometimes considered. But while steel is a practical choice for models of 1½ in. scale and larger, it is definitely not recommended for smaller boilers. This is mainly due to the problem of corrosion, as steel boilers, in certain conditions, can rust very quickly, especially if the feed water used is at all acidic. Even on 1½ in. scale boilers, both barrel and plates should be an absolute minimum thickness of ⅛ in., while 5/32 in. or 4mm. is certainly desirable.

Another disadvantage of the steel boiler is the difficulty of flanging the metal, while if flanges are dispensed with, all joints have to be welded, and this calls, in most cases, for qualified assistance. All in all, then, copper should be the model engineer's choice.

Stainless steel has been suggested for model locomotives boilers, and some boilers have been constructed entirely in this metal with apparent success. Nevertheless, there seems no advantage in the use of stainless steel as it is generally at least as expensive as copper and sometimes more difficult to obtain in small quantities. Further, it is a difficult metal to braze, calling for special fluxes etc. Its greater strength for a given thickness is really no advantage, as most steam locomotives are on the light side, so that a lighter boiler will result in a lower adhesive weight.

BRAZING EQUIPMENT

At one time, the principal source of heat for the brazing of model boilers, at least as far as the amateur was concerned, was the paraffin (kerosene) blowlamp. The largest size in general use was of 5 or 6 pint capacity, and this size was capable of producing enough heat to deal with most boilers in the ¾ to 1 in. scale range.

But few model engineers today would wish to resort to paraffin blowlamps, the very large sizes being somewhat frightening things to use!

Another type of brazing equipment that is well worth considering is the Air/Town Gas outfit. An air/gas blowpipe having a burner tube of around 1 in. dia. and provided with an adequate air supply, can comfortably cope with locomotive boilers up to 1 in. scale. The air supply will be from either a rotary blower, driven by an electric motor of about ¼ h.p., of from a compressor.

Perhaps the most popular and certainly the most convenient source of heat for brazing is the bottled gas equipment, generally using propane. Propane blowlamps can be obtained up to a heat output of around 180200 B.T.U., involving a gas consumption of 145 ozs per hour. But such a large blowlamp is not necessarily the most suitable for boiler brazing, whatever the size of the boiler; the flame is so large and the heat so great that the work becomes uncomfortable, to say the least; the large flame also tends to obscure the point to which the brazing alloy is to be applied.

For boilers from ½ in. to 1 in. scale, the most suitable propane blowpipe would be one of about 87000 B.T.U., with a gas consumption of around 70 ozs. per hour.

At normal room temperatures, the gas pressure in a propane cylinder is between 100 and 142 p.s.i. (7-10 kp/cm^2). The burners, however, work on a pressure between 14 and 56 p.s.i., so that a pressure reducing valve must be used, and this is generally combined with a hose failure valve; this is a valve which automatically cuts off the gas supply in the event of hose breakage.

Although small gas cylinders can be obtained from the manufacturers of propane blowpipes, these are too small for boiler work in the ½ to 1 in. scale range, and the model engineer is advised to obtain one of the large industrial propane cylinders from the local agent or garage. These large cylinders are generally supplied on a rental and exchange basis.

After the model engineer has equipped himself with a suitable brazing torch, a brazing stand or forge will be required. A convenient size of locomotive boiler up to the larger ¾ in. scale sizes would be around 30 in. long x 15 in. wide x 10 in. deep, the side nearest the operator being left open. Such a brazing stand can be quickly made up using C.R.C.A. steel sheet about 16 SWG thick, bolted to steel angles, to bring the base up to a reasonable working height, say about 2 ft. 6 in. It is a good plan to cut a circular hole in the middle of the floor of such a diameter that the barrel of the largest boiler contemplated may be put through, this hole being normally covered by a flat plate. The idea of this is so that the boiler can be set up vertically when brazing the smokebox end, tubes

A circular-firebox locomotive by J. Andrews.

An experimental boiler for a 3/4in. scale "Pacific" by Arthur Hughes (U.S.A.).

etc., the bulk of the boiler being held below the level of the floor.

The brazing stand should be further fitted with some firebricks at the back and sides to deflect the heat back on the boiler being worked upon. A supply of coke is also useful when dealing with the heaviest parts of the boiler where the most heat is required.

Other items for boiler brazing include a large pair of steel tongs for lifting the boiler when hot – these can be home-made – and a length of steel rod, about 1/4 in. dia. sharpened at one end, which will be found useful for breaking up flux "bubbles" and to ensure free flow of the brazing alloys in use.

Equally important is some form of "pickling" tank, for dunking the boiler or parts thereof after brazing. A large rubber bucket can be used for the smaller boilers, while quite large rectangular plastic containers can be obtained from such stores as Woolworths etc, which can be used if care is taken. The acid for pickling should be Sulphuric. This can generally be obtained from the larger chemists. The commercial quality concentrated acid should be asked for, and this is diluted with water in the ratio 1 acid to 10 to 20 water. It is most important that the acid is added to the water, *never* the other way round, otherwise a severe explosion may result.

One of the most useful tools for model boiler work is the bending rolls. Al-though these can be obtained commercially, the smallest size available is usually too large for model boilers up to 1 inch scale. However, bending rolls are not at all difficult to make, as shown on page 26.

Another useful tool for model boiler making is the metal shears. Although a regulation "guillotine" is of very great assistance for cutting sheet metal without appreciable distortion, this type of machine may be beyond the resources of many model engineers. The ordinary hand lever shearing machine is, however, quite moderately priced or alternatively a suitable machine can be made in the workshop without much difficulty. The two cutting blades can be made from tool steel or ground flat stock, and hardened after all machining, drilling etc, has been done. The design of the frame of the machine should be such that the sheet metal being cut can be pushed forward in a straight line and continuous motion without fouling the frame. As the pivot pins of the lever, the connecting links and the cutting blade are subject to considerable stress, they should be made of a high carbon or nic-kel-chrome steel and of generous proportions.

Although with modern silver-soldering methods of boiler construction, not a great number of rivets are used, nevertheless a selection of rivet punches and "dollies" will be required. Standard

G.W. type taper-barrel boiler by the author. Note tube arrangement.

single punches and dollies can be obtained ready-made quite cheaply, but to get the best results in boiler riveting, builders are advised to make their own drawing-up punches and three snap punches for each rivet diameter (in most cases, the only diameters required will be $^3/_{32}$ in. and $^1/_8$ in.) The drawing shows what is required. The length of the punches can be about 4 in., and they can be made from silver-steel, with the "business" ends hardened and tempered to a dark straw colour. The top end should be well chamfered. For good riveting, the bodies of the dollies should be as heavy as possible, though slender ones are often unavoidable for certain positions.

A useful shape of dolly for small boiler work is one of an oblong shape, the snaphead recess being close to one corner. This will be found useful when riveting plate crown stays to fireboxes and similar operations. Another useful tool is the rivet jammer; this consists of two sets made from hexagon steel: one has an external thread, say $^3/_8$ in. BSF, cut upon its body, while the other is drilled and tapped to match so that the overall length of the two when assembled can be adjusted with spanners. The snap recesses can be cut in the lathe and then finished off by hitting with a hardened steel ball, the recesses being afterwards case-hardened.

When making rivet punches, the depth of the recesses should be made slightly less than the thickness of the heads of the rivets in use; this will prevent the punch from damaging the sheet metal around the rivet head. All sharp edges on both punches and dollies should of course be removed for the same reason.

Hammers for riveting should be of the ball-pein type, the flat ends of which should have slightly rounded edges; they will vary in weight between $^1/_2$ lb. and $1^1/_2$ lb. according to the size of the work being dealt with. Their working faces should be kept bright and smooth.

Other tools for boiler work include strong tongs for handling the boiler while hot, or for putting parts of the boiler into the pickle tank. These tongs can be home made from flat mild steel strip, the ends being heated to red and twisted through 90 deg.

SILVER SOLDERS AND BRAZING ALLOYS

It should be understood that there is no hard and fast dividing line between the silver solders and the various brazing alloys; it is mainly a question of their melting temperatures. Generally speaking, those alloys containing the highest proportions of silver are the most expensive, but as against this, are the ones that melt at the lower temperature and therefore are the most useful to the amateur boiler maker.

It is quite possible to build a thoroughly sound copper boiler using one type of silver solder only – the last two boilers made by the author involved the use of Messrs Johnson Matthey's

Easyflo No. 2. This is an excellent silver solder as it not only melts at a comparatively low temperature (about 608 deg. C. or a dull-red) but it is very ductile, highly penetrative and has good corrosion resistance, as well as having a high ultimate tensile strength. It will form fillets of reasonable size, not too large nor too small, on the work and its only possible drawback is that it contains a proportion of cadmium, which means that the user must be careful to ensure really adequate ventilation while brazing is in progess, as the fumes given off when this material is heated are dangerous.

There are occasions when a silver solder which forms a larger fillet has an advantage, the builder can then use such alloys as Johnson Matthey's Argoflo, Argoswift or Argobond, which have melting ranges of 607-650, 607-685 and 616-735 (deg. C) respectively. All these alloys require the use of a flux and the same manufacturer's Easyflo flux should be used in each case.

When alloys of higher melting temperatures are required – for instance when making up superheater elements – C.4 alloy (melting range 740-780) or B.6 (790-830) may be employed. If these two alloys are used on stainless steel, Tenacity 4A flux is to be preferred.

It is sometimes said that if a single silver solder is used for all the joints in a locomotive boiler, then when fixing some of the later joints, the joints made first will become melted and spoilt. However, this very rarely happens. This is because of a phenomenon known as liquation. Take the case of an alloy of rather low silver content and long melting range in contact with a capillary passage or gap between two pieces of metal to be brazed together. The work is in the process of being heated; when the temperature reaches the solidus of the brazing alloy, some of the alloy melts and runs into the gap, away from the un-melted part of the alloy. The un-melted part is now no longer in contact with the liquid that has run away, and it has a different composition from that possessed by the original complete alloy. Consequently the melting temperature of the solid part robbed of its liquid is higher than the quoted liquidus temperature of the original alloy. As a result, it either remains at the mouth of the joint as a costly and possibly unsightly fillet, or the temperature has to be raised much higher than it was originally.

For the caulking of stays, where these are not silver-soldered, the use of a high-melting-point soft solder, such as Comsol (melting at about 295 deg.C.) can be recommended. Ordinary soft solder such as plumber's should not be used, except on boilers having working pressures below 50 p.s.i.

THE DESIGN OF MODEL LOCOMOTIVE BOILERS

Most model steam locomotives being built today are made more or less to scale, so that the overall size of the boiler is immediately limited. This is perhaps just as well, as we do not want to go back to the "Greenly era" where outsize boilers were considered essential!! The builder of the "free-lance" engine can of course please himself as regards overall dimensions; he will however be well advised to design the boiler in proportion.

When building a scale, or near to scale, model of some full-size locomotive, the builder will not go far wrong if he makes his boiler to scale externally, with the possible exception of the length of the firebox. As the model locomotive engineer is not restricted, as is his full-size counterpart, as to weight on the track, it is a good plan to increase the length of the firebox somewhat, while keeping the tube length constant. This generally means extending the firebox further into the cab, but within reason, this is no disadvantage. Over-long tubes, however, are to be avoided, especially when it is realised that firebox heating surface is much more valuable than tube heating surface.

Of course if the prototype locomotive was known as an indifferent steamer, the above advice may not apply, but where the full-size engine was one of the Churchward, Collet, Stanier or Gresley designs, a scaled down version will not be far out.

One method of reducing tube length is to set the smokebox tubeplate further in, though this should not be overdone or it may be difficult to gain access to the main steam pipe connections and the blower union. As a rough guide, the smokebox tubeplate could be set in by an amount equal to one quarter of the diameter of the barrel; anything more than this may cause difficulties.

Having now determined the overall dimensions of the boiler, the next matter

FIG. 120

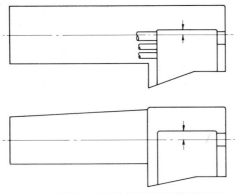

SHOWING THE RECOMMENDED HEIGHT OF THE FIREBOX
CROWN ABOVE BARREL CENTRE LINE

to be decided is at what height to put the crown of the inner firebox. It is generally convenient for the purpose of comparison to dimension the height of the crown from the longitudinal centre-line of the barrel. As the steam space of a Belpaire firebox is greater than that of a round-top of similar length, it follows that the firebox crown can be placed a little higher in the Belpaire type. Further, if the boiler has a taper barrel and a Belpaire firebox, both the steam and water spaces are relatively greater at the firebox end than in the corresponding parallel barrel/roundtop boiler, thus the crown of the firebox may again be placed a little higher. The following approximate heights of firebox crown above barrel centre-line can be recommended:-

3in. dia. parallel barrel, round-top boiler	11/32in.
3in. dia. parallel barrel, Belpaire type boiler	3/8in.
3in. dia. (at front end) taper barrel, Belpaire	15/32in.
4in. dia. parallel, round top	7/16in.
4in. dia. parallel, Belpaire	1/2in.
4in. dia. taper, Belpaire	5/8in.
4½in. dia. parallel, round-top	1/2in.
4½in. dia. parallel, Belpaire	9/16in.
4½in. dia. taper, Belpair	11/16in.
5in. dia. parallel, round-top	9/16in.
5in. dia. parallel, Belpaire	5/8in.
5in. dia. taper, Belpaire	13/16in.
6in. dia. parallel, round-top	5/8in.
6in. dia. parallel, Belpaire	3/4in.
6in. dia. taper, Belpaire	15/16in.

THE FIREBOX

The shape of the outer firebox wrapper can now be considered. The four basic shapes of the firebox are the round-top narrow type, the lower part going down between the frames of the engine, the Belpaire narrow type, the round-top wide type (generally called the Wootten type) where the lower part of the firebox spreads out nearly the full width of the locomotive, and the Belpaire wide type. Well-known examples of the Wootten firebox are seen in the Great Northen "Atlantics" and the L.N.E.R. "Pacifics". Examples of the Belpaire wide type can be seen in the L.M.S. "Pacifics" and the British Railways "Britannias".

When dimensioning the width of the narrow type of firebox, allowance must be made for the thickness of the stay heads on each side, and also a small amount to allow for expansion when hot.

In most model boilers, the foundation ring is generally made from square copper bar, but in nearly every case, it is an advantage to increase the water space at the front, that is between the throatplate and the firebox tubeplate – to at least 25% more than the width of the other parts of the foundation ring. As the use of square bar at the front would work out unnecessarily heavy, rectangular bar can be used. For a typical 3½ in. gauge locomotive boiler therefore, the front section of the foundation ring might be of 3/8 in. x 1/4 in. section, and the sides and rear section of 1/4 in. square.

The crown of the inner firebox in a round-top boiler may be made curved, convex to the pressure in the boiler; apart from being stronger than a flat plate, a curved plate has a slightly greater heating surface. In a Belpaire firebox where the outer wrapper is flat on the top, it is generally convenient to make the crown of the inner firebox flat to match, but if the outer wrapper is slightly radiused, the inner wrapper should follow suit.

The position and size of the firehole are important considerations in a coal-fired boiler. If made to scale, the firehole would be much too small for easy firing, especially on the run. Even in a ½ inch scale boiler, the firehole may be as much as 1½ in. diameter, or of an oval shape of similar area. Although a little heating surface may be lost by a large firehole, this is not likely to have any appreciable effect. It is advisable to place the firehole fairly high up in the backhead, so as to enable the driver to observe the state of the fire without having to bend very low; a high firehole is also easier to use especially in tank locomotives, and it makes staying of the backhead easier.

The strength of a model boiler is of course of great importance. For a given thickness and diameter, a length of seamless solid-drawn tube will make the strongest barrel. If the barrel has to be made from flat sheet rolled up, the beginner will be well advised to adopt a silver-soldered seam, using a good-quality alloy such as Easyflo No. 2.

To arrive at the right thickness of metal to be used for the boiler barrel, the following simple formula can be recommended:-

$$A = \frac{D \times WP \times F}{S \times T \times 2}$$

Where A is the thickness required in inches.
D is the diameter of the barrel in inches.
WP is the desired working pressure in lbs. per sq. in.
F is a factor of safety.
S in the ultimate tensile strength of the material in lbs. per sq. in.
T is a temperature allowance

The factor of safety has been taken at between 6 and 10, but 8 is generally thought to be adequate.

The ultimate tensile strength of copper is generally taken as 25,000 p.s.i. For mild steel 60,000 is acceptable and for stainless steel 70,000.

A temperature allowance is necessary for copper boilers as copper has diminished strength at high temperatures; T may be taken as 0.8.

The above formula only applies to copper boilers, and for steel boilers an additional allowance must be made for

corrosion. For plate thicknesses under $\frac{1}{4}$ in. the thickness should be doubled, and for plate thicknesses over $\frac{1}{4}$ in. the thickness should be multiplied by $3/2$.

It should be emphasised that if boilers are built up entirely by riveting, an additional allowance should be made; for a double riveted barrel seam for instance, the thickness of both barrel and cover strap should be increased by around 50%.

The formula for the thickness of barrels should not be used for fire-tubes or superheater flues, as it would give tubes of far too thin walls. The following thicknesses of tubes are therefore recommended:-

Outside diameter	Thickness Copper tube	Thickness mild steel	Thickness stainless steel
$\frac{1}{4}$ or $5/16$"	22 swg	--	26 swg
$3/8, 7/16, 1/2$"	20 swg	--	24 swg
$5/8, 3/4, 7/8, 1$"	18 swg	16 swg ($1/16$")	20 swg
$1\frac{1}{8}, 1\frac{1}{4}, 1\frac{3}{8}$	16 swg	16 swg	18 swg
$1\frac{1}{2}$"	16 swg	13 swg ($3/32$")	16 swg

STRENGTH OF BOILER PLATES

The outer firebox wrapper, when made separately from the barrel, should never be made of material thinner than the barrel. In fact, if the wrapper is of the Belpaire type, it may be made very slightly thicker with advantage, as this reduces the amount of staying without adversely affecting steaming. The inner firebox wrapper may however be made slightly thinner than the barrel, provided that it is adequately stayed. The smokebox tubeplate, the firebox

G.W.R. pannier tank in $3/4$in. scale by G. Marden.

backplate and the firebox tubeplate should be approximately 50% thicker than the barrel, to the nearest $1/64$ in. In fact the firebox tubeplate may be even thicker than this with advantage as it is subjected to the maximum heat of the fire as well as the abrasive effect of combustion. The backhead may be some 50% thicker than the barrel material.

It is most important that bushes are fitted to the boiler for every fitting – water gauges, check valves, safety valves, etc. It is bad practice to try to tap the sheet metal directly even if it is as thick as $1/8$ in. The bushes in copper boilers may be of copper or bronze, with a slight preference for bronze as this metal takes threads better. Brass should never be used in boiler construction.

THE TUBES AND FLUES

There is a definite relationship between the diameter and length of a boiler tube, whatever the size of the boiler. An examination of the most successful full-size locomotive boilers shows that the length of the tubes divided by the square of the internal diameter works out at between 50 and 70. Similarly, it has been found that most successful model locomotive boilers seem to follow the same rule. So for model boilers, the following formula can be recommended:-

$$d = \sqrt{\frac{L}{65}}$$

where d is the internal diameter of the tube and L the distance between tubeplates, both measured in inches. The formula cannot of course be used exactly, as it is generally only possible to obtain tubes to the nearest $1/16$ in. diameter. So for tubeplates that are from 6in. to 8 in. apart, $3/8$ in. o.d. tubes may be used, and for tubeplates that are from 9 to 11 in. apart, $7/16$ in. o.d. tubes can be recommended.

The size of the superheater elements is governed by two main considerations: the diameter must be small enough to ensure that all the steam passing through the element is properly heated, and there must be sufficient cross-sectional area in the elements to prevent wire-drawing. Reference to successful full-size locomotive boilers is again helpful. Generally speaking, the shorter barrel boilers give the least trouble as far as superheat temperature is concerned. For model locomotive boil-

Inner firebox and tubes on one of the author's boilers.

Opposite, stages in construction of the firebox for a Midland "Single" by Mr. Thornton of British Columbia.

ers of any scale, the following formula may be used safely:-

$$\text{External diameter} = \sqrt{\frac{L}{275}}$$

For all practical purposes, the overall length of the element may be taken as twice the distance between tubeplates.

To find a suitable size of superheater flue for the elements, it is only necessary to add sufficient clearance for the passage of the gases around the elements. The following table gives suitable sizes of superheater flues:-

Element, outside diameter	Flue inside diameter
$3/16$ in.	$1/2$ in.
$7/32$ in.	$9/16$ in.
$1/4$ in.	$11/16$ in.
$5/16$ in.	$27/32$ in.
$3/8$ in.	1 in.
$7/16$ in.	$1\,1/8$ in.
$1/2$ in.	$1\,1/4$ in.

The total cross-sectional area of the superheater elements must be sufficient

to prevent wire-drawing. The main steam pipe (from regulator to superheater) should be made at least one-quarter of the cylinder bore (for a two-cylinder engine). As a guide, the total cross-sectional area of the superheater elements should be about 25% greater than that of the main steam pipe.

There are three ways in which the tubes can be arranged in the tube plate:- as a horizontal diamond pattern, in a vertical diamond pattern or in a square pattern. The horizontal diamond arrangement is most often used in small boilers as it enables the maximum number of tubes to be used in the rather limited space available. The circulation of the water is however slightly better in the vertical diamond arrangement and better still in the square (or "marine") pattern. The superheater flues are best placed in the top row for three reasons:- it allows for easier flue sweeping, the possibility of the flues becoming blocked by particles of ash etc. is reduced, and the temperature of the gases is higher towards the top of the tube plate.

Whatever arrangement of tubes is adopted, they should not be placed too close together. In $3/4$ in. scale boilers, there should be at least $7/64$ in. of water space between every tube; in 1 in. scale boilers, at least $1/8$ in. should be allowed for.

Sometimes, the whole bank of tubes and flues are given a slight rise from firebox to smokebox tubeplate. This can be recommended as it makes the operation of sweeping the tubes a little easier. It may also assist the draught very slightly.

STAYING

The general rule in staying a locomotive type boiler is that all flat or nearly flat surfaces must be supported, and in fact all surfaces not self-supporting will require stays.

In locomotive boilers, there are three principal types of stays:- Longitudinal stays, to support the flat ends of the boiler, that is the smokebox tubeplate and the backhead. Crown stays, to support the top or crown of the inner firebox. Side stays, to support the flat sides, front and back of the firebox.

In full-size locomotive boilers, there are also palm stays, but these are not

Right: Horizontal diamond tube arrangement.

Left: Vertical diamond tube arrangement

Right: Square or Marine tube arrangement.

FIG. 121

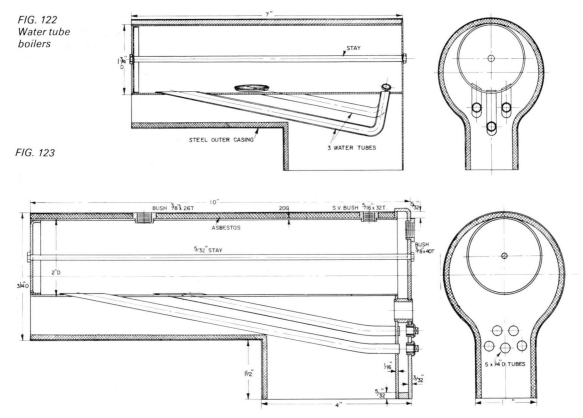

FIG. 122
Water tube boilers

FIG. 123

STAY

STEEL OUTER CASING

3 WATER TUBES

BUSH ³⁄₈" x 26T

20G

ASBESTOS

S.V. BUSH ⁵⁄₁₆" x 32T.

BUSH ⁷⁄₈ x 40T

⁵⁄₃₂" STAY

2"D

3¼"D

1½"

4"

5 x ¼" D. TUBES

generally used in model locomotive boilers below 2 in. scale.

Longitudinal stays are used where the firebox outer wrapper is separate from the barrel, the two being joined by some kind of throatplate. In most model boilers, these stays are fitted so that they run the full length of the boiler, from the smokebox tubeplate to the backhead, and they are arranged just above the inner firebox and tubes. Two to five may be used, according to the size of the boiler, and one is generally a hollow tube used to carry the blower steam from the control valve on the backhead to the blower nozzles in the smokebox.

In some model boilers of the round-top type, it is often possible to make the outer firebox wrapper from the same material as the barrel. Thus if seamless tube is used for the barrel, a vertical cut can be made at the throatplate and another, longitudinal, cut along the bottom of the tube from the rear end to meet the first cut. The metal can then be bent outwards (after annealing) to the shape of the wrapper required. Boilers built in this way do not need longitudinal stays at all, but if they are omitted, it is important to see that the flat surfaces of the smokebox tubeplate and the backhead, above the level of the inner

FIG. 124

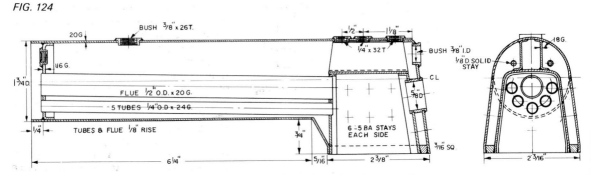

BUSH ³⁄₈" x 26T.

20G

16 G.

1¾"D

FLUE ½" O.D. x 20G.

5 TUBES ¼" O.D. x 24G.

TUBES & FLUE ⅛" RISE

BUSH ³⁄₈" I.D

⅛" D. SOLID STAY

18 G.

C.L

6 - 5 BA STAYS EACH SIDE

¼" x 32 T

6¼"

5⁄₁₆"

2³⁄₈"

2³⁄₁₆"

GAUGE 'O' LOCOMOTIVE BOILER FOR PROPANE FIRING

138

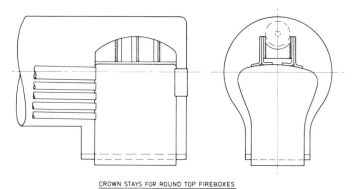

CROWN STAYS FOR ROUND TOP FIREBOXES

FIG. 125

firebox, are adequately strengthened; a simple way of achieving this is to fit a curved plate, of fairly thick metal, to the inside, across the area that requires to be stiffened. This plate should be held by a couple of gunmetal screws and then brazed to the plate before the tubeplate or backhead is fitted to the boiler. The screws make certain that the stiffening plate does not become loose and fall inside the boiler during later brazing operations.

Longitudinal stays may be made from monel metal or drawn bronze; copper can be used, but is not so strong and does not take threads so cleanly. Opinions differ as to the best way of fitting longitudinal stays; the "traditional" method is to use threaded nipples at both ends, these nipples being threaded both inside and outside at the same pitch, while the ends of the stays are also threaded to match. The advantage of this method is that should a stay break in service, it is easily removed and a re-

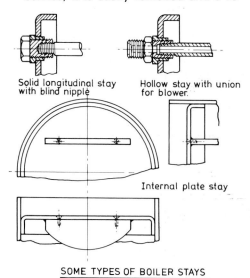

Solid longitudinal stay with blind nipple

Hollow stay with union for blower.

Internal plate stay

SOME TYPES OF BOILER STAYS

FIG. 126

placement fitted. Another method is to thread both ends of the stay but to dispense with nipples; a clearing hole is drilled in the backhead and a tapped hole in the smokebox tubeplate. The stay is then screwed home into the smokebox tubeplate (from the firebox end) and nutted up on the outside. A nut is then put on the other end – which should protrude through the backhead. Finally, both ends are given a touch of best-grade silver-solder, this being done after the main brazing operations on the boiler have been carried out.

Some boiler builders fit these stays with no thread at all, relying on silver-soldering at both ends, though this is a method than can only be recommended for experienced workers.

At least four different types of crown stays are used in model locomotive boilers:- 1. Direct rod stays. 2. Fabricated plate-girder stays. 3. Fabricated stays not connected to the outer wrapper. 4. Sling stays.

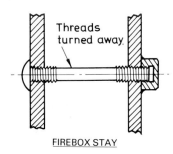

Threads turned away.

FIREBOX STAY

FIG. 127

On many full-size boilers, sling stays were fitted near the front end of the firebox, the remainder of the crown being supported by rod stays. The reason for this was to give a certain amount of flexibility to allow for the unequal expansion and contraction which takes place, especially during steam raising and closing down periods. This was important in steel boilers, but is not so in copper boilers as copper is so much more ductile than steel.

The direct rod stay is an excellent type to use in Belpaire boilers where both the outer wrapper and firebox crown are flat, or nearly so, and approximately parallel to one another. But this type of stay should always be made from monel metal or drawn bronze, never from brass or cast metals. When fitting rod stays, the outer wrapper may be threaded to a larger size than the thread in the crown,

FIG. 128

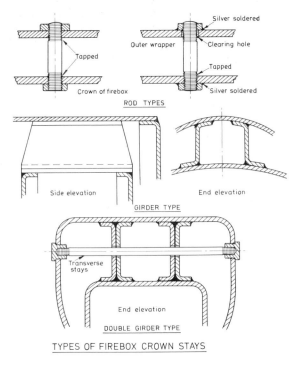

Rod Types

Silver soldered
Outer wrapper
Clearing hole
Tapped
Silver soldered
Tapped
Crown of firebox

ROD TYPES

Side elevation   End elevation

GIRDER TYPE

Transverse stays

End elevation

DOUBLE GIRDER TYPE

TYPES OF FIREBOX CROWN STAYS

Firebox drilled for side stays, showing extra long tap.

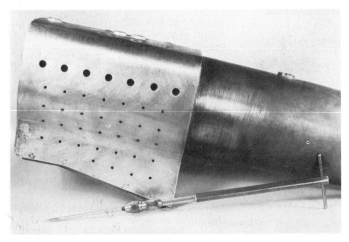

silver-solder MUST be used on the outer end, to ensure strength and steam-tightness.

Rod stays are not ideal for round-top boilers as it is impossible to arrange them to lie at right-angles to the part of the plate which they are supporting, at least on the outer wrapper. This applies particularly to the outer rows. The fabricated plate girder stay is the most popular type for round-top boilers, though it is not at all necessary to attach this type of stay to the outer wrapper, which is always rather a difficult operation especially in long fireboxes. The drawing shows the type of crown stay which the author now adopts for round-top boilers. It has the great advantage that all silver-soldering is carried out on the top of the inner firebox before this is assembled inside the outer wrapper, so that it is easy to see whether the soldering is sound before the firebox is no longer so easy of access. The design is sometimes criticised on the grounds that if the crown is not attached to the outer wrapper, the whole of the pressure on the crown is transferred on to the foundation ring. But in an all-silver-soldered model boiler, the foundation ring is probably the strongest part and can easily resist such pressure. In any case, many full-size boilers have been built on this principle, and being in steel with riveted joints, there might have been some question as to their safety, but such boilers have been tested to well over 300 p.s.i. without trouble.

As mentioned earlier, sling stays are not really necessary in model boilers made in copper and they have the disadvantage of involving the use of screws, studs or rivets inside the boiler. Stays which involve the fitting of pins or screws *inside* the boiler should be avoided.

The side stays in locomotive boilers are very important. Although copper is often used for these, monel or drawn bronze is to be preferred; copper is weak in tension and does not take too kindly to being threaded.

Some professional model boiler makers use ordinary copper rivets for side stays, fixing them by the use of the oxy-acetylene torch. This method should not be used by the amateur. For one thing, there is always the danger of burning the metal; for another, it is difficult to keep the inner and outer firebox wrapper at the correct distance apart while the heat

but to the same pitch. The stay can then be screwed straight in from the outside, and nutted up internally and externally, the nuts on the outside being thin; both should be run over with best silver-solder.

Another method of fitting rod stays is to thread both ends of the stay to the same diameter and pitch, but to drill the holes in the outer wrapper clearance size. The stay is then put through these clearance holes and screwed into the crown. Nuts are put on both ends as before, but note that with this method,

Rod-type crown stays on firebox for Columbia boiler being built by Bert Perryman.

Tubeplate and backhead with internal plate stays.

plates to be supported, and if the inner firebox wrapper is thinner than the outer wrapper, this is the factor to be considered. The following stay sizes can be recommended:-

Thickness of inner wrapper	Stay diameter and thread
3/64" or 18 SWG	5 BA
1/16" or 16 SWG or 1.6mm	5 BA
3/32" or 13 SWG or 2.5 mm.	4 BA
1/8" or 10 SWG or 3 to 3.5 mm.	3/16" x 40t.
5/32" or 4 mm.	1/4" x 32t.
3/16" or 5 mm.	5/16" x 32 or 26t.

The pitch of side stays will depend on the above and also on the working pressure of the boiler. The following pitches will be found satisfactory for working pressures from 80 to 100 p.s.i.:-

Thickness of wrapper	Pitch of stays
3/64"	9/16"
1/16"	11/16"
3/32"	7/8"
1/8"	1 1/16"
5/32"	1 5/16"
3/16"	1 1/2"

is being applied, leading to distortion; this may of course be dealt with to some extent by fitting a few screwed stays at strategic points.

Undoubtedly, the best type of side stay for the beginner is one that is threaded through both plates and nutted on the inside; the heads and nuts may then be run over with either a good-grade silver-solder or a high-melting-point soft solder. The nuts may be ordinary commercial brass ones though "Cap" (i.e. "blind") nuts made from bronze are better. To improve the screwed stay still further, the threads between the plates may be turned away; this makes the stay more flexible and more resistant to corrosion.

The diameter of the side stays used should be related to the thickness of the

The top row of side stays should be placed as high as possible though below the radiused corners of the inner firebox, the other rows being put in at regular intervals. Further stays will be required between the lower part of the firebox tubeplate and the throatplate, the top row of these being placed fairly close to the underside of the barrel, though not so close as to cause difficulty when drilling. Once the holes are drilled, there should be no trouble in tapping them if a special long tap wrench is made up, long enough to allow the handle of the wrench to come beyond the end of the barrel.

Finally, stays will be required between the firebox backplate and the backhead. In large boilers, there may be quite large areas of unsupported flat surface on either side and possibly above the firehole, so that stays will be required here as well as the usual rows below the level of the firehole.

Belpaire fireboxes require transverse stays to support the flat sides of the outer wrapper above the level of the inner firebox. They may be fitted by means of internal/external threaded nipples, as described for longitudinal stays,

141

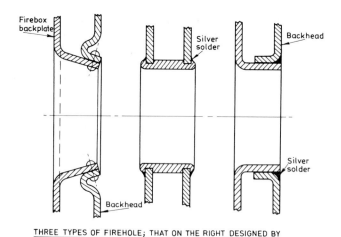

THREE TYPES OF FIREHOLE; THAT ON THE RIGHT DESIGNED BY
Mr K.N.HARRIS

FIG. 129

or they may be screwed into the wrapper on one side of the boiler and nutted outside, nutted on the other side and then run over with silver-solder.

FIREHOLE RING

For copper boilers, a turned firehole ring is recommended. This saves having to flange either the firebox backplate or the backhead. Thick-walled copper tube can be obtained for this ring, which is turned down at each end to form a step and can then be inserted in the hole in the firebox backplate and flanged over, making a very strong job. If an oval firehole is preferred, the turned ring can be squeezed oval in the vice before assembly and the plates cut to suit.

Four types of firehole door are in general use:- the plain hinged door with the

hinges on the side, either right or left-handed, the sliding door, the "butterfly" door, and the drop-down door.

The side-hinged door has the big disadvantage that it is inclined to swing shut just as the fireman's shovel is about to shoot the coals through; this seems to happen particularly when the train is at full speed, resulting in the coals being deposited on the footplate!

The sliding door, much used by the ex-G.W.R. and L.M.S., is a good design for models; in fact it consists of two doors sliding in runners above and below, the lever being connected so that the doors move in unison. It can generally be opened and closed by a judicious tap with the firing shovel. To prevent the lower runner of this type of door from becoming jammed with coal dust, one side of this can be left open immediately under the door.

The "butterfly" firedoor consists of two doors which are pivoted to a frame above the firehole; each half door has a toothed sector at its upper end. These sectors work together, thus transmitting any movement of one half door to the other.

FIREGRATES

Grates for model boilers are sometimes built up from mild steel strips, but these burn out quickly and cannot therefore be recommended. Sometimes, patterns are made and the grates cast in iron. This has the advantage that the firebars are easily shaped to the proper profile, with adequate taper, and once

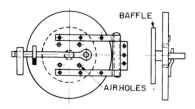

ROUND HINGED DOOR

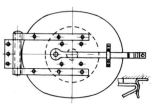

OVAL HINGED DOOR

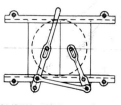

SLIDING TYPE DOOR

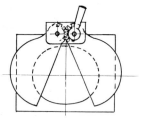

BUTTERFLY TYPE DOOR

FIG. 130

FIREDOORS

FIG. 131

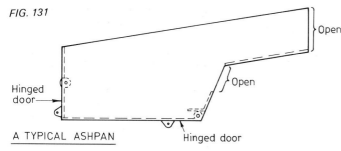

Open

Open

Hinged door

A TYPICAL ASHPAN

Hinged door

the pattern has been made, further castings can be obtained as the grates become burnt out.

But stainless steel is really the best material to use for grates, provided that the firebars are properly shaped and that both the cross supports and spacers are of the same metal. Ready-made stainless steel grates can now be obtained for many of the more popular types of locomotive.

The grate should be fitted so that it can be dropped quickly in emergency; this can usually be arranged by allowing the grate to rest on top of the ashpan, the ashpan being supported by one or more pins or shafts fitted across the frames, which can be pulled clear when necessary, allowing both ashpan and grate to fall clear. In wide type fireboxes, the grate may be made in two halves or even in three parts, the centre section being allowed to drop as required. The gaps or air spaces in grates are best made somewhat wider than the thickness of the firebars; for instance, if the firebars are $1/8$ in thick at the top, the air gaps could be $3/16$ in.

ASHPANS

Thermic syphon and firebox, another example of Mr. B. Palmer's work.

A properly designed ashpan helps the fire to burn evenly over its whole area,

while at the same time preventing hot ashes from falling on to the track and perhaps damaging the sleepers. The shape of ashpans varies a great deal, depending on the proximity or otherwise of driving or coupled axles, or in the case of "Atlantic" and "Pacific" locomotives, the presence of trailing wheels and axles. The rear end of the ashpan is usually left open, though it is always worth while fitting a "damper door" controlled by a lever in the cab, whenever space allows. If the ashpan has to be shallow, some air gap may be necessary at the front end, though care should be taken to prevent ashes from getting into the inside motion or axleboxes.

COMBUSTION CHAMBERS

Where the boiler has, of necessity, a very long barrel, and particularly if it has a wide firebox, a combustion chamber generally improves steaming. Very often such a chamber is fitted with a number of water tubes, which improve circulation to some extent while also acting as stays. If no such water tubes are fitted, the metal used in its construction would have to be considerably thicker than the other parts of the firebox, unless some other type of staying is adopted. But many model engineers no longer favour combustion chambers in the smaller scales owing to the inaccessibility. Should a leak occur anywhere in the combustion chamber, it is almost impossible to reach it for repair. A better method of dealing with long-barrel boilers is to fit one or more thermic syphons.

THERMIC SYPHONS

Full-size American locomotives with large boilers were invariably fitted with thermic syphons, generally two, sometimes three or more. The advantages claimed for such syphons were that circulation was much improved, steam raising was speeded up and there was less danger of the crown of the firebox becoming uncovered due to too low water level. These advantages also apply to model boilers, particularly those of 1 inch scale and larger. At one time it was thought that fitting such syphons would cause too violent a circulation and perhaps priming, but the author's 5 in gauge G.W.R. 2-6-2 tank

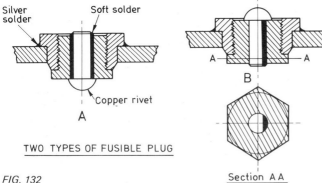

Silver solder — Soft solder — Copper rivet

TWO TYPES OF FUSIBLE PLUG

A   B   Section A A

FIG. 132

locomotive fitted with a thermic syphon in 1963 showed none of these failings, and also proved a very fast raiser of steam.

The pinciple behind the syphon is that water is allowed to flow through a comparatively small inlet sited at the bottom of the firebox tubeplate (where circulation is usually sluggish) and the syphon is so designed that its cross-sectional area increases all the way upwards towards the crown of the firebox, where its outlet is arranged; thus while the rate of water passing upwards from the front part of the foundation ring is very rapid, the rate decreases quickly towards the top of the firebox.

As the sides of the syphon are generally flat, or nearly so, side stays are fitted similar to those in the other parts of the firebox.

BRICK ARCHES

Brick arches would appear to be essential fitments in full-size locomotive boilers. Whether they are essential in model boilers is open to argument. However, several model engineers have fitted brick arches to their boilers, although they have generally been made of stainless steel sheet rather than firebrick. Reports indicate a definite improvement in steaming, although whether they have much effect, at least in boilers up to 1 inch scale, at preventing excessive ash build up in the smokebox is open to doubt.

The chief difficulty with brick arches, whether made of firebrick or some other refractory material or even of stainless steel sheet is how to fit them in the firebox and prevent them becoming loose in service. Sometimes, some of the firebox side stays may be extended further into the firebox to provide a kind of ledge on which the brick arch may rest.

FUSIBLE PLUGS

If the locomotive boiler has any soft solder in its construction, some kind of fusible plug should be fitted. This is a device containing a low melting-point metal which will melt if the temperature of the firebox crown should rise considerably due to a dangerously low water level. The usual type of fusible plug used in model boilers consists of a threaded bronze plug fitted internally with a loose copper rivet held in position only by soft

The top and firebox views of a thermic syphon by the author.

solder, and so arranged that if the solder melts, due to excessive heat on the firebox crown, the rivet will fall clear and release the pressure in the boiler.

BOILER CONSTRUCTION

To come now to actual construction of the model boiler, most builders make a start on the barrel. If the barrel required is a parallel one, a seamless solid-drawn tube should be considered, This will save a good deal of time and the builder is generally assured of a truly circular barrel, making connection to the smokebox reasonably easy.

If the design is of a "round-top" firebox, the seamless tube may also be used to form the outer firebox wrapper. The tube is cut by a hacksaw cross-wise at the throatplate and a longitudinal cut made from the rear end along the bottom centre-line of the barrel to meet the first cut at right-angles. After annealing, the two sides are pulled out and bent to the required shape to form the outer firebox wrapper.

Sometimes, the above method does not provide a deep enough firebox, so that extensions have to be added, these being made from the same thickness of sheet as the barrel itself, and secured by means of a cover strap, riveted in place and afterwards silver-soldered. However, it is not necessary to add these extensions to *both* sides. If the longitudinal cut is offset to one side, the wrapper on the side furthest from this cut can be opened out to form the full depth required, leaving only the other side needing the extension. It is not necessary to become involved in difficult calculations to determine where to make this offset longitudinal cut; it can be determined quite easily by pasting some thick paper on the barrel, opening this out and cutting with scissors, when it will be seen where to make the required cut in the tube itself.

The flanged throatplate required for a parallel-barrel, round-top firebox boiler is very simple, very much easier to make than a regulation throatplate.

Another method of boiler construction is to use seamless tube for the barrel proper and to bend up the outer firebox wrapper from flat sheet copper (after adequate annealing of course). The connection is then made by a proper throatplate, or a simple throatplate plus a turned ring can be used. The latter method is generally used for a Belpaire firebox.

If the barrel of the boiler is to be rolled up from sheet copper, two methods for joining the edges are in general use. The edges of the sheet are brought together and a cover strap of a least the same thickness as the sheet placed along the full length of the barrel, but allowing for the width of the flange of the smokebox tubeplate, which will be inserted later on. Although it is customary to place this cover strap on the inside of the barrel, there is no reason why this should be so, and from many points of view, it is better placed on the outside and away from the bottom of the boiler. In any case, it should be held in place by a few copper rivets and then silver-soldered, using a free-running alloy such as Easyflo No.2. It should be emphasised that this joint is a very important one from the point of view of the strength of the boiler, so it should be dealt with carefully.

The other method of joining the edges of the sheet is shown in Fig. 136 on page 147; after cutting and fitting the castellated edges, the seam is lightly

145

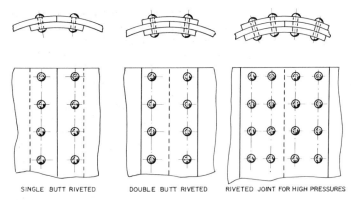

SINGLE BUTT RIVETED DOUBLE BUTT RIVETED RIVETED JOINT FOR HIGH PRESSURES

FIG. 133

hammered over a round mandrel of suitable diameter and then silver-soldered, no rivets being necessary.

As regards the actual operation of silver-soldering, the important thing to remember is that all the parts to be joined must be really clean, and this is best insured by rubbing them with coarse emery cloth and then inserting them in the "pickle" tank for at least ten minutes, afterwards washing in hot water before applying the flux; the operator's hands should be kept well away from the actual area of the joint.

The aim should then be to bring the parts to be joined up to a dull red heat as quickly as possible, that is to such a heat

that when the silver-solder is applied to the joint, it immediately melts and flows freely even if the flame is momentarily removed. If the solder should be applied too soon, it will merely form into little balls which run off the joint and are wasted. Most boiler builders arm themselves with a steel "scratch-rod", merely a length of rod about $3/16$ in. diameter and a foot or so long, with the end bent at right-angles with a sharp point. This can be used to break up any blobs of hardened flux, but will be found to be seldom necessary if the above advice is followed.

After each stage of silver-soldering, the job should be immersed in the pickle for about 20 minutes, then lifted out and thoroughly washed in hot water and "Vim". It will then be nice and clean to handle and it will be possible to examine the job for possible missed places. Needless to say, if any parts of a joint appear doubtful, they must be properly dealt with before proceeding to the next stage. This means thoroughly cleaning the offending spot, re-fluxing and re-heating.

TAPER BARRELS.

A straightforward taper barrel – one where the taper is uniform and continuous from smokebox to firebox – is not too difficult to tackle, even for the beginner. Although it is possible to produce a taper barrel from a seamless round tube, by annealing and stretching, such a method is best left to the expert sheet metal worker. The best method for the average amateur is to roll the barrel from sheet. It is quite possible to calculate the exact size and shape of the flat sheet to form a taper barrel after rolling, though as most such barrels have all the taper on the top, the underside being horizontal, this is not quite so easy as it sounds.

The beginner may proceed as follows:- roll up a dummy taper barrel from thin cardboard, the edges being overlapped and glued together using any quick-drying glue. To lay the cardboard out in the flat to start off with, the required diameter at the small end and the large end are taken off the drawing, and the circumference at each point calculated by the usual formula – Circumference = $\pi \times D$. A longitudinal centre-line AB (Fig. 137) is now drawn and the two circumferences CD, EF, set off at 90 deg. at a dis-

FIG. 134
Rivet details

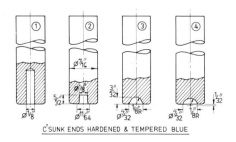

C'SUNK ENDS HARDENED & TEMPERED BLUE

BARE RIVET FIRST FORMING SECOND FORMING FINISH

RIVET DETAILS

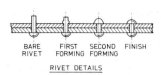

T	D	P	L
$1/16$"	$1/8$"	$3/8$"	$3/16$"
$3/32$"	$5/32$"	$1/2$"	$1/4$-$7/32$"
$1/8$"	$3/16$"	$9/16$-$5/8$"	$5/16$"
$1/4$"	$1/2$"	$1\,1/4$"	$3/4$"
$5/16$"	$5/8$"	$1\,1/2$"	$15/16$"
$3/8$"	$3/4$"	$1\,3/4$"	$1\,1/8$"
$7/16$"	$13/16$"	$1\,7/8$"	$1\,7/32$"
$1/2$"	$7/8$"	2"	$1\,5/16$"

T	D	P	C
$1/4$"	$1/2$"	2"	$1\,1/8$"
$5/16$"	$5/8$"	$2\,1/2$"	$1\,1/4$"
$3/8$"	$3/4$"	$2\,5/8$"	$15/16$"
$7/16$"	$13/16$"	$2\,3/4$"	$1\,3/8$"
$1/2$"	$7/8$"	$2\,7/8$"	$1\,1/2$"

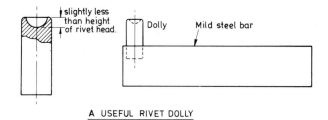

slightly less than height of rivet head.

Dolly   Mild steel bar

A USEFUL RIVET DOLLY

FIG. 135

A RIVET JAMMER

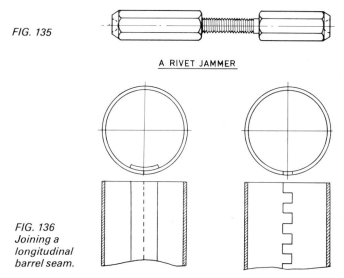

FIG. 136
Joining a
longitudinal
barrel seam.

with scissors, allowing a small overlap for glueing; it is then rolled up and glued together. If the taper barrel is one with a horizontal base, the ends can now be squared up with the scissors, checking with a square on a surface plate or other flat surface.

When the cardboard dummy barrel is complete and to correct dimensions, it is cut and opened out and used as a template for marking out the metal sheet. Once again, a small cutting allowance may be made on the width of the material, 1/16 in. being sufficient for barrel up to 4 in. dia., other barrels in proportion.

The ends of a parallel barrel may be squared off in the lathe. The author's usual method is to plug the ends with discs of wood. The discs need to be a close fit and in the centre of one a steel bolt can be fitted, a centre being drilled in this so that tailstock support can be given to the outer end.

Having completed the barrel and attached it to the outer firebox wrapper, the various flanged plates can be put in hand. For the normal locomotive boiler, these will comprise the smokebox tubeplate, the firebox tubeplate, the firebox backplate (sometimes called the firebox doorplate) the throatplate and the backhead.

The formers for flanging these plates are sometimes made from mild steel, about 1/4 in. thick, but this is a very laborious process and hardly necessary if only one boiler is contemplated. A hardwood such as oak or beech can be used, or a combination of a thin steel plate attached to hardwood, in which case the steel need not be thicker than 1/8 in. and the wood 1/4 in. to 3/8 in. according to the scale of the boiler being built. Another possible material for formers is a plastic such as Bakelite or Tufnol. The edges of all plate formers for copper plates should be rounded off at a minimum radius of 3/32 in. according to the size of the plate. (Formers for steel plates should allow for a radius double that for copper). The sheet material is cut to size, allowing for the width of the flange and for the thickness of the sheet itself; it is then well annealed, clamped to the former and the flange beaten over with a hammer. A hammer with a hardplastic face will be found ideal for this job, as the ordinary steel-faced hammer is inclined to mark the work rather severely. The plate must be annealed im-

tance apart equal to the required length of the barrel, plus a small allowance for trimming (about 1/16 in. per inch of barrel diameter).

Lines are now drawn from C to E and from D to F. Now draw lines EG and FH at 90 deg. to CE and DF respectively as shown. The required edge of material is then given *approximately* by the curved line EJF which can be drawn in by a suitable trammel. There is no need, if working in cardboard, to draw a similar arc at the smaller end.

The cardboard template is now cut out

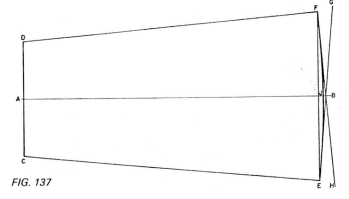

FIG. 137

Brazing the combustion chamber tubeplate.

mediately it shows signs of going hard – a thick plate may require annealing three or four times before flanging is complete.

Smokebox tubeplates should always be flanged over formers large enough in diameter to leave the flanges somewhat oversize, the plate may then be chucked in the lathe and turned to the exact size required to fit closely the inside of the barrel.

A Belpaire throatplate for a 7¼in. gauge locomotive by Alec Farmer.

In locomotive work, the throatplate of a Belpaire type firebox is always the most difficult plate to make. If the boiler is a small one, ¾ in. scale or smaller, and of the all-brazed variety, it is not essential to flange the throatplate forwards to receive the rear end of the barrel as well as to the rear for attachment to the outer firebox wrapper, though some additional means can be provided to increase the area of the joint into which the silver-solder can penetrate – i.e. by means of a turned ring. For larger Belpaire boilers, the throatplate should be double flanged to take the barrel and the outer firebox wrapper. A metal former is first cut out on its outside only for the flanging on the wrapper side of the plate, after which the partly completed throatplate is removed from the former and a hole cut in the former in the required position and to a diameter slightly greater than the *inside* diameter of the barrel at the firebox end. This can be done on the lathe, the former being held in a 4-jaw chuck.

A circular hole is now cut in the throatplate of a diameter equal to the hole in the former less twice the flanging allowance. After further annealing, the partly flanged throatplate is again clamped to the former and flanged forwards, into the hole cut in the former. Finally, the throatplate is returned to the lathe for light turning to receive the rear end of the barrel.

Throatplates for round-top boilers can be made in much the same way, though as mentioned previously, if the firebox wrapper is made from an extension of the barrel, only a very simple throatplate will be required – provided that the joint between the throatplate and the barrel can be silver-soldered.

In many boilers, the two firebox plates can be flanged over the same former, though as the tubeplate is often deeper than the firebox backplate, the former should be made to accommodate this.

Having completed all the flanged plates, the next item to tackle is the inner firebox. To measure the length of sheet copper required to make the wrapper, a good dodge is to use a length of soft iron wire about ⅛ in. dia. This can be wrapped around the firebox tubeplate, then straightened again and measured; a similar method can be used for the firebox backplate. To bend the wrapper to the required shape, a bending rolls is the ideal tool, but if one is not available, it is not difficult to get the required bends by using round bars of mild steel of suitable diameter, clamped in the bench vice and supported at the outer end as required. The copper must of course be well annealed beforehand and it may be necessary to reanneal during the bending process, "offering up" the wrapper to check the fit against the flanged plates.

Having got the wrapper to a good fit all around the flanged plate, the latter can be marked out and all tube and flue holes drilled, say 1/8 in. dia. to start with. This plate can then be clamped to the smokebox tubeplate and used as a jig for drilling the latter, not forgetting a possible rise in the tubes from firebox to smokebox. The tube holes are then opened out, and finished with a reamer, the reamer being put through only about half way along the "lead", so that the holes are left a few thou undersize. The holes in the smokebox tubeplate, however, should be finished to size and very lightly countersunk on both sides of the plate.

The firebox wrapper is now riveted to the firebox tubeplate, using just enough rivets to hold it closely, ready for silver-soldering. The crownstays are made up and attached to the crown of the firebox, again using only the minimum number of rivets. The assembly so far is now silver-soldered.

The tubes may now be taken in hand. As it is most important that the silver-solder penetrates the joint when fixing the tubes to the tubeplate, a good plan is to file three or four small nicks in each hole, this being done with a triangular needle file. The tubes are cut to length and their ends lightly turned down in the lathe to such a diameter that they can just be twisted into their holes; the slight "shoulder" left will prevent any chance of the tubes slipping right through when being heated. The tubes should also be thoroughly cleaned and annealed before fitting.

The firebox assembly is now set up with the tubeplate horizontal, the tubes standing up vertically. The outer ends of the tubes can be supported by pushing on the smokebox tubeplate. Plenty of flux should be used for the operation of fixing the tubes and silver-solder wire will be found convenient as this can be wrapped around the base of every tube before heating is started. When heating, the flame should be applied mainly from the inside and kept continually on the move so that there will be no danger of burning the thin tubes. On reaching a dull red heat, the solder should flow freely throughout the tubes. A little more silver-solder may be fed in from the outside, to make doubly sure of a sound joint. After pickling and washing, it should be possible to see a silvery ring around every tube on the *inside* of the firebox.

The foundation ring is generally made from four separate pieces of copper bar. The front section is fitted first, when the alignment of the inner firebox in the outer wrapper can be checked. If all is well, the front section can be riveted, two rivets being enough for most small boilers. The two side sections of the foundation ring are next fitted, but only bolted in position temporarily. Meanwhile the backhead is prepared, its bushes brazed in position and the firehole ring cut out. The firebox backplate is inserted and also bolted in position, the backhead being pushed up against it so that the hole required in the firebox backplate can be marked out. The firebox backplate is now removed and the firehole ring, previously turned in the lathe from thick-walled copper tube, inserted and flanged over on the inside and brazed in place.

At this stage, the smokebox tubeplate can be prepared, any bushes being brazed to it before it is pushed home into the barrel, where it can be secured with a few gunmetal screws around the periphery of the barrel. The ends of the tubes and flues may now be lightly expanded, this being done by a couple of taper drifts of suitable diameter. The smokebox tubeplate is now silver soldered, for which the boiler is set up vertically with the barrel protruding through a hole in the floor of the brazing stand (as mentioned earlier).

If it is desired to silver-solder the firebox side stays, and those between the throatplate and the firebox tubeplate, now is the time to do this before the firebox backplate is finally fixed. When drilling for these stays, it is important to try to keep the drill square to the *inner* plate, at the expense to some extent of the hole in the outer plate; if this is not done, the drill may wander when it meets the inner plate and spoil the job.

The stays are turned in the lathe, threaded as required, leaving a rounded head. This is only partly parted off, so as

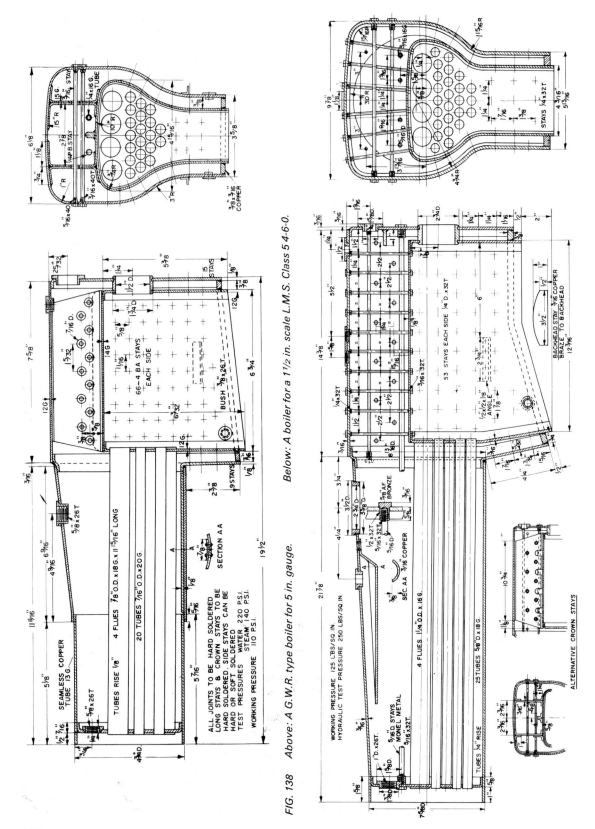

FIG. 138   Above: A G.W.R. type boiler for 5 in. gauge.

Below: A boiler for a 1½ in. scale L.M.S. Class 5 4-6-0.

to leave the stock material as a "handle" by which the stay can be screwed right home in the boiler, when the stock is twisted off and returned to the lathe for the next stay. The head left in the boiler is then filed and smoothed over with coarse emery cloth, leaving a neat finish. When all the stays that can be fitted at this stage are screwed home, they are nutted up on the inside of the firebox. Although ordinary brass nuts can be used here, to make a really good job, "blind" or cap nuts, turned from gunmetal bar, are much to be preferred.

If the boiler is a Belpaire one, the transverse stays can now be fitted and nutted up, after which the firebox backplate can be silver-soldered in position. Although the stays between this plate and the backhead are generally fitted after the backhead has been put in place and silver-soldered, it is possible, and in fact not at all difficult, to fit these stays to the firebox backplates beforehand and braze them in position, clearance holes being drilled in the backhead to match. But if this method is adopted, these stays must be nutted on the outside and silver-soldered, this being done when the final heating is tackled.

When the backhead is being fitted for keeps, the rear section of the foundation ring is cut and fitted. If any small gaps are found anywhere around the foundation ring, these may be plugged with slivers of copper driven in place. Where the firehole ring protrudes through the backhead it is gently flanged over, care being taken not to distort the plate, though support on the back of the ring should help to prevent this

The last and biggest heating job involves silver-soldering the foundation ring and the backhead, including the firehole ring and the stays protruding through the backhead, if fitted as described above. If there is any doubt about the heating facilities available, it is wise to use a silver-solder of the lowest melting point on this job, care should also be taken to conserve the heat as much as possible – by packing coke around the outside of the firebox to within a few inches of the foundation ring (the boiler being laid on its back to start off with) while the inside of the firebox can also be filled with coke, though in this case it is wise to put some asbestos sheet inside to protect the crown and the ends of the tubes. Care should also be taken to ensure that no

dust from the coke gets near the seams that are to be silver-soldered.

The flame from the blowpipe should be worked right round the foundation ring until the whole glows a dull red, when the silver-solder is applied and this should be fed in continuously right round until the starting point is reached. Immediately the foundation ring is finished to the builder's satisfaction, the boiler is "up-ended" while still hot and the backhead dealt with. This leaves only one or two bushes to fit, such as those near the bottom of the firebox for blow-down valves; those in the barrel should have been fitted and brazed before the firebox was dealt with, but if not, now is the time to fix them while the boiler is still hot.

Builders using stays which are screwed through both outer and inner plates can now caulk them with a high-melting point soft solder. A liquid flux is best for this, such as Baker's fluid. A generous amount is brushed over all stay nuts on the inside and the solder applied to every one individually, for which the boiler will only have to be heated to some 320 deg. C., or roughly half the temperature required for the silver-solder. After this, the heads of the stays on the outside are dealt with in a similar manner, when the boiler should be ready for the hydraulic test.

Wherever possible, boiler builders should have their boilers tested by official boiler testers of their local model engineering society, but if this is impossible, the only requirements are a large pressure gauge, reading up to at least 300 p.s.i. (on no account should one of the small "model" pressure gauges be used), a hand pump, say of $\frac{3}{8}$ in or $\frac{1}{2}$ in. dia. ram, and a container or tray filled with cold water, into which the pump is placed. All bushes must be carefully plugged, the regulator and dome bushes securely blanked off, using washers or gaskets as necessary, while one of the safety valve bushes can be used for the attachment of the test pressure gauge. A check or non-return valve can be fitted to one of the smaller bushes on the backhead, and the pipe from the hand pump fitted up to this.

The boiler is now completely filled with cold water, all air being excluded, when it will be found that just a few strokes on the hand pump will bring the pressure up. The pressure should be brought up gradually, watching for

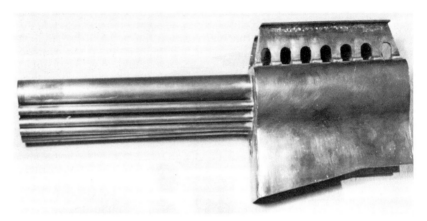

Boiler for a ³/₄in. scale Jubilee by the author.

leaks. Sometimes a leaking bush may be mistaken for an actual leak in the boiler, so this should be watched for! When the final test pressure, which must not be higher than twice the working pressure, is reached, it should be held for at least 15 minutes, and if all is well, the pressure can be let down and the boiler passed for service.

Regular hydraulic tests should be carried out on all model locomotive boilers, preferably every other year. Subsequent tests need not be carried out at higher pressures than 1½ times working pressure. It is also important that steam tests are carried out, so that the safety valves can be seen to be reliable and capable of releasing all the steam the boiler can generate, however hard the fire is worked. Generally speaking, the safety valves should not permit a rise of more than 10% over working pressure however hard the boiler is worked.

A final, repeated word on boiler brazing or silver-soldering. Many silver-solders contain cadmium and the fumes of this when heated are dangerous; every care should therefore be taken to provide plenty of ventilation during brazing operations.

Brazing a large 7¹/₄in. gauge boiler, using propane.

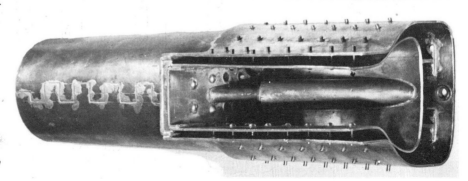

Underside of boiler with thermic syphon by the author.

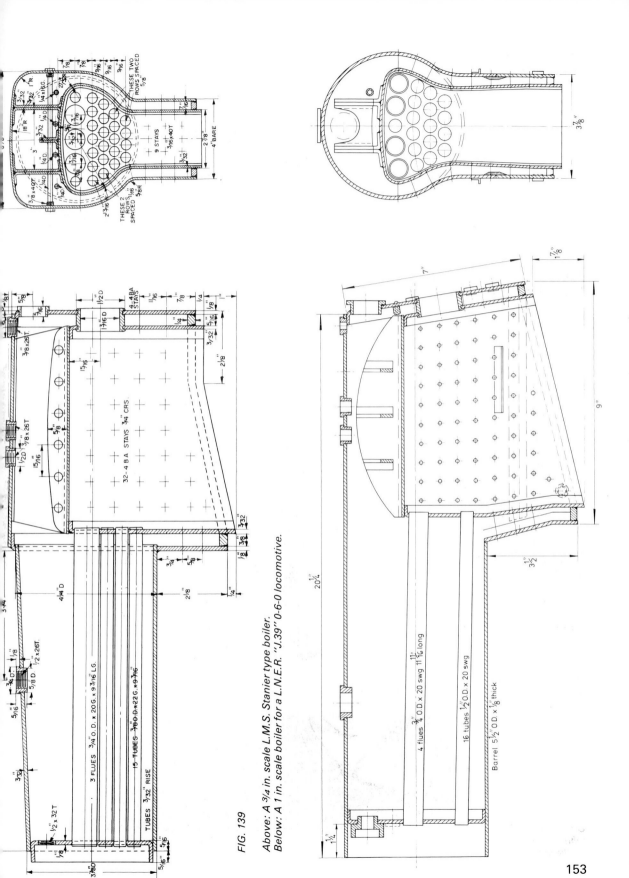

FIG. 139

Above: A 3/4 in. scale L.M.S. Stanier type boiler.
Below: A 1 in. scale boiler for a L.N.E.R. "J.39" 0-6-0 locomotive.

153

CHAPTER EIGHTEEN

Smokeboxes, superheaters, boiler fittings

SMOKEBOXES

The smokebox of model locomotives up to about 1 inch scale is generally made from brass or copper tube; steel can also be used, though unless adequate precautions are taken against rust, steel can be troublesome. If it is decided to us steel, it is worth having the smokebox plated or galvanised, after which it can be painted with one of the heat-resisting paints as used on motor-car exhausts.

The smokebox can sometimes be screwed direct to the end of the boiler barrel, the two tubes being made to "telescope" together. Where this is not possible, a turned ring made from a casting in gunmetal can be used. On the older types of locomotives, the smokebox was generally somewhat larger in diameter than the boiler barrel, even when the latter has been fitted with the usual lagging and cleading, and in these cases, a turned ring is essential and often it is of quite an ornamental shape. If no casting is available for this ring, it can be made by bending up square brass or copper bar, after annealing, and silver-soldering the join, afterwards turning the ring in the lathe.

It is important that the join between the smokebox and the boiler barrel is quite air-tight otherwise steaming will be adversely affected; this can be assured by smearing the mating surfaces with plumbers' jointing or one of the Hermetite compounds before final assembly.

The front of the smokebox is usually fitted with a turned ring to which is attached a hinged door giving access to

Unfinished G.E.R. "Claud" in 5in. gauge by Len Labram.

the tubes etc. This turned ring may, in small smokeboxes, be made a tight push fit into the smokebox tube, so that the full internal diameter of the latter may be free for the purpose of sweeping the tubes, attention to the superheaters etc. Although castings are often used for the smokebox door, with the hinge straps cast on, the drawback here is that the front cannot be turned in the lathe, so that separate hinge straps are preferred. Brass blanks are often used for this door, rather than castings, these being dished after annealing and then turned in the lathe. The door hinges are generally made from square mild steel or nickel-silver, and held to the door by small rivets, either round head or countersunk, according to the prototype modelled.

It is most important that the smokebox door should be quite air-tight, and in fact the whole smokebox, otherwise the boiler will not steam. The gaps inevitably left around the blast pipe and the steam pipes to the cylinders where these pass through the bottom of the smokebox should be carefully plugged with a putty made by kneading asbestos with water. A removable crossbar is generally fitted across the inside of the door ring, a rectangular slot in which is engaged by the "dart", thus enabling the door to be tightened up by the usual handles on the outside. The inner of these two handles has a square hole in its boss, to match the dart, while the outer handle is tapped anything from 6 to 2 BA according to the scale of the locomotive.

In locomotives smaller than 1 in. scale, difficulty is often experienced in coupling up the various pipes inside the smokebox due to the small internal diameter; one way of overcoming this is to make the smokebox in two halves, split horizontally exactly on the centre-line. This enables all the pipes etc, inside the smokebox to be put permanently in place without having to grope through the front at all. The smokebox tube can be split by means of a very thin slitting saw or by hacksawing, but if too much metal is "lost" in the cutting, it may be necessary to make up for this by silver-soldering a thin strip of metal to one cut edge; another method is to use a fine metal fretsaw, which requires patience as such saw blades are very fragile, though the result is good.

The two halves of a split smokebox can be held together by means of a hori-zontal lap strip on each side, closely spaced countersunk screws being used, and the adjoining surfaces treated with jointing compound on final assembly.

Smokeboxes of the larger-boilered locomotives are generally fitted with a "petticoat" pipe, this being an extension of the chimney inside the smokebox. In smaller models, this may take the form of a length of tube belled out at the bottom, the chimney being made a tight push fit over the upper part of it. On some engines, the arrangement of blast pipe and petticoat makes access to the tubes for sweeping difficult. A petticoat which can be quickly removed through the smokebox door overcomes this, the lower portion being held in place by a screw (preferably of stainless steel) set at an angle to the horizontal. Care should however be taken to see that the correct alignment of the petticoat pipe and the blast pipe are not upset, as this is most important for good steaming, as mentioned in Chapter 4.

SUPERHEATERS

In the early days of the model steam locomotive, smokebox superheaters consisting of a row of small diameter tubes located between the "wet" header and the cylinders were often adopted. These became known as "gridiron" superheaters. They cannot be recommended as they do not provide any superheat at all, in fact they are no more than steam driers, and have the big dis-advantage that they clutter up the smokebox and make tube sweeping almost impossible.

Many model locomotives have been built with the so-called "hairpin" or flue-tube superheaters. These are generally made from copper tube and a shaped block of solid copper or gunmetal is used at the extreme end to give some protection from the extreme heat of the fire. This type of superheater, although giving reasonable results, makes tube sweeping somewhat difficult and is also inclined to become blocked, especially if the locomotive is in continual steam for lengthy periods.

Undoubtly, the most effective superheater for model locomotives is the firebox "radiant" type, first used by the late Bill Crebbin in the late 1920's. Although copper can be used for this type of superheater, it will not have a very long life before becoming burnt out.

bend'' may take the form of a solid piece of stainless steel, with the joints welded or brazed.

As stainless steel tube is difficult to bend, a good plan is to use this tube for the straight parts and copper tube for the radiused ends, where the elements are connected to the ''wet header'' and to the branch pipes to the cylinders. The connection between the two metals may be made by lightly turning the ends of each and slipping over a thin sleeve, which may be made of copper or bronze, the ends being silver-soldered and ''faired off'', so as to cause the minimum restriction to the passing of the gases from the fire.

The smokebox and pipework of the author's 3¹/₂in. gauge Jubilee.

Mild steel tube is sometimes used, and can have a fair life before extreme rusting sets in. But the ideal material to use for superheaters is stainless steel; the tube should be solid-drawn and may be

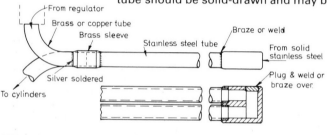

FIG. 140

RADIANT TYPE SUPERHEATER

Lower part of a divided smokebox (author's Jubilee).

of quite light gauge. The extreme end of a firebox superheater may be right over the fire ending in the rear top corner of the firebox where it will not interfere with the fireman's shovel. The ''return

BOILER FITTINGS – SAFETY VALVES

The safety valves are perhaps the most important fittings on the locomotive boiler. Except on the very smallest models, at least two safety valves should be provided.

The safety valves should be so designed that however hard the boiler is worked, the pressure in the boiler will not rise to higher than 10% above the normal working pressure. This is not so easy as it sounds if the valves are to be anywhere near ''scale'' size and shape! Perhaps one solution would be for the locomotive builder to equip himself with two sets of safety valves, one set intended for working under steam, and another, true to scale but dummy, for exhibition purposes only. Of course the owner would have to be careful not to forget to change over before putting his engine into steam!

In designing a safety valve, it should not be forgotten that the area *above* the valve seating is as important as the area of the seating itself. So often one sees a model locomotive fitted with safety valves with adjusting nuts have three or four tiny holes for the escape of the steam which are clearly quite inadequate, and therefore extremely dangerous. Another point to bear in mind is that if ball valves are used, the diameter of the seating must not be too close to the diameter of the ball, otherwise the ball may stick until the pressure has risen to a dangerous level.

As to the area of the valve seating, this is best based partly on the grate area of the boiler and partly on the working pressure. As many model safety valves

156

FIG. 141

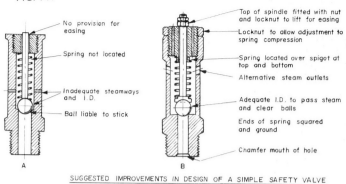

No provision for easing

Spring not located

Inadequate steamways and I.D.

Ball liable to stick

A

Top of spindle fitted with nut and locknut to lift for easing

Locknut to allow adjustment to spring compression

Spring located over spigot at top and bottom

Alternative steam outlets

Adequate I.D. to pass steam and clear balls

Ends of spring squared and ground

Chamfer mouth of hole

B

SUGGESTED IMPROVEMENTS IN DESIGN OF A SIMPLE SAFETY VALVE

FIG. 142

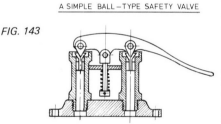

Ball $\frac{7}{32}\emptyset$

$\frac{3}{8}'' \times 26T$

ream $\frac{5}{32}''\emptyset$

A SIMPLE BALL—TYPE SAFETY VALVE

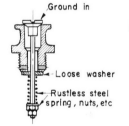

Ground in

Loose washer

Rustless steel spring, nuts, etc

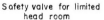

Safety valve for limited head room

FIG. 143

Ramsbottom type safety valve

FIG. 145A

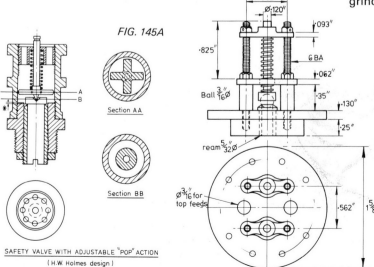

Section AA

Section BB

SAFETY VALVE WITH ADJUSTABLE "POP" ACTION
(H.W. Holmes design)

use ball valves, the following table of suitable valve seatings and diameters of throughways may be found helpful. They are for working pressures between 90 and 110 p.s.i. and refer to TWO safety valves.:-

Grate area sq. in.	Seating diameter in.	Diameter of ball. in.	Minimum dia. of throughway. in.
6	$3/32$	$1/8$	$5/32$
9	$1/8$	$5/32$	$7/32$
12	$9/64$	$3/16$	$15/64$
24	$3/16$	$1/4$	$5/16$
36	$9/32$ (or $3/8$)	$11/32$	$29/64$ (or $15/32$)

Where two or more safety valves are used, they should be adjusted to the same pressure. If one is set to blow off at a higher pressure than the other, it may never blow and may become stuck as a result.

Stainless steel wire is generally used for safety valve springs. However, better results can usually be obtained by making them from ordinary piano wire. Although this wire will rust in time, rusting can be kept at bay if the springs are frequently removed and greased after the run. To make a good quality spring, do not be tempted to take a tension spring and pull it out to make a compression spring. The spring should be wound in the lathe, spacing the wire at a suitable pitch, with the wire kept under proper tension. After a suitable length has been wound, both ends should be squared off and softened by holding against the grinding wheel.

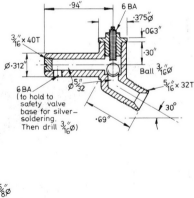

G.W.R. TYPE SAFETY—VALVES & TOP—FEEDS

FIG. 144

157

bronze, bronze on monel, or stainless steel on bronze. (Fig. 145a)

The thread of the safety valve by which it is screwed into the boiler should be fairly coarse, 26 t.p.i. being ideal for locomotives from ½ in. to 1 in. scale.

REGULATORS

The regulator is of course the main steam stop valve of the locomotive. It must control the passage of the steam to the cylinders so that the driver has full control over his engine at all times. It

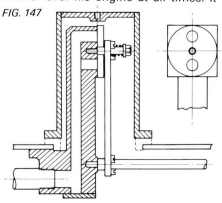

FIG. 147

STROUDLEY TYPE REGULATOR

Safety valves with a "pop" action are preferred by some model engineers. Although a "pop" valve can be made using a ball, the results are usually disappointing. To obtain a good "pop" action that is not too fierce and a shut-down without too great a loss of pressure, a flat valve on a sharp-edge seating should be used. The drawing shows a type of "pop" safety valve which should give good results; the two dimensions marked with an asterisk are somewhat critical and may need some experiment to obtain the desired action. The valve should be made of a different metal from its seating, for instance gunmetal on phos/

must have a gradual opening, yet at the same time be capable of passing all the steam required by the cylinders when fully open.

For small models, the simple screw-down type of valve may be considered; this type of valve will not stick if made of the right materials and handled properly. It is also very easy and quick to make and will not leak steam. The only real drawback of the screw-down regulator is that it requires rather a large amount of handle opening, though the use of a coarse thread, or even a two-start thread, will generally overcome this.

Another type of regulator in common use is the so-called "disc in a tube" variety. For a domeless boiler, this type can be made with a large number of very fine holes for the entry of the steam. The disadvantage of the disc regulator is that it tends to leak steam after a time due to fine particles or "hardness" in the water getting between the valve and the port face.

For a "pull-out" regulator, a simple sliding valve on a horizontal seating can be used. The body of the regulator should be of such a size and shape that it

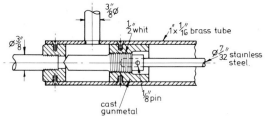

FIG. 145   SIMPLE SCREW—DOWN REGULATOR

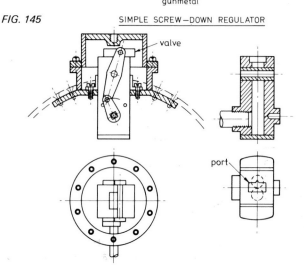

FIG. 146   SLIDE—VALVE REGULATOR

Boiler front end and superheater elements.

complicated than those described so far. It is not suitable for very low domes, but for the older types of locomotive with large domes it is ideal. As there is always the danger of some of the pins in this type of regulator working loose in service, it is essential that some positive method be adopted to prevent this, such as wiring them together.

For Great Western Railway boilers, a smokebox regulator is often used, and for many American and Colonial types of locomotive, a smokebox regulator may be of the poppet valve type, with an external operating rod running alongside the boiler. Although full-size American locomotives had poppet valve regulators with a large number of valves, for models up to $3/4$ in. scale, one such valve will be found sufficient, while for locomotives of 1 in. scale and larger, two valves may be used, one a pilot valve of smaller bore than the main valve and arranged to open slightly before the main valve.

A more elaborate slide-valve regulator is one based on the L.M.S. Stanier type. It is suitable for quite low domes and can be arranged to give a large opening without becoming too bulky.

All screws used in regulators, whether used inside the steam space or on the outside of the boiler, should be made of either bronze or stainless steel, with a preference for the former. On no account should commercial brass or mild steel screws be used.

The shape of the regulator handle is very much a matter of personal choice, the older type, working vertically in a quadrant being very easy to operate unless the cab roof is low, while the more modern type suits a long low-built cab. It is important to ensure that the handle is a secure fit on the operating rod, either a squared fitting being used, or a small cotter and nut.

Where a sight-feed lubrication system is specified, the regulator handle will require an extension to operate this; it is fully described in a later chapter.

can be introduced into the boiler through the dome bush, and bolted to the underside of the barrel, after which the main steam pipe is screwed into it from the smokebox end. The operating rod is then inserted through a bush on the backhead, having on its end a wide-jawed fork which is able to embrace the regulator body and the operating levers situated on either side. Although the pressure of the steam will keep such a valve down on the port face, it is a sensible precaution to fit a light plate spring, made of thin phos-bronze sheet, to bear on the top of the valve.

The so-called "Stroudley" type of regulator is a good one, though rather more

FIG. 148

SIMPLE PULL-
OUT REGULATOR

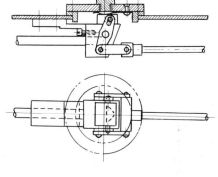

FIG. 149

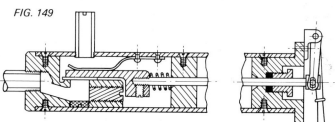

PULL OUT REGULATOR, double–handle design.

WATER GAUGES

All coal-fired boilers should be provided with at least one water gauge. Small water-tube boilers for gauges "0" and "1" may be fitted with two "try" cocks in lieu, one cock being placed a little above normal water level and the other a little below. Two water gauges are often fitted to locomotives of one inch scale and above (Great Western models excepted, as the full-size G.W.R. locomotives were fitted with one gauge only).

Where possible, the water gauge should be arranged with a vertical glass. On round-top boilers this can generally

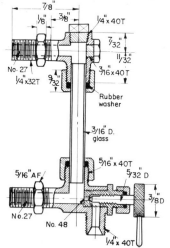

FIG. 150
Simple water gauge.

be achieved by fitting an "elbow" shaped bush to the outer firebox wrapper, so that the top water gauge fitting can line up vertically with the bottom fitting. While the top fitting may be placed as high on the backhead as convenient, the bottom fitting should be placed so that when the water level is flush with

the top edge of the gland nut, there is still a little water over the top of the crown of the inner firebox. In allowing for this, it should be remembered that a small bore water gauge always shows the water level as slightly higher than it actually is, due to capillary attraction.

A glass of reasonable bore is advisable, i.e. $3/16$ in. dia. minimum for $3/4$ in. scale locomotives, $1/4$ in. dia. for 1 in. scale, or $5/16$ in. dia. for $1\frac{1}{2}$ in. scale. The bore of the water and steam ways should be made slightly greater than the bore of the glass, and the connections into the boiler kept on the short side, as the connections only tend to collect scale. Cleaning plugs are advised for both ways into the boiler and a blow-down valve of not too small a bore so that a good rush of water can be passed when it is required to clean the glass.

Glass breakages do occur sometimes, although these are generally due to mis-alignment of the fittings, or overtightening of the gland nuts. As a glass breakage can be a nuisance or even dangerous, a protective screen is sometimes fitted. This may take the form of a piece of mica in a metal frame which can be clipped on to the two gland nuts, or a piece of flat glass in a similar frame may be fitted, perhaps on small hinges so that it can be swung out of the way when required. The shut-off cocks fitted to full-size water gauges are not essential in small models and would have to be very much out of scale to be of practical value in any case.

An excellent design of water gauge with offset fittings, known as the Cottam gauge, can be recommended for models of 1 in. scale and above. With this gauge, both the steam and water ways into the boiler can be shut off almost instantaneously by the use of a key, so that the glass can be changed without having to drop the fire. The usual blow-down valve is also fitted.

Water gauge fittings should be carefully lined up, using a length of silver-steel rod of the same diameter as the glass, before the glass is tried in place. The fittings and gland nuts should always be made appreciably larger in the bore than the glass itself. Rubber washers are normally used, these being made from thick rubber tube. These washers can be parted off with a razor blade while mounted on a length of metal rod. When the glass is inserted, it should be noted whether there is

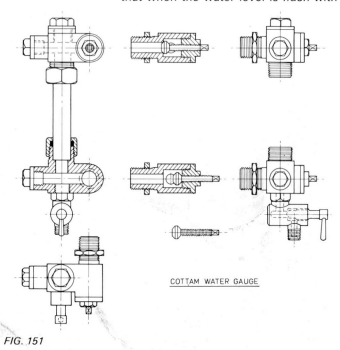

COTTAM WATER GAUGE

FIG. 151

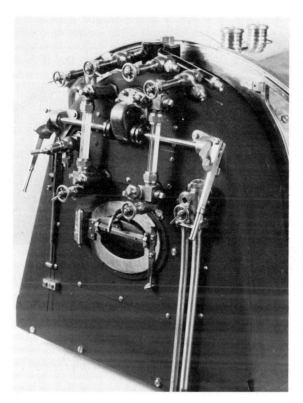

Above left, backhead fittings by George Thomas. Above right, footplate of Len Labram's 5in. gauge G.E.R. "Claud". Below left, cab view of the late Louis Raper's fine "Dean Goods" and, below right, of the late H.A. Taylor's 3¹/₂in. L.M.S. 4-6-0.

Backhead of 5in. gauge 2-8-0 by B. Palmer of Durban. Note water gauge column.

the ball is restricted according to the duty involved; for instance, where mechanically-driven pumps are fitted, the lift of the ball may be restricted to about one-eighth of the ball diameter, for slow speed pumps or hand-operated pumps, the lift may be about one-sixth of the ball diameter, while for use with injectors, the lift can be made about one-third of the ball diameter.

The usual method of making the actual seating for the ball is to first use a drill of suitable size, follow this with a reamer, put through slowly and carefully; the upper chamber is then opened out with a drill and "D" bit of diameter somewhat larger than the ball to be used, to allow plenty of clearance for the water to pass the ball. A steel ball of the same diameter as the stainless ball to be used in the valve is then placed on the seating and given a sharp tap by means of a light hammer and a piece of brass rod. However, this method is somewhat hit and miss, and a better way is to make a proper guide for the brass rod, which should have a small depression or centre on its end, to locate the ball fair and square.

Although a little more work, a check valve with the seating made as a separate turning is a better proposition, as the seating can be finished in the lathe at an angle so that a sharper edge is presented to the ball. This also helps to prevent foreign matter from getting between the ball and its seating.

Check valves for use with injectors require a less restricted water way than the usual type of valve. The vertical type shown in the drawing can be recommended and is not difficult to make.

The best position for the admission of the feed water into the boiler is on top of the barrel and not too close to the firebox. On Great Western locomotives, the "top-feed" took the form of quite an elaborate series of trays through which the water was delivered in a number of very fine streams. In this way the feed water was heated thoroughly before it could come into contact with the metallic surfaces of the boiler. The trays also helped to prevent foreign matter and hardness deposits getting into the boiler, as they could be removed for cleaning.

In model boilers, it is not necessary to go to such lengths as the above arrangement, but the water can with advantage be directed towards the front of the bar-

enough room for the glass to expand lengthwise. Finger pressure should be sufficient to tighten the gland nuts; spanners should not be used.

CHECK (CLACK) VALVES

Check valves, also known as Clack valves, are non-return valves which are fitted on all water pipes feeding water into the locomotive's boiler. They are also used on lubrication oil delivery pipes. In the majority of model locomotives, they are simple valves fitted with a single stainless steel or bronze ball. The lift of

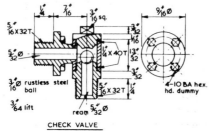

CHECK VALVE

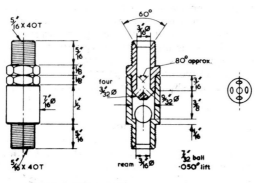

VERTICAL CHECK VALVE

FIG. 152

162

FIG. 153
The essential
parts of a small
pressure gauge.

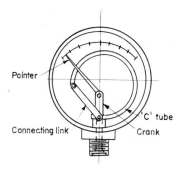

more easily to quantity production rather than hand work, though the final assembly calls for some "watchmaking". The basic component is the "C" tube. This is generally made from thin phosphor-bronze or hard brass sheet, closed and soft soldered at the ends to render it steam-tight. One end of this tube is soldered to the union fitting and a connection between the two made by carefully drilling through one wall of the "C" tube. The other end of the "C" tube is connected by a very light linkage to the pointer. When pressure is applied, the "C" tube tends to straighten itself out, thus moving the pointer across the scale. Calibration is carried out against a large gauge of known reliability.

The making of the "C" tube is clearly the most difficult part of a pressure gauge. Some model engineers have found that the "C" tube can be made from bronze rod, which is turned and drilled in the lathe and then mounted on a mandrel of silver-steel for final turning, to reduce the walls of the tube (which it has now become) to anything from 3 to 5 thou. according to the scale or size of the gauge. The embryo "C" tube is next annealed (this has to be done very carefully owing to its thin walls) and its centre part flattened by rolling a piece of round steel rod along it against a flat plate, leaving the ends round.

Pressure gauges are sometimes made with geared drive. A very fine pinion is used, plus a sector to match. Suitable gears can be obtained from scrap watches, the pinion being around $1/16$ in. dia. for a small pressure gauge, while the sector would have to be cut from an un-pierced gear of around $3/8$ in. dia. The pointer can be filed from a piece of sheet metal, but this is not easy and another possibility is to use a watch second hand. To make a good dial requires some photography, a dial being first drawn in Indian ink on stiff white paper, this being then photographed giving the necessary reduction in size.

The pressure gauge should have a range at least 50 per cent higher than the normal working pressure of the boiler and must be fitted to a "U" or syphon pipe to protect the internal mechanism from unnecessary heat. Although steam pressure gauges can generally be obtained in sizes as small as $3/4$ in. dia., it should be remembered that the larger the gauge, the more likely it is to be reliable.

rel through a series of small holes, or on to a single tray with a slight slope forwards and downwards towards the front.

Although on full-size locomotives the top-feed fittings normally contained the check valves, one on each side, this is not good practice on model locomotives, as there is too much restriction to the flow of the water. This would not matter much where pumps are used, but cannot be recommended in conjunction with injectors. The best place for check valves when injectors are used is at the side of the boiler, a vertical straight-through type of valve being used, with unions top and bottom, so that the valve can be quickly and easily removed for cleaning without disturbing anything else.

If top-feed is objected to because the model is of some prototype which did not have this method of boiler feed, the check valves can be placed in the side of the barrel, fairly near the front end. This was the usual position adopted on the Southern Railway. Most L.N.E.R. locomotives had the check valves on the backhead. This is not the ideal position, especially if the pumps are used. However, if they are of ample bore and fitted with internal pipes directing the water forward, they will be satisfactory. However, if internal pipes are used, it is most important to arrange that the pipes are easy to remove for cleaning, as they will tend to become obstructed in time due to impurities in the water (especially in "hard" water districts).

PRESSURE GAUGES

The making of the steam pressure gauge is not usually attempted by the model engineer as this is a fitting which, though simple in principle, lends itself

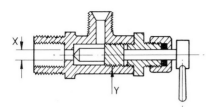

FIG. 154

VALVE FOR BLOWERS OR INJECTOR

X — $\frac{3}{32}''\varnothing$ for blowers, $\frac{1}{8}''\varnothing$ for injectors.
Y — 40T for blowers, 32T or 2 BA for injectors.

STEAM BLOWERS

A steam blower is an essential fitting on any coal-fired locomotive. Without a blower, when the engine is standing, the fire would quickly die out as its combustion depends entirely on an induced draught up the chimney.

Locomotives fired by methylated spirit lamps and paraffin (kerosene) blowlamps or high-pressure gas burners also require blowers, to avoid the possibilities of a blowback, though the draught does not have to be nearly so fierce as when solid fuel is used.

In small models, the blower usually consists of an auxiliary blast pipe fitted with a fine diameter jet laid alongside the main blast pipe, the jet being directed to the middle of the petticoat pipe or chimney. On larger models, the blower will be more elaborate, having two, three or four fine jets, equidistant around the main blast pipe. Mr. D.E. Lawrence's blower design embodies four separate and removable jets which are screwed into the main blast pipe top at a slight angle of inclination towards the centre, thus filling the petticoat completely and leading to rapid steam raising without too great use of steam. The jets are drilled No.80 drill size for models up to 1 in. scale, while No. 75 or 76 will be found satisfactory for 1½ in. scale locomotives.

The steam for the blower should be taken from as high a point on the boiler as possible, the usual place being the "fountain" or manifold on the top of the firebox at its rear corner. Steam is led from this fitting to a screw-down valve with a fairly fine thread and then into a thick-walled tube through the boiler (thus acting also as a stay) and ending at the smokebox tubeplate with a union fitting, from which the steam is finally taken to the blast pipe top, as described above.

Whatever design of blower is adopted, it is important to ensure that the jets are not easily knocked out of alignment, when sweeping the tubes etc.

SNIFTING VALVES

All locomotives fitted with piston valves or with slide valve cylinders with the valves on top should be provided with a snifting or "anti-vacuum" valve. It should be so arranged that the air is drawn into the wet header, thus when the regulator is closed and the engine is coasting, cool air is drawn through the superheater elements, preventing them from overheating. If no snifting valve is fitted, the action of the pistons, when the regulator is shut, would create a partial vacuum in the superheater and steam pipes, with the danger that ashes and grit might be sucked down the blast pipe, with severe effects on the cylinders.

On L.N.E.R. models, the snifting valve is generally placed on the top of the smokebox, just behind the chimney. Gresley designs used a single large valve, while Great Eastern engines were sometimes fitted with two snifting valves in this position. On some Southern Railway locomotives, two snifting valves were used, one on each side of the smokebox, with an inter-connecting pipe across the inside of the smokebox. On many Great Western and L.M.S. locomotives, the snifting valve was situated in the lower part of the smokebox, just above or to the rear of the saddle. If this position is chosen, a pipe can be taken from the inside of the snifting valve to the wet header, the pipe

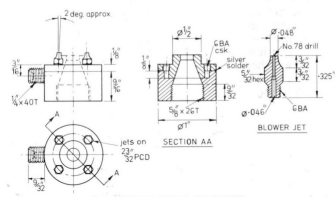

FIG. 154A

BLAST NOZZLE WITH 4-JET BLOWER

FIG. 155

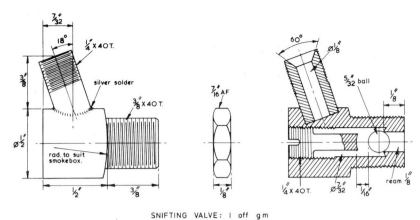

SNIFTING VALVE: I off g m
ball rustless steel

FIG. 156

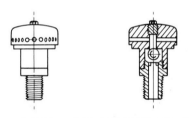

S.R. TYPE SNIFTING VALVE

FIG. 157

L.N.E.R. TYPE SNIFTING VALVE

being laid inside and close to the wall of the smokebox, so as to avoid the blast pipe and steam pipes to the cylinders. This pipe should be of adequate bore, as should be the snifting valve itself. A $3/16$ in. dia. thin-walled pipe should be about right for a 1 in. scale locomotive.

When fitting snifting valves, great care should be taken to ensure that there is no leak of steam, where the valve is attached to the header, and also that there is no possibility of air getting into the smokebox, otherwise the steaming of the locomotive will be impaired.

BLOWDOWN VALVES

All locomotive boilers should be fitted with at least one, and preferably two, blowdown valves. They should be located as low down in the firebox as possible, the best position being at the front corner of the foundation ring. Where the layout of the driving or coupled wheels permits, a good plan is to provide a large opening, circular or rectangular, in the main frames on both sides of the locomotive through which the blowdown valves can be screwed home in bushes fitted to the firebox. They can then be operated easily from the outside.

Unless only distilled water is used in the boiler (an inconvenient and expensive business) solid matter from the water will gradually become deposited all over the inside of the boiler, but particularly around the lower part of the firebox and on the foundation ring, where circulation tends to be sluggish. This trouble applies particularly in districts where the water is hard, but if the blowdown valves are used regularly, im-

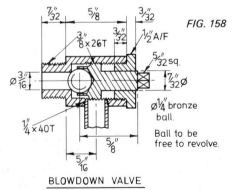

FIG. 158

BLOWDOWN VALVE

mediately after a run, such deposits will be much slower in forming and the boiler will remain in good condition for longer periods before removal from the frames for proper cleaning.

The usual type of screw-down valve is not ideal as a blowdown valve, as the coned end of the valve spindle quickly

A three-chime whistle.

FIG. 159

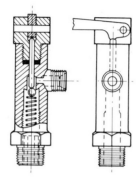

VERTICAL WHISTLE VALVE

emitted would be a very poor one, of small volume and much too high a pitch. On some full-size railways, the pitch of the whistle used was high (some readers will remember the ear-splitting note emitted by some Great Northern Railway and L.N.E.R. locomotives) and in such cases, the problem can be solved by using a long thin-walled brass tube about ⅜ in diameter for a ¾ in. or 1 in. scale locomotive, the whistle being fitted out of sight underneath the footplate just inside the valance edging. A pipe is then taken from a whistle valve on the backhead.

To give a more mellow note, such as that emitted by whistles on the old Great Western Railway, it is suggested that the tube be at least ¾ in. dia. and 5 to 6 in. long. The length which gives the best note can be determined by experiment, by using a sliding end piece which can be adjusted while the whistle is tried out using steam from the boiler at normal working pressure. When the desired

becomes scored through the passage of the "foreign matter", even if made of stainless steel. The author therefore always uses a type of blowdown valve which incorporates a revolving ball. The ball is arranged loose in its "cage" but without shake, and is so positioned that the rush of steam from the boiler causes it to revolve and thus to equalise wear.

In large model locomotive boilers, washout plugs should also be provided, in the corners of the firebox and at other strategic points. In steel boilers, bosses for these may be welded on, to give greater depth of thread. The plugs themselves may have a standard taper thread.

STEAM WHISTLES

The difficulty in a model steam whistle is to obtain a realistic note, at the same time keeping the overall dimensions within reasonable limits. If the whistle is made to scale proportions, the note

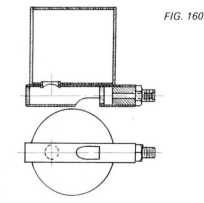

FIG. 160

FIG. 161
A typical
steam turret

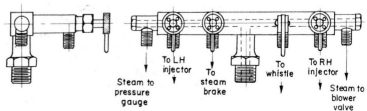

Steam to pressure gauge

To LH injector

To steam brake

To whistle

To RH injector

Steam to blower valve

note is obtained, the sliding end piece is soldered in position and any excess tube cut off.

Wherever the whistle is fitted, it is important to remember that the opening must be arranged at the bottom of the whistle, and the outer end of the tube set very slightly higher than the entry end, so that if any water should condense in the tube, it can run out through the opening.

A deep toned whistle (or hooter) suitable for L.M.S. Stanier models and models of Caledonian prototypes can be made by using a short whistle tube of the type described above and fitting to it a soundbox. The soundbox can be made

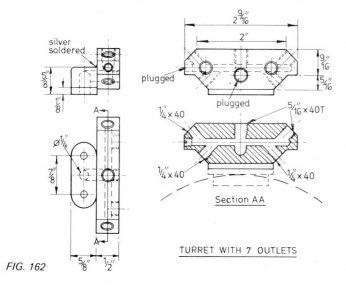

silver soldered

plugged

plugged

$\frac{1}{4}'' \times 40$

$\frac{5}{16}'' \times 40T$

$\frac{1}{4}'' \times 40$

$\frac{1}{4}'' \times 40$

Section AA

TURRET WITH 7 OUTLETS

FIG. 162

of tube of length approximately equal to its diameter, the diameter being about three times the diameter of the whistle. The soundbox is arranged on top of the whistle tube, with an inter-connecting hole of diameter somewhat less than the diameter of the whistle, so that the jet of steam is blown straight across this inter-connecting hole. The exact size of the various components of this type of whistle is best determined by experiment, using steam from the locomotive's own boiler.

An added touch of realism can be obtained, when using one of the "outsize" whistles, by fitting a scale size dummy whistle in the usual position on the boiler, and running a very small diameter pipe from the whistle valve to the dummy. Thus when the whistle valve is operated, a fine jet of steam will issue from the dummy whistle.

TURRETS OR MANIFOLDS

A turret or manifold is a combination fitting arranged on the top of the firebox at the extreme rear end, generally within the cab space but not necessarily. It will contain a number of branches to supply steam, as dry as possible, to various fittings, such as the steam blower, the steam valves for the injectors, steam valve for steam brakes, pressure gauges, etc. etc. The fitting generally also contains the whistle valve. This is not only for convenience in arranging the various pipes, but also it saves making a large number of holes in the boiler.

As far as the whistle valve is concerned, this is often quite a simple fitting containing a small stainless steel ball on a suitable seating which can be pushed off this seating against the pressure of a small compression spring to allow steam to pass to the whistle.

A small turret can be attached to the boiler in the usual way by being screwed into a bush (which is silver-soldered into the boiler during the boiler's construction). If so, the thread should not be too fine, nor should the orifice be too small, as steam has to pass to a considerable number of fittings at one and the same time. A suitable thread for 3/4 in and 1 in. scale locomotives would be 3/8 in x 26t.

Sometimes the turret is too wide and unwieldy to be screwed home. It should therefore be provided with a flange fitting, the flange on the turret matching an oval bush fitted to the boiler, with the usual steam-tight gasket fitted in between.

BOILER EXPANSION JOINTS

Although not strictly a boiler fitting, the boiler expansion joint or clip is an important item in the locomotive. On nearly all full-size and certainly all model locomotives, the smokebox is attached rigidly to the engine frames, and as the front end of the boiler barrel is equally firmly attached to the rear of the smokebox, it follows that the boiler as a whole will expand towards the rear of the locomotive as it becomes heated. Thus the rear end of the boiler cannot be attached rigidly to the frames, but allowance must be made for this expansion.

On narrow-type locomotive boilers, where the lower part of the firebox goes down between the frames, expansion can be taken care of fairly easily by fixing

167

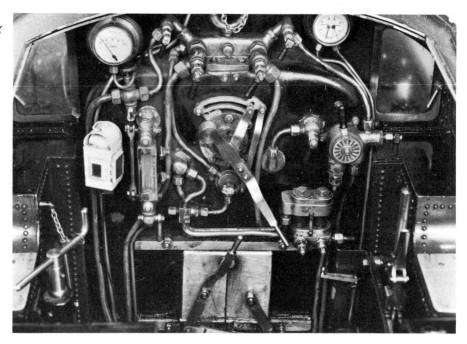

Backhead layout of Roy Amsbury's 51XX class G.W. tank.

This excellent 2-6-2 tank by Roy Amsbury has cab fitting as close to scale as possible, consistent with driving, with a pressure gauge and speedometer made by the builder (see above).

a length of angle to each side of the firebox so that one leg of each angle rests on top of the engine frames, at such a height that the boiler as a whole is level. A further angle, of the same length, is then clamped on top of the first, using three or four steel screws into tapped holes in the frame. This angle will then hold the boiler down firmly while allowing it to expand. The angle fitted to the boiler may be of brass, but the screws used to attach it should preferably be of bronze and their threads should be treated with plumber's jointing or similar material, to prevent leaks.

On wide-firebox boilers, the problem is sometimes more difficult, as the firebox is generally immediately above

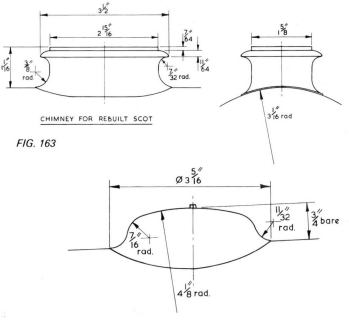

CHIMNEY FOR REBUILT SCOT

FIG. 163

DOME FOR REBUILT SCOT

FIG. 164

FIG. 165

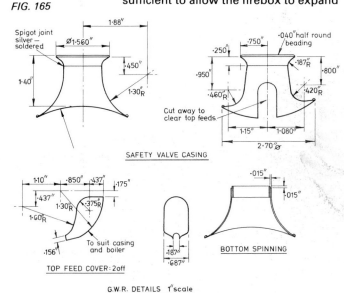

Spigot joint silver — soldered

SAFETY VALVE CASING

Cut away to clear top feeds

·040" half round beading

TOP FEED COVER: 2 off

To suit casing and boiler

BOTTOM SPINNING

G.W.R. DETAILS 1" scale

and move longitudinally without causing any trouble. On some wide-firebox type locomotives, a similar method can be adopted, but the sheet metal can be attached to the lower edge of the backhead.

CHIMNEYS AND DOMES

The chimneys and domes fitted to model locomotives are often made from gunmetal castings, though brass rod may be used for the very smallest gauges and scales. A chucking spigot may or may not be provided, but if it is, it should be on the top and sufficiently long to enable it to be gripped safely for turning or fly-cutting. If there is no chucking spigot, it should be possible to hold the casting firmly enough by gripping in the 4-jaw and setting to run true; the inside can then be bored. After boring, the underside may be hand filed to fit the curvature of the smokebox. However, a more accurate method is to fly-cut the underside in the lathe.

For fly-cutting, a brass mandrel should be turned up, a push fit into the bore of the casting, leaving about 2 in. above the top of the casting. Two flats are now filed on the extension part of the mandrel, the chimney is soft-soldered to it, and the mandrel clamped under the lathe toolholder at centre height. The cutter, held in the 3-jaw chuck and supported additionally by the tailstock, is set out to describe a circle equal to the diameter of the smokebox. Light cuts must be taken, the saddle being moved longitudinally, and the cutter revolved at a fairly slow speed.

After the underside has been attended to, the brass mandrel is un-soldered from the casting, and the outer part of the mandrel turned circular again. The chimney is then mounted on the mandrel once more and the outside and top finished to shape. For this, a lathe tool similar to a parting tool with the cutting edge quite square but with both corners slightly radiused will be found suitable, though for some chimneys, a similar tool but with sharp corners will be found invaluable.

It will be appreciated that it is not possible, assuming normal lathe turning methods, to complete the machining of the bases of either chimneys and domes. In most cases, the model locomotive builder attempts to file this part, the chimney or dome being

trailing wheels or a trailing truck in the case of a 4-6-4 or 4-8-4 type locomotive, and there are no easily located points on the main frames for attachment of angles as in the case of narrow-type fireboxes. One solution is to fix to the bottom edge of the throatplate a piece of thin sheet metal, preferably stainless steel, the full width, or nearly so, of the throatplate, and attach this sheet metal to a cross stretcher fitted to the frames, the flexibility in the sheet metal being sufficient to allow the firebox to expand

Boring the smokebox for the chimney.

top of the chimney, but at the other end, the arbor is left about the same amount short. Thus mounted, one end of the arbor can be held in the 3-jaw while the other end can be reached by the tailstock centre. The job is now machined in the usual way up to where the concave curves prevent the lathe tool going any further.

The job is next mounted on an angle plate on the vertical-slide with its horizontal axis accurately at right-angles to the lathe spindle. The Carrig jig consists of a spindle of diameter a nice working fit inside the arbor on which the chimney is mounted, this being attached rigidly to the angle plate. To this spindle is fitted a vertical stop or guide, which can be made from a ¼ in. bolt of suitable length with its head turned to provide a narrow rubbing edge to work against the outer edge of the previously fly-cut base of the chimney being machined.

The chimney is held by a lathe carrier which is attached to the projecting part of the arbor on which the chimney is mounted and it is pressed by hand on the spindle of the jig so that the chimney base is kept hard against the stop while the whole chimney is carefully and slowly turned by hand counter-clockwise during the machining of the base. The machining is done by an end-mill of convenient size held in the 3-jaw or in a collet and rotated slowly. The

screwed down to a short piece of tube of the same diameter as the smokebox (or boiler barrel as the case may be) and the filing being done with needle files used on the right-hand side of the chimney with strokes away to the right, so that if the file slips, it will not score the finished turned part. However, a Mr. Frank Carrig of the Melbourne S.M.E.E. has shown how the bases of chimneys and domes can be finished entirely in the lathe, eliminating all filing.

In the Carrig method, the chimney is mounted on an arbor a light press fit, the arbor being drilled and reamed to a suitable diameter, and it is made long enough to project at least ½ in. from the

A 7¼in. gauge Isle of Man Railway 2-4-0 by Vince Bentley (U.S.A.) with a fine dome.

chimney casting is adjusted by the vertical-slide so that the cutting edge of the end-mill is just above the finished diameter of the chimney by the thickness of a piece of paper when the cutting edge is above the centre-line of the chimney.

The first cut should be a small one, with the cutter brought to the base of the chimney by moving the cross-slide with the saddle locked. When the machining reaches the edge of the chimney base, this should be left as slightly thicker than a knife-edge, with a final touch up by emery cloth, the latter being done with the chimney held between centres. A final mirror finish can be obtained, if desired, by polishing on a rag buffing wheel held for convenience in a bench drilling machine.

When dealing with both chimneys and domes, it is essential that a large and accurate drawing of the fitting and the boiler or smokebox top be made so as to ascertain the distance the sides go below the top and to decide the radius to which the sides of a dome can be machined to get the knife-edge at the base when the base is the correct diameter. The castings should therefore be checked beforehand to find out if they can be machined to the required dimensions.

Sometimes it is found that, due to the lack of any chucking spigot, it is difficult to hold a dome casting. One method is to hold it in a clamp made of hardwood

such as beech or oak. The clamp is split longitudinally and held in the 4-jaw chuck and bored in situ to take the dome casting which can then be bored. The dome is then transferred, in its hardwood clamp, to the vertical-slide for fly-cutting the base, after which it can be pressed (lightly) on a brass mandrel for turning the outside, before tackling the base as described previously.

Chimneys are generally made a tight hand push fit over the petticoat pipe and may not require any further fixing, although to follow full-size practice, small hex-head or round-head bolts may be used, four or six as per prototype. Domes can generally be held by a single bolt through the top into a tapped hole in the inner dome.

CHAPTER NINETEEN

Lubrication, pumps, injectors, brakes

CYLINDER LUBRICATION

The principal types of cylinder lubricator in use on model locomotives are the hydrostatic, with or without sight-feed, and the mechanical.

The simple displacement lubricator is generally used on Gauge "0" and "1" locomotives. One reason for this is the lack of complication, and the fact that such a lubricator can be made smaller than the mechanical type. However, it is not a reliable type. In the displacement lubricator, the steam is arranged to condense on the surface of the oil; the water so formed, being heavier than oil, sinks to the bottom of the container. The oil thus rises until it reaches the level of the outlet, when it flows into the steam chest. But the action of such a lubricator is seldom regular and it sometimes "gulps" a large quantity of oil into the cylinders on the regulator being shut, due to the sudden drop in pressure in the steam pipes and steam chests.

Displacement lubricators should not be placed too close to the cylinders so that they may keep cool in service. They should be fitted with a separate inlet pipe for the steam and outlet pipe for the oil and a small needle valve for adjustment. They should also be provided with a drain valve at the bottom of the container to allow the condensed water to escape.

The sight-feed lubricator was perfected by the old Great Western Railway, and although this type of lubricator is based on the displacement principle, the details are much more elaborate. The steam is taken from a turret on the top of the backhead. The regulator handle is provided with an extension connected to a controlling valve which is so arranged that oil is admitted to the cylinders just before the regulator allows the steam to reach them. The steam for the lubricator is taken from a small cock on the turret, from which coiled pipes act as a condenser on the inside of the cab roof; the oil rises and flows to the sight feed control valve. The oil for the regulator flows through a small pipe forwards to the smokebox. The oil supply for the cylinders flows through small pipes to the controlling valve mentioned previously, and is picked up by the steam from the cock on the turret in this

FIG. 166

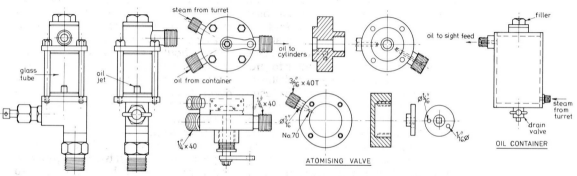

SIGHT FEED FITTING

SIGHT FEED LUBRICATION SYSTEM

valve, from which it is carried forward to the cylinders.

Matters are so arranged that when the locomotive fitted with the Swindon sight-feed lubricator is coasting, a little steam and oil is fed to the cylinders. When the regulator is fully closed against its stops, the lubricator feeds a few more drops of oil and then stops altogether; thus a small quantity of oil remains in the pipes ready to be fed to the cylinders when the engine is started again.

Model lubricators made on the Swindon principle have been successfully made in sizes down to ¾ in. scale.

In spite of the success of the sight-feed lubricator on Great Western locomotives, most other railway locomotives were fitted with mechanical lubricators. Mechanical lubricators are equally popular on model locomotives; two main types are in general use, the oscillating cylinder type, popularised by the late 'LBSC" and the fixed cylinder type, based on the Wakefield type.

Most model locomotives of ¾ in. scale are fitted with single ram lubricators, feeding the oil to two cylinders. Locomotives having three or four cylinders are better fitted with twin ram lubricators to ensure that each cylinder receives its fair share of oil. Where a single-ram lubricator feeds oil to two cylinders, it is important to ensure that the length and shape of the pipes carrying the oil to each cylinder are as near as possible identical, otherwise the oil will naturally take the easier path.

One advantage of the mechanical lubricator over other types is that the amount of oil fed to the cylinders is roughly proportional to the speed of the locomotive. However, the trouble is (with the usual oscillating or fixed cylinder type) that if the ram is properly fitted and the lubricator well made, far too much oil is supplied, and the excess oil is thrown out of the chimney or finds its way on to the wheels and eventually on to the track with annoying results. One method which has been tried is to provide a by-pass arrangement, with the intention of varying the amount of oil actually fed to the cylinders. A needle valve using a very fine thread and having the cone ("needle") of very fine angle has been tried, but is only partially successful, as however much the needle valve is adjusted, if it is opened at all, all the oil tends to find its way to the by-pass.

Perhaps the best method of controlling the amount of oil fed is by making the lubricator with an adjustable stroke to the ram. The author's design incorporates this feature and has proved very successful. An external handwheel fitted to a screw raises or lowers an eccentric which actuates the ram, thus the amount of oil fed can be varied at will from zero to the full capacity of the ram and cylinder.

Mechanical lubricators should be fitted with two check or non-return valves, one being fitted to the lubricator itself

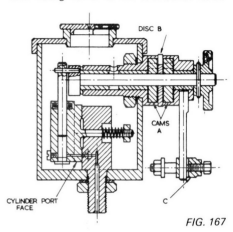

FIG. 167

SECTION THRO LUBRICATOR & DRIVE AT 'Y'Y'

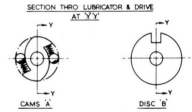

MECHANICAL LUBRICATOR

and the other to the steam pipe or steam chest. Where possible, the oil delivery should be made against the flow of the steam from the superheaters, as this helps to break up the oil into fine particles. Small ball-type check valves are suitable, the ball being kept on its seating by a light compression spring. The spring should not be allowed to bear directly on the ball or it may have a tendency to push the ball to one side. It is a good plan to fit a slightly stronger spring to the check valve on the lubricator than to the check valve at the steam pipes as the latter is subjected to full boiler pressure when the regulator is fully open. It might be thought that two spring-loaded check valves would be a rather severe load for the lubricator to overcome, in

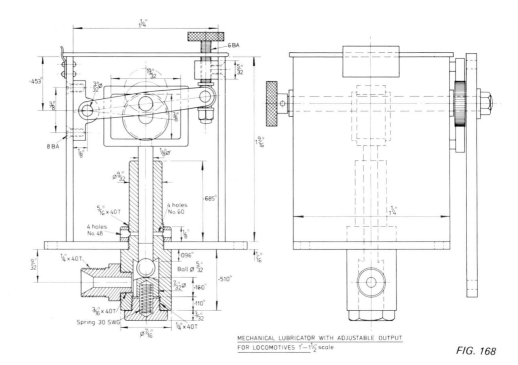

MECHANICAL LUBRICATOR WITH ADJUSTABLE OUTPUT
FOR LOCOMOTIVES 1"—1½" scale

FIG. 168

addition to the pressure of the steam. However this is not so. Test have shown that mechanical lubricators of the type described, given good workmanship, can deliver oil at pressures as high as 400 to 500 lbs. per sq. inch.

Mechanical lubricators seldom fail in service. When they do, the trouble is nearly always due to the check valve or valves not seating properly. Of course, care must be taken to ensure that the oil used is absolutely clean and of a suitable grade. A graphited oil should not be used in these small lubricators, but a proper grade of steam cylinder oil such as Shell Valvata or a similar grade by a well known maker.

As regards the check valves used with mechanical lubricators, there is an alternative to making these with the usual metal seating for the ball; this is to use instead a synthetic-rubber "0" ring. Such a check valve is less likely to fail due to minute particles of dirt or grit getting between ball and seating. It is important, however, to ensure that the "0" ring cannot be forced upwards with the ball, it must be restrained by a definite circular projection immediately above it.

Another point worth mentioning in connection with mechanical lubricators concerns the method of driving the ram. This is normally done by an eccentric as mentioned previously, the return mo-

tion of the ram being effected by a compression spring. A better method is to use a "scotch crank" giving a positive drive.

It has been the custom for some time to fit the mechanical lubricator between the frames just ahead of the smokebox. Although this position ensures that the lubricator will be out of sight, and therefore the outward appearance of the locomotive is not spoilt by the out-of-scale size of the oil container, this position is actually a very bad one. For one thing, it is very difficult to prevent dust and ashes from the smokebox getting into the oil container when the tubes are being swept, or even when the smokebox door is only opened for adjustments. It is also difficult to reach the driving and ratchet mechanism for cleaning and adjustment, while if the lubricator is fitted with a needle valve or some other means of adjusting the output, this too is difficult to reach.

Probably the best position for a lubricator from the point of view of operation and maintenance is that generally adopted on the full-size locomotive, i.e. on the running board just behind the cylinders. While this position may offend advocates of strictly scale appearance, at least in the smaller gauges, the advantages of easy maintenance, cleanliness, and also the ease with which the

FIG. 169
A simple type
of mechanical
lubricator.

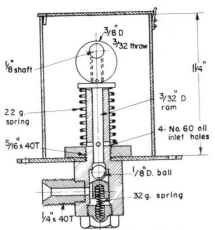

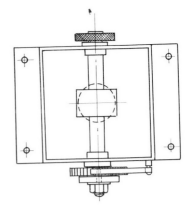

driving mechanism may be fitted up, may outweigh the disadvantage mentioned.

When lubricators are fitted between the main frames, the drive is generally taken from an eccentric and strap mounted on a convenient coupled axle. Sometimes the drive can be taken from some convenient point on inside valve gears, or from the crosshead through a reducing linkage. Lubricators mounted on the running board are usually driven from the expansion link of a Walschaerts valve gear, or from a lug attached to the radius rod or eccentric rod. The drive has also been taken from the main crosshead on the outside of the locomotive, again through a reducing linkage, while in models such as the larger Great Western Railway prototypes with outside cylinders and inside valve gears, the drive may very conveniently be taken from the valve crosshead.

GENERAL LUBRICATION

All bearings and rubbing or sliding surfaces of the model steam locomotive should have adequate lubrication. Even in 1/2 in. scale locomotives, the bosses of coupling and connecting rods and some of the larger valve gear levers and links may be provided with proper oil boxes, the latter generally having a fine hole at the bottom of the oil reservoir communicating with the bearing itself, while on models of 1 inch scale and larger, the lubrication arrangement may follow full size practice more closely.

The lubrication of driving and coupled axleboxes is obviously most important. Whenever space permits, an oil recess may be provided underneath the axle journal and proper felt pads fitted. Oil boxes can be mounted on the running board, on wheel splashers, on the fronts of side tanks or on the insides of cab side

Lubricator drive and pipework to crosshead gland and valve stems. Note also valve gearbox. (B. Palmer).

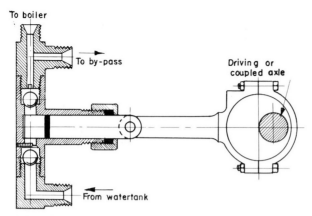

To boiler

To by-pass

Driving or coupled axle

From watertank

FIG. 170 An axle-driven feed pump.

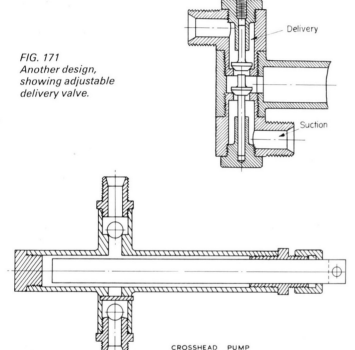

FIG. 171
Another design,
showing adjustable
delivery valve.

Delivery

Suction

FIG. 172

CROSSHEAD PUMP

sheets, with pipes leading to the bearings concerned. These pipes may be of copper and $1/16$ in. diameter for models up to $3/4$ in. scale, $3/32$ in. dia. for locomotives of larger scales. Inside the oil boxes, small trimmings can be fitted. Trimmings for small models should not be made from worsted as the strands are too coarse for the purpose. A better material to use is fine silk- covered electric wire; this is twisted up tightly and bent into the shape of a hairpin, the shorter leg of the trimming is then put into the oil box and the longer leg fed down the pipe, leading to the axlebox or hornblock as required.

For locomotives above $1\frac{1}{2}$ in. scale, a proper mechanical system may be considered, the lubricator being of the mechanical type, as described for cylinder lubrication.

The lubricating oil for the bearings for a model locomotive should not be too light; if it is, it will be flung about and eventually find its way on to the track, leading to wheel slip etc. A fairly heavy oil applied sparingly will be found satisfactory, in fact it is worth considering the use of a light grease of lubricating quality for the oil boxes of such parts as coupling and connecting rods, as these parts are "flung about" at high speeds and a light oil would very quickly be lost.

BOILER FEED

Water feed pumps are not often used in full-size locomotive practice; the axle-driven or crosshead pump will not of course feed water when the locomotive is standing, which can be a big disadvantage even on a model locomotive, resulting in the very un-railwaylike practice of filling the boiler with a hand pump! Nevertheless, many model locomotive builders like to fit a mechanically-driven pump of some kind, as if it is fitted with a bypass arrangement, this can be set to give a constant feed to the boiler on continuous runs, with possibly an injector for standby or for "topping up".

Most pumps for small scale locomotives are mounted between the frames, the pump body being either cast integral with a suitable frame stay or a separate pump body is bolted to a cast frame stay. The pump ram is usually driven by an eccentric mounted on one of the driving or coupled axles as convenient. In this case, the eccentric rod should be as long as possible, to avoid unnecessary angularity which causes wear on the gland or end of the pump barrel. The ram too should be made of reasonable length.

Another method of driving this type of pump is to arrange for the eccentric rod to drive on to a link suspended from some suitable point on the main frames above the pump, and to fit a short link connecting the eccentric rod to the ram.

On locomotives above ¾ in. scale, it is a good plan to use two pumps, set at approximately 180 deg. to one another, rather than a single large pump. This will be found to equalise the thrust of the rams to some extent, eliminating jerkiness in running.

Those making feed pumps should avoid making the ram with a so-called "anti-airlock pin", this being a small diameter extension on the leading end of the ram which is arranged to enter a passage into the valve box, the passage being somewhat larger in diameter than the pin. Such a design can only lead to restriction towards the end of the stroke, and a much better method is to arrange for a plain-ended ram to pass right through between the suction and delivery valves.

The valves used in small boiler feed pumps are generally of the simple ball type, either rustless steel or bronze balls being used. The lift of the balls should be restricted to about one-sixth of the ball diameter.

Many locomotive builders prefer a crosshead pump to an eccentric-driven pump, as the drive is direct, and provided the ram is carefully lined up, wear on the gland is negligible. Crosshead pumps can be situated either outside or inside the frames, the stroke being of course the stroke of the engine, while the bore will be between one-fifth and one-sixth the diameter of the cylinders (for a two-cylinder locomotive).

Where models of G.W.R. locomotives are concerned, a good plan is to fit the crosshead pump in the position occupied by the vacuum pump on the full-size locomotive; this can usually be done with very little alteration to the external appearance of such a pump.

All feed pumps should be fitted so that they can be removed from the engine for maintenance without too much difficulty. Too often one finds eccentric-driven pumps fitted between the frames in such a way that it is impossible to reach their screw-heads without dropping the driving and coupled wheels. The posi-

tion of the fixing screws for these pumps should therefore be carefully determined on the drawing board, so that they are easily accessible from the outside.

When a model locomotive fitted with the conventional type of feed pump is laid up for some time, it often happens that the ball valves stick to their seatings and the pump fails to function. This is generally due to furring action which occurs with normal tap water, especially in hard water districts. However, the trouble can sometimes be cured without having to dismantle the pump by giving the valve box a light but sharp tap with a small hammer. Apart from occasionally cleaning the valves and their seatings, the only maintenance required on pumps is the adjustment of the glands (which should have a positive locking device to prevent the nuts from slackening back in service), greasing of the pins and oiling of the eccentric straps, and the renewal of the gland packing material, which may be of the graphited-yarn type, or a synthetic-rubber "0" ring may be used. At longer intervals, the gland nuts and the pins will require renewal; the ram itself, if made of stainless steel, should have quite a long life.

It is difficult to specify exact dimensions for feed pumps for model locomotives, as the capacity required depends on the size of boiler, cylinders, etc, and also whether the engine is likely to be used mainly on continuous tracks or on short "up-and-down" lines (where somewhat greater pump capacity will be needed), but the following may be taken as a rough guide:-

½ in. scale
Small engines:-one pump ¼" bore x ⅜" stroke, capacity 0.0184 cu. in. or crosshead pump ⁵/₃₂" x 1" stroke. (0.0192 cu. in.)
Large engines:- one pump ⁵/₁₆" x ⁷/₁₆" (0.0336 cu. in.) or crosshead pump ³/₁₆" x 1⅛" (0.0216 cu. in.)

¾ in. scale
Small engines:- one pump ⁵/₁₆" x ⁷/₁₆" (0.0336 cu. in.) or crosshead pump ⁵/₃₂" x 1½" (0.0288 cu. in.)
Large engines:- Two pumps ⁵/₁₆" x ⅜" (0.0576 cu. in.) or crosshead pump ⁷/₃₂" x 1⅝" (0.0611 cu. in.)

1 in. scale engines.
Small engines:- Two pumps ⁵/₁₆" x ⅜"

Opposite, a crosshead feed pump on a G.W.R. 2-6-2T (K. D. Hornsby).

177

FIG. 173

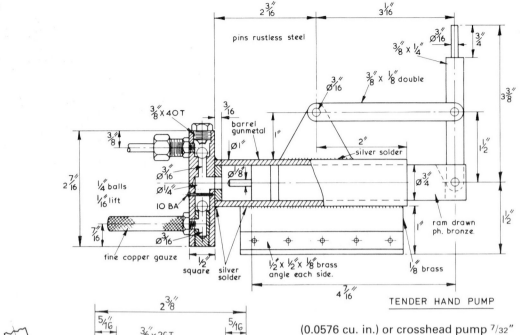

TENDER HAND PUMP

FIG. 174

HIGH–CAPACITY HAND PUMP

FIG. 175

A DOUBLE-ACTING FEED PUMP

(0.0576 cu. in.) or crosshead pump $^7/_{32}$" x 2" (0.0752 cu. in.)

Medium-sized engines:- Two pumps $^3/_8$" x $^1/_2$" (0.1104 cu. in.) or crosshead pump $^1/_4$" x 2$^1/_4$" (0.1105 cu. in)

Large engines:- Two pumps $^7/_{16}$" x $^9/_{16}$" (0.1692 cu. in.) or crosshead pump $^5/_{16}$" x 2$^3/_8$" (0.822 cu. in.)

1½ in. scale engines

Medium-sized engines:- Two pumps $^1/_2$" x $^5/_8$" (0.2456 cu. in.) or crosshead pump $^5/_{16}$" x 3$^1/_4$" (0.2494 cu. in.)

Large engines:- Two pumps $^9/_{16}$" x $^3/_4$" (0.3729 cu. in.) or crosshead pump $^3/_8$" x 3$^1/_4$" (0.3591 cu. in.)

Suitable pipes for suction, delivery and bypass for the above pumps may be as follows:-

½ in. scale pumps:- $^5/_{32}$ in. dia. 24 or 26 SWG.

¾ in. scale:- $^3/_{16}$ in. dia. 22 or 24 SWG.

1 in. scale:- $^7/_{32}$ in. dia. 22 or 24 SWG.

1½ in. scale:- ¼ in. dia. 22 SWG.

The water suction pipes from tenders or side tanks to the feed pumps should always be fitted with filters. These should be as large as possible and of the finest mesh copper or brass gauze and made easily removable for cleaning. The by-pass pipe should be as direct as possible and no longer than necessary, while the by-pass valve or cock must be of reasonable bore, otherwise there will

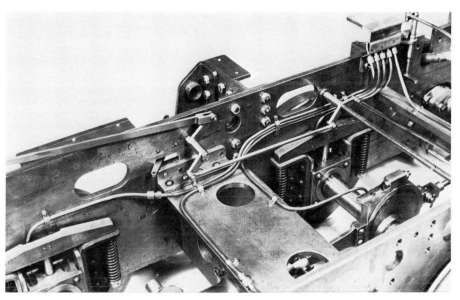

Lubrication arrangements on the 1½in. scale I.O.M. locomotive shown on page 170.

be unnecessary losses through friction when the pumps are not feeding the boiler.

Where synthetic-rubber "0" rings are used for packing in feed pumps, care should be taken to see that the correct amount of "pinch" is given to the ring and also that the groove for the ring is of the correct length to allow the cord to expand sideways and to move a trifle in the groove.

Suggested sizes of "0" rings for feed pumps, together with suitable groove sizes are as follows:-

Ram dia.	Cord dia.	B.S. No.	Groove width	Groove depth.	Outside dia.
⅛ in.	.070"	006	.090"	.065"	¼"
5/32 in.	.070"	007	.090"	.065"	9/32"
3/16 in.	.070"	008	.090"	.065"	5/16"
7/32 in.	.070"	009	.090"	.065"	11/32"

Due to the small diameter of the rams in the above sizes the groove is of course cut in the cylinder, not the ram.

¼ in	.070"	006	.090"	.065"	¼"
5/16 in.	.070"	008	.090"	.065"	5/16"
⅜ in.	.070"	010	.090"	.065"	⅜"
7/16 in.	.070"	011	.090"	.065	7/16"
½ in.	.070"	012	.090"	.065"	½"
9/16 in.	.103"	110	.125"	.098"	9/16"
⅝ in.	.103"	111	.125"	.098"	⅝"
11/16 in.	.103"	112	.125"	.098"	11/16"
¾ in	.103"	113	.125"	.098"	¾"

The grooves for the above sizes of ram are cut in the ram and not in the cylinder.

When fitting "0" rings, it is important to make sure that both ram and bores are smooth and that no sharp edges are left which might cut the "0" ring. The ring can be gently stretched to get it into its groove.

To measure the width of the groove for the "0" ring, use a small diameter drill shank plus feeler gauges. To measure the depth of the groove, use a straight edge across the gap.

STEAM FEED PUMPS ("DONKEY" PUMPS)

Model locomotives are sometimes fitted with steam feed or "Donkey" pumps. These are basically miniature steam engines complete with simple valve gear and fitted with a small lubricator, the pump ram being generally connected directly to the steam cylinder piston rod. They may be single or double acting, though the latter is much to be preferred and may be fitted with one or two cylinders.

Although donkey pumps are most fascinating both to build and operate, they cannot be regarded as efficient as boiler feeders compared with either axle-driven or crosshead pumps or injectors.

INJECTORS

At one time, the model injector was considered a somewhat unreliable item of locomotive equipment. But this is certainly not true today, in fact hundreds of satisfactory injectors are now operating

FIG. 176

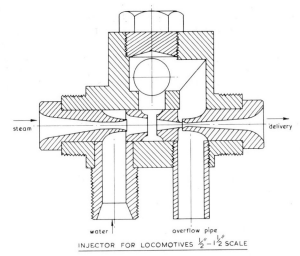

INJECTOR FOR LOCOMOTIVES ½″–1½″ SCALE

on locomotives as small as 2½ in. gauge.

In many respects, an injector is easier to make and erect than a pump, although its manufacture calls for very careful workmanship. The pipework necessary with injectors is also less elaborate than that required with pumps.

The main advantages of an injector over a pump are as follows:- An injector can be operated equally well while the locomotive is stationary; it can be fitted in a position that is really accessible and can be removed for cleaning or adjustment in a few minutes. An injector is more efficient than a pump, as the feed water put into the boiler is hot and there are no appreciable losses in friction as there are no moving parts. The only real drawback to an injector is its inability (without complicated additional parts) to handle hot water; thus on tank engines, injectors are sometimes unreliable unless the water carried in the side tanks is extremely well insulated from the heat of the boiler. Very hot weather can also sometimes be a hazard to good injector operation.

There are three distinct processes in the working of an injector. First, the pressure energy of the steam has to be converted into kinetic energy, this then has to be imparted to the feed water, when it is again turned back into pressure energy, the feed water being given a higher pressure than that in the boiler. When an unbroken column of fluid is moving through a closed chamber, its velocity and pressure are interchangeable. Thus if the cross-sectional area of the chamber is increased, the velocity of the fluid passing through it is reduced, and vice versa, though there is always some loss through skin friction etc. With the lowering of the velocity, the pressure is increased, so that the column of water is able to enter the boiler against the pressure in it.

A typical injector consists of three cones: the steam cone, the combining cone and the delivery cone, each cone being mounted in line inside the body of the injector. Steam from the boiler is admitted to the steam cone, while the feed water is admitted between the steam and combining cones. A non-return valve is fitted above the combining cone, leading to an overflow pipe.

In the steam cone, the aim is to convert as much as possible of the pressure energy of the steam into kinetic energy. This is done by admitting the steam into a cone which first converges to speed up the flow of the steam, and then diverges, so that the steam is expanded until its pressure is lower than atmospheric.

Both the inside and the outside of the steam cone should be highly polished, where the steam and water make contact with it, and the nozzle should be machined to a knife edge in small injectors. The nozzle should be arranged to protrude into the larger end of the combining cone by an amount equal to the smallest internal diameter of the delivery cone, or slightly less. This last should be qualified by saying that the gap left between the nozzle of the steam cone and the entrance to the combining cone should not be so small that the smallest particle of dirt or foreign matter blocks it.

Although the combining cone can be made in one piece, the two piece cone is probably more efficient. The angle of the combining cone is not very critical, but about 9 deg. is generally satisfactory.

In some model injectors, a large gap is left between the nozzle of the steam cone and the entrance to the combining

FIG. 177

PROPORTIONS OF CONES FOR INJECTOR

cone, and the amount of water fed into the boiler is controlled by throttling the supply from the tender or side tanks. This, however, is bad practice, as an injector should be arranged to work properly with both the steam and water valves fully open. The outlet end of the combining cone should have some of the metal around the actual orifice removed, so as to allow plenty of space for the starting overflow.

The function of the delivery cone is to accept the high velocity column of water and condensed steam from the combining cone, where it is at low pressure, and to slow it down and increase its pressure to a higher figure than that in the boiler. The entry into this cone must be well radiused so as better to receive the water from the combining cone, and this part must also be highly polished for good performance.

The output of a small injector of this type can be obtained approximately from the following formula:-

$$\text{Output in ounces per minute} = \frac{d^2}{40}$$

where d is the internal diameter of the throat of the delivery cone in thousandths of an inch.

Although the lifting properties of an injector are not essential in model locomotive work, there are definite advantages in the use of an injector that is capable of lifting, even though it is fitted below the level of the water in the tender or side tanks. Thus any leakage from the check valve on the boiler will pass out of the overflow, and even if the injector becomes overheated, the water besides flowing into the injector through gravity will be picked up by the suction of the lift, and the fitting will be quickly cooled down again. To ensure lifting properties, the first part of the combining cone must be sufficiently long for it and the steam cone to act as an ejector, so that a partial vacuum is formed in the water space.

The body of a model injector may be cut from solid brass or a brass casting of good quality used. As much of the unwanted metal as possible should be cut away, so that if the injector does get overheated, it will cool down quicker. The external diameter of the various cones, where these fit into the body, should be very carefully turned, the steam and delivery cones being made a nice hand push fit, while the combining cone should be a fairly tight fit. When drilling the cones, a drill somewhat smaller than the minimum diameter of the cone should be put through first, followed by the appropriate reamer.

The necessary reamers can be made from silver-steel, using a file in the lathe, the lathe being run at a high speed. Using the angles of the cones given in Fig. 177, the following data may be found useful:-

6 deg. = $1\frac{1}{4}$ in. per foot = $\frac{5}{64}$ in. to a point in $\frac{3}{4}$ in. length.

9 deg. = $1\frac{7}{8}$ in. per ft. = $\frac{5}{32}$ in. to a point in 1 in. length.

13 deg. = $2\frac{3}{4}$ in. per ft. = $\frac{5}{32}$ in. to a point in $\frac{11}{16}$ in. length.

The above figures are close approximations, but quite accurate enough for the purpose. When filing the taper, the whole length should not be filed at once, but a short length filed first to a greater angle and the file gradually worked back, finishing with a dead-smooth flat file of greater width than the length of the taper. When filing the flat, a start should be made at the thick end, and only very light pressure used. Heating for both hardening and tempering should only be done indirectly. If the flame were to be directed on to the end of the taper, this part of the reamer would be spoilt very quickly.

FITTING UP INJECTORS

However well made the injector, the pipework, valves etc, involved in the fitting up of the injector can make or mar its performance. The author believes that many injectors have been blamed for poor performance when the real culprit has been the steam valve, the water valve, or even the pipework.

An injector shoud, as mentioned previously, be mounted below the level of the tender or side tanks, where it will keep cool and be readily accessible. The overflow pipe should be short and arranged so that it can be easily seen by the driver. The steam pipe should have adequate bore, so that there is a minimum drop of steam pressure at the steam cone. The steam should be collected from a high position on the boiler, such as from the turret or manifold, and the steam valve must have a good bore and be quick-acting, using a thread of

comparatively coarse pitch. The water valve should also be of large bore and quick-acting, and it is most important that it be fitted with a gland, so that no air is drawn in with the water.

A fine filter, using the finest possible gauze, is an essential fitting in the tender or side tanks as the most common cause of small injectors failing is the clogging of the fine cones due to foreign matter in the water. The filter should be much larger than is usually seen in ¾ and 1 inch scale locomotives and it should be arranged as low as possible, so that part of it does not become uncovered by the water if the water level in the tender is accidentally allowed to get very low.

The delivery pipe from the injector to the boiler should be as direct as possible, though not too short, and any bends found necessary should be of as large a radius as possible. The check valve on the boiler must have rather more valve lift than if used with pumps. For instance, if the check valve uses a ball, a lift of .020 to .025 in. is adequate for pumps, but for injectors, the lift should be .040 to .050 in. according to the size of check valve and injector. Furthermore, although the boiler check valve is often placed on the side of the barrel, a better scheme from the maintenance point of view is to use top feeds, but to place a vertical type check valve below the top feed, outside the barrel and just above

running board level where it is immediately available for cleaning or adjustment.

Suitable steam and delivery pipes for injectors are as follows:-

For injectors with delivery cones .014 in. to .018 in. — ⅛ in. thin walled.
For injectors with delivery cones .019 in. to .022 in. — ⁵/₃₂ in. thin walled.
For injectors with deliver cones .023 in. to .028 in. — ³/₁₆ in. thin walled.
For injectors with delivery cones .029 in. to .036 in. — ⁷/₃₂ in. thin walled.

Injectors fitted to tank locomotives are not generally so reliable as on tender locomotives, as it is difficult to keep the water in the side tanks sufficiently cool. To avoid this trouble as far as possible, the side tanks should be well lagged and there should be a small air gap between the tanks and the boiler barrel. An additional water tank can also generally be fitted underneath the coal space in the bunker, this tank being connected to the side tanks by "balance pipes" of fairly large diameter. The water for the injectors can then be drawn from this bunker tank, which is likely to be somewhat cooler than the water in the side tanks. It also helps if a large bore water cock is fitted to the bottom of the bunker tank, so that the water in the whole system can be drained out rapidly if it has become too hot for injector operation.

When trying out a new injector, if it is found that hot water comes out from the overflow, but does not go into the boiler, it is probable that it would do so if the pressure was raised. Thus the fault may be corrected by either increasing the size of the steam cone or by advancing the steam cone further into the combining cone.

If on the other hand, when first turning on the steam supply, one gets hot water, but on further opening the steam valve, this does not go into the boiler but gives instead a mixed spray of water and steam, the trouble can probably be corrected by either reducing the size of the steam cone, or by withdrawing the steam cone slightly from the body of the injector. Once the injector is feeding correctly, it will generally continue to do so even if the boiler pressure drops to say half its normal figure. The knocking-off point can usually be delayed by partly closing the water valve.

Should the injector fail through dirt in the cones, the usual sign of this would be for steam plus a little water to be blown out from the overflow.

Injectors should be removed frequently for cleaning, and in this connection it should be remembered that if the cones are made of brass, they should be treated with care, as the application of hard steel wire, or similar devices, to clear the cones could very easily score the polished surfaces, resulting in loss of performance. The best way to clean injector cones is to wash them in a very dilute acid such as acetic acid, followed by a thorough wash in hot water.

Regarding the proportions of the cones in small injectors, as mentioned previously, the easiest way is to base all dimensions on the throat diameter of the delivery cone. Referring to Fig. 177 for working pressures 80-110 lbs. per sq. in. where A is the throat diameter of the delivery cone:-

$$B = A \times \tfrac{3}{2} \qquad G = J \times \tfrac{1}{10}$$
$$C = A \qquad\qquad H = A \times \tfrac{7}{2}$$
$$D = A \times \tfrac{5}{4} \qquad J = A \times 14$$
$$E = A \times 15 \qquad K = A \times 18$$
$$F = A \times 6$$

For any given injector, increasing the diameter of the steam cone, without altering the diameter of the other cones, will make the injector suitable for a lower pressure. Decreasing the diameter of the steam cone will make the injector suitable for higher pressure.

While the actual angle of the diverging part of the steam cone need not be altered for different working pressures, the higher the pressure, the greater the ratio between the area of the throat of this cone and the area of its exit.

A splendid G.W.R Dean "Single" by the late A. Heyden.

LOCOMOTIVE BRAKES

On model locomotives below 1 inch scale, brakes are fitted more for appearance than for actual use in stopping the train. This is because the weight of the locomotive is generally very much less than the weight of the train. If the brakes on these small scale engines were used, the result would be the locking of the wheels, resulting in the engine sliding along the track and probably wearing flats on the tyres.

When driving small locomotives, therefore, the driver is well advised to rely upon brakes fitted to his passenger car and to other cars in the train, if any. Such brakes can be strongly built without difficulty. Hand brakes are, however, useful on the locomotive itself, in case it has to be left unattended on the track at any time.

On large and heavy 1½ in. scale locomotives, the steam brake is worth considering, although rather slow in action due to condensation of the steam in a cold brake cylinder. For reliable results on models of 1 inch scale and larger, either automatic vacuum or a Westinghouse brake system may be considered. Either system can be fitted to the passenger cars for continous braking.

THE STEAM BRAKE

In the steam brake, the brake blocks are actuated by means of a steam cylinder located between the frames, generally below the driver's footplate. Steam is taken from a suitable high point in the boiler via a quick-acting driver's valve in the cab. The brake blocks are strongly hung from the engine frames and cross rods which are generally of flat section connect each pair of hangers. The cross

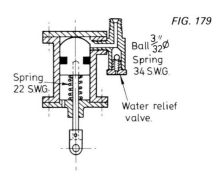

FIG. 179

A STEAM BRAKE CYLINDER

beams are turned circular on their ends on which the hangers pivot.

For a non-compensated brake system, central pull rods are sometimes used, attached to each cross beam by forked joints with adjustable turnbuckles between each fork. In a compensating system, the pull rods are duplicated and pull against short compensating levers, these levers being connected by a short link to the adjacent brake beam and to the next pull rod and their other end. In this way, the actual force applied to each of the brake blocks of the locomotive is approximately equal.

The steam brake cylinder is generally fitted with a packed piston, similar to the traction cylinders, but not more than half the diameter of the latter. An automatic drain valve is fitted just above the head of the piston; this valve remains shut under steam pressure, but when steam is cut off, condensation creates a slight vacuum and the pressure of the atmosphere opens the valve. Alternatively, a very light spring may be arranged under a ball type valve, to lift the ball off its seating when steam is shut off; the spring must not, of course, be strong enough to lift the ball against steam pressure.

Steam brake cylinders should be of fairly light construction and situated, whenever possible, close to the ashpan. In this way, they can be kept fairly hot and the trouble of condensation kept to a minimum.

The operation of steam brakes can be improved to some extent if the driver's valve incorporates a proportional inlet valve. In the drawing, the driver's handle operates an eccentric which bears on a round pin or plunger. This plunger works in a packed gland and has a collar on its lower end which engages with a compression spring, made of hard phosphor-bronze or stainless steel. This spring in turn bears, via a cup-shaped

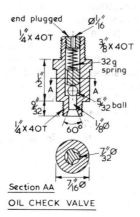

FIG. 178   OIL CHECK VALVE

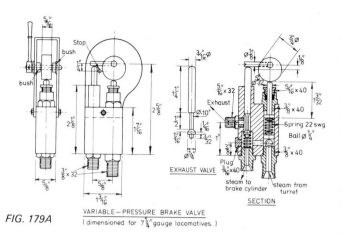

FIG. 179A

VARIABLE—PRESSURE BRAKE VALVE
(dimensioned for 7¼" gauge locomotives.)

component, on the top of a ball valve, controlling the entry of boiler steam to the valve. A cross-connection is made, just above the seating of the ball valve, to a second chamber containing the exhaust valve. By means of a second valve, the steam in the brake cylinder and in any pipework between the cylinder and the valve can find its way out. This second valve is operated by the reverse action of the driver's handle through a grub-screw fitted to the eccentric, this grub-screw thus doing a double duty as it also locks the eccentric to the shaft on which the driver's handle is fitted.

The "full-on" position of the driver's handle is at 90 deg. to the vertical in a clockwise direction looking at the drawing; in this position, the eccentric has moved round sufficiently to enable the steam pressure to push the compression spring right up, allowing nearly full boiler pressure to pass to the brake cylinder. But if the handle is only moved a short way round, the ball will only just lift from its seating, and the pressure reaching the cylinder will be lower.

To get the best possible performance from a steam brake, it would be necessary to fit a steam jacket to the brake cylinder itself.

In the smaller scales, it is important to be able to drop the grate and ashpan of the model locomotive without delay in the event of emergency, as for instance if the water level has been inadvertently allowed to get dangerously low. With the normal arrangement of brake rigging, this is often impossible. It is, however, generally possible to dispense with the brake beam which lies underneath the ashpan of the locomotive. In this case, the push rods are run close be-

hind the driving and coupled wheels and just below the frames; the hangers which are now left without a cross-beam may be connected to short links brazed on the pull rods. In this way, all the space below the ashpan is left clear, so that instant removal of grate and ashpan is possible.

VACUUM BRAKES.

Vacuum brakes are of two types, the "simple" and the "automatic", the automatic vacuum brake being the system favoured by most of Britain's railways.

Vacuum is measured in inches of mercury below atmospheric pressure in the same way that boiler pressure is measured in pounds per square inch above atmospheric pressure. A perfect vacuum is absolute zero pressure or 30 in. mercury on the vacuum gauge. The pressure of the atmosphere at sea level is approximately 15 lbs. per sq. in. so that 1 in. of mercury represents about ½ lb. per sq. in.

Although strictly speaking it is the pressure of the atmosphere which provides the power for the vacuum brake, it is sometimes more convenient to deal in so many inches of vacuum. In the "simple" vacuum brake, the brake is applied by the creation of a partial vacuum by means of an ejector and it is released by the admission of air through the driver's brake valve. The chief disadvantage of this system is that any leakage, such as the loss caused by a disconnected hose between vehicles, renders the brake useless. This difficulty is overcome in the automatic vacuum brake, where a partial vacuum is maintained during the whole time the train is running, and the brake is applied by the driver's valve admitting air to the system. The brake is also applied automatically in the event of leakage or ejector failure through low steam pressure.

On locomotives, the partial vacuum for operating the brakes is usually obtained by an ejector, though on some full-size locomotives, such as Great Western engines, a crosshead pump was used. The ejector has the advantage of simplicity as it has no moving parts. It is somewhat similar to an injector though is easier to make; it comprises a steam cone, an exhaust cone and a non-return valve. As working pressures on most model locomotives are considerably lower than on full-size locomotives,

FIG. 180

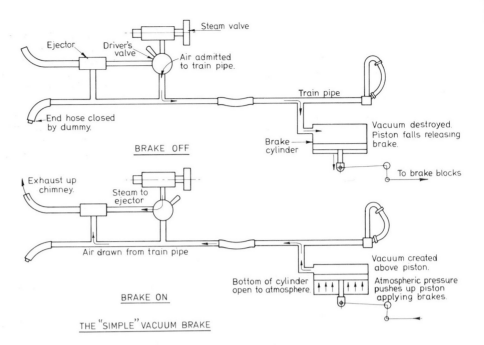

THE "SIMPLE" VACUUM BRAKE

it is usual to work at a lower figure for vacuum, the general figure for full-size locomotives being 21 in. of mercury.

The steam supply for the ejector can be brought through 1/8 in. or 5/32 in. dia. thin-walled copper tube, while the exhaust is better catered for by tube about 1/4 in. dia. The exhaust is led to the smokebox and the orifice is arranged alongside the blast pipe, the pipe being left full bore, with no nozzle, so as to re-duce back pressure.

The driver's brake valve may be a sim-ple disc valve; its main function is to control the flow of air for the brake, but additional ports can be arranged in the valve face to control the air supply or the steam supply to the ejector.

In full-size practice, two ejectors are generally used, a small one for maintain-ing the vacuum economically and a larger one for creating the vacuum

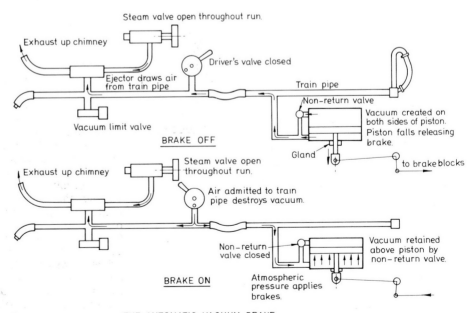

THE AUTOMATIC VACUUM BRAKE

FIG. 181

186

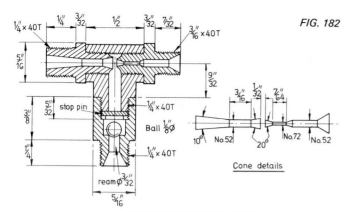

FIG. 182

EJECTOR FOR VACUUM BRAKES

Cone details

10°   No.52   20°   No.72   No.52

ing valve may be used, which will limit the vacuum and hold it steady even though the boiler pressure varies. A suitable limiting valve can be made in the form of a diaphragm valve. In this, rubber sheet is used for the diaphragm and by means of a ball valve and suitable springs, when the vacuum created reaches a pre-determined figure, air is admitted above the diaphragm until the desired amount of vacuum is obtained.

FIG. 184

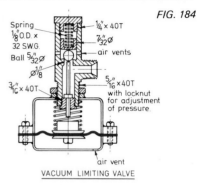

VACUUM LIMITING VALVE

quickly. The steam supply to the ejectors is often controlled by two separate screw-down valves, while another method is to have the small ejector controlled by a screw-down valve but to control the large ejector with the driver's brake valve. In model locomotive work, one ejector is generally sufficient, but if two are used, the driver's valve may be used for controlling the large ejector. Again, in full-size work, the ejectors, steam valves and application valve are often combined in one fitting.

As the vacuum created by the ejector varies with the steam pressure, a limit-

The brake cylinder (in the automatic vacuum brake), in addition to providing the force to actuate the brakes, stores on the reservoir side of the piston the vacuum which has to be maintained the whole time the train is in motion. Thus there must be no leakage on the reservoir side of the piston; however, the effective volume of the reservoir can be increased quite easily by fitting an additional and separate reservoir. In full-size practice, large diameter but very short pistons are used, with suitable packing and glands, but for small gauge models, it is probable that diaphragm type vacuum cylinders are easier to make, using rubber sheet as mentioned in connection with limiting valves. A spring-loaded non-return valve is fitted to retain the vacuum above the piston.

The size of the brake cylinder required for good braking depends on several factors: the normal working vacuum, the reduction in volume in the reservoir or reservoirs when the brakes are applied, the leverage of the brake rigging and the proportion of the load to be braked. To take an example, suppose that a model passenger car (or driver's car) together with the weight of the driver comes to 200 lbs., and we take 50% of this as the proportion of the load to be braked. Suppose also that the leverage of the brake rigging amounts to 5 to 1, then the pull required from the brake cylinder would be 20 lbs.

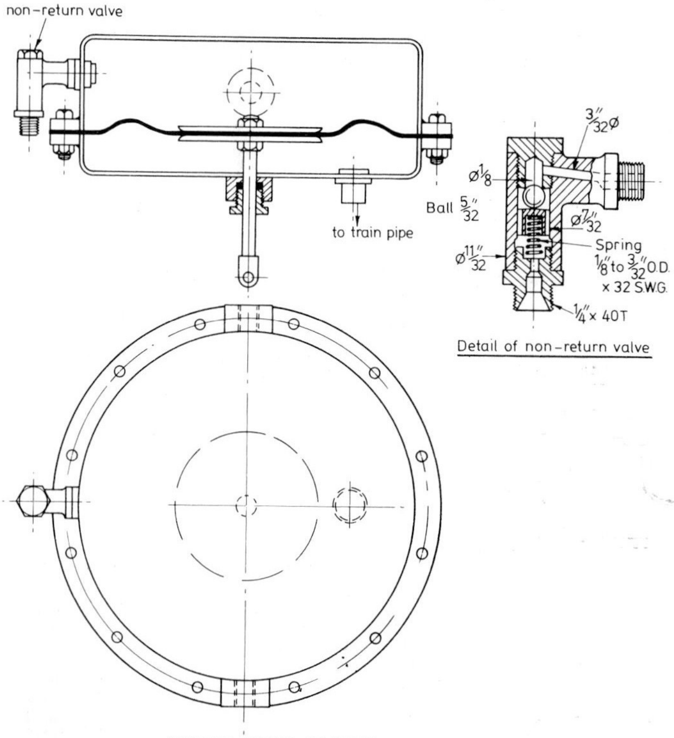

non-return valve

Detail of non-return valve

to train pipe

VACUUM BRAKE CYLINDER

FIG. 183

187

Steam-driven air compressor for Westinghouse brake system.

A wider view of the compressor, mounted on the l.h. running board of Basil Palmer's Indlovu *(see page 182)*

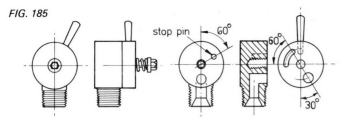

FIG. 185

SIMPLE BRAKE VALVE FOR AUTOMATIC VACUUM BRAKE

A diaphragm type brake cylinder of 4½ in. diameter has a total area of 15.9 sq. in., but its effective area might be taken as 11 sq. in. To find the pull exerted by the brake cylinder we would need to know the final pressure. This can be measured by a vacuum gauge or can be calculated from the volume of the reservoir, or the volume of the reservoir plus any additional reservoir in use.

$$\text{Final pressure} = \text{Initial pressure} \times \frac{\text{Initial volume of reservoir}}{\text{Final volume of reservoir}}$$

Suppose the train pipe vacuum to be 8 in. mercury, which is equal to 11 p.s.i. absolute (approx). Suppose that the initial volume of the reservoir to be 20 cu. in., and the final volume to be 17 cu. in. Then the final pressure will be:-

$$11 \times \frac{20}{17} = 12.94 \text{ p.s.i. abs.}$$

12.94 p.s.i. abs. gives us 2.06 p.s.i. available from the atmosphere. If the effective area of the brake cylinder is 11 sq. in., the force available area of the brake cylinder is 22.7 lbs. approx. If the leverage from the brake rigging is 5 to 1, then the total force available for braking, ignoring friction, is 113.5 lbs.

In deciding the size of the brake cylinder, it should be remembered that in the piston-type cylinder, the effective area may be taken from the full internal diameter, whereas in the diaphragm-type cylinder, only about 70% of the area should be taken.

A release valve, to destroy the vacuum in the cylinder or reservoir should the need arise, is a useful fitting. It may be fitted either direct to the brake cylinder or to any convenient point along the train pipe. If fitted to the driver's vehicle, it should be placed so that it can be easily reached by the driver.

The train pipe, for vacuum brakes, may be made from ³/₁₆ in. dia. copper tube, with the flexible connections between vehicles made from rubber tube; the vehicles should be coupled closely, to avoid snatching of couplings as far as possible. Both the limiting valve and the vacuum gauge may, if desired, be fitted to the driver's car, rather than on the locomotive. Vacuum gauges, however, can now be readily obtained as small as ¾ in dia., reading to 15 or 30 ins. mercury.

AIR BRAKES

An alternative to the vacuum brake is the Westinghouse or compressed air brake. In this system, an air pump, directly coupled to a steam cylinder, compresses air which is then stored in a brake reservoir on the locomotive. A brake cylinder, which can be much smaller than that used with the vacuum brake, is fitted to the locomotive and to each of the vehicles in the train. On opening the driver's valve, the compressed air operating on the pistons in the brake cylinders applies the brakes almost instantaneously.

An air pump governor is normally fitted, attached to the steam pipe leading from the locomotive boiler to the steam cylinder, and so arranged that when the pressure in the air reservoir reaches a pre-determined figure, the steam supply to the pump is automatically cut off. A lubricator is also required, to lubricate the air pump.

The compressed air brake may be considered for large scale locomotives, though it is considerably more complicated than the vacuum system.

CHAPTER TWENTY

Platework, tenders, tanks, fittings

LOCOMOTIVE SUPERSTRUCTURES

In full-size practice, locomotive superstructures are mainly built up from mild steel sheets from ⅛ in. to ¼ in. thick, bolted, riveted or welded to angle, tee or channel sections. Very little wood is to be found, though it was generally used for cab footplates, upon which the driver and fireman stood at the controls. On some of the older engines, wood was also used for cab roofs, buffer beams and brake blocks. Where wood was used for buffer beams, the wood was often covered on each side by fairly thin steel plate, in fact the main frames were sometimes built up in a similar "sandwich" method in the early days of the steam locomotive. Where wood is used for the cab floor in models, care should be taken that the planks are well defined and that the grain of the wood is not too obvious. In most cases, the planking should be laid "fore and aft" rather than across the cab.

On model locomotives of 1½ inch scale and larger, steel is nearly always used for such parts as running boards, cab sides and fronts, wheel splashers, tender floors, sides, ends and top decks, also for the side tanks of tank locomotives. In such cases, a thin brass or copper tank is generally used in tenders and side tanks to carry the water and so avoid rusting problems.

Brass is generally used for all "platework" on models up to 1 inch. scale, though the running boards of 1 inch scale locomotives may be of mild steel for the extra strength gained. But the big advantage of brass is that beadings and small details may be soft sol-

dered rather than riveted, while this metal is certainly to be preferred for tender bodies and side or saddle tanks, thus avoiding a separate inner tank of some non-rusting metal. Nickel-silver (German-silver) has been used for the smaller gauge model steam locomotives as it has all the advantages of brass while being somewhat stronger and retaining paint better; its high price, however, may deter most enthusiasts from using this material.

Generally speaking, 22 SWG metal will be found strong enough for most of the superstructure of Gauge "1" model locomotives, 20 SWG for ½ in. scale models, 18 SWG for ¾ in. scale models, 16 SWG or 1/16 in. for 1 inch scale and 13 SWG or 3/32 in. for 1½ in. scale locomotives. As much sheet metal is now only available in metric thicknesses, the following approximate equivalents may be found useful:-

4.5mm (.177")	–	6 SWG or 3/16" approx.
4.0mm (.158")	–	8 SWG or 5/32" approx.
3.0mm (.118")	–	10 SWG or ⅛" approx.
2.5mm (.098")	–	13 SWG or 8/32" approx.
2.0mm (.078")	–	14 SWG approx.
1.6mm (.062")	–	16 SWG or 1/16" approx.
1.2mm (.047")	–	18 SWG approx or .048"
0.9mm (.035")	–	20 SWG approx or .036"
0.7mm (.027")	–	22 SWG or 1/32" approx.

The footplate or running board edging, or valance (sometimes called the "hanging bar") is generally made from hard brass angle, which may be screwed, or screwed and soft soldered, or riveted to the running board. Where ornamental curved end sections are required, especially those which butt up against the buffer or drag beams, sheet material is generally employed, this being blended into the angle on the straight sections.

The cab front or spectacle plate of the locomotive may be made in two pieces, the division being made on the vertical centre-line; this will be found easier than attempting to make it in one piece and also permits an easier removal of the boiler, should this become necessary for boiler tests etc. It is usual to mount the spectacle plate on top of the firebox cleading rather than attempt to butt the lagging and cleading accurately up against this plate. The spectacle plate of tank locomotives can sometimes be made in one piece as this may be built up from the level of the top of the tanks, rather than from footplate level as on tender engines.

Cab roofs are often cut away quite considerably, even in tender locomotives, to give better access to the firedoor and backhead fittings. In the author's opinion this is rather a pity as the appearance of the locomotive is spoilt. However, a good solution to this problem is to fit a large sliding hatchway in the cab roof which can be slid forward while the driver is at the controls, leaving a U-shaped gap. Tank locomotives call for special treatment in this respect; on the larger tank engines, the whole of the back of the cab and possibly the upper part of the bunker can be made removable for driving. On models of very small tanks, contractor's engines, etc. the fuel is often carried in a special compartment in the front of the vehicle carrying the driver, the back of the bunker being left completely open for firing.

WATER TANKS

The side tanks of even small gauge locomotives should be arranged to hold water, and where possible, an additional water tank can be fitted below the coal space in the bunker. Apart from the advantage of the greater water capacity, the extra water provides more weight for adhesion (incidentally giving the tank locomotive some advantage over the tender locomotive, which has to haul its coal and water in a separate vehicle!).

The three tanks are connected by large diameter "balance pipes", so that they can be filled quickly through one manhole. The connections between the tanks are usually made by flanged joints, though on small models, rubber tubes may be used, which are quite satisfactory in service and easily removed when required. Air vents are fitted to each tank, the bunker tank having a specially tall one, to allow air to be displaced by the water and to prevent coal dust from entering. Other details usually found on side tanks include lifting lugs and rings and fire-iron racks; a bar is also often fitted joining the two tanks, passing over the boiler barrel.

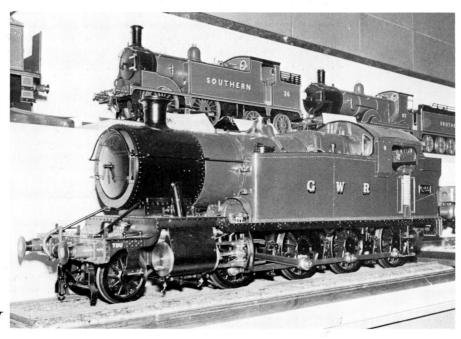

Fred Cottam's 5in. gauge G.W.R. 2-8-0T at the Model Engineer Exhibition.

On locomotives up to 1½ in. scale, a substantial hand pump may be fitted for use in emergency; such a pump is also very useful for boiler testing. In side tanks, the hand pump should be fitted at such a height that an extension handle may be attached to it through a slot in the top of the tank, the slot having a cover plate which is put into position when the pump is not in use. The suction pipe of the hand pump is arranged to draw water from the bottom of the tank through the usual fine gauze filter. An additional removable filter may also be fitted in the tank filler or manhole with advantage.

On side tanks above ½ in. scale, anti-surge plates or baffles may be fitted to reduce the surge of the water when the locomotive is braking or accelerating. If it is desired to fit injectors to tank locomotives, every endeavour should be made to insulate the side tanks from the heat of the boiler, while if a bunker water tank is fitted, the water for the injector may be taken from this, rather than from the side tanks, as mentioned in an earlier chapter.

TENDERS

A locomotive tender is designed to carry the fuel and water required by the engine, and as far as British prototypes are concerned will run on six or eight wheels, although some of the early and smaller types of locomotives were supplied with tenders running on only four wheels. Modern six-wheel tenders invariably had outside frames with the springing gear below running board level, though some early tenders had the

High capacity hand pump by the author

leaf springs much higher, above running board level.

The eight wheel tenders were sometimes bogie vehicles as on the Southern Railway "Lord Nelson", or rigid wheelbases as on the Gresley "Pacific" tenders and the Drummond tenders on the L.S.W.R. where some tenders had inside frames.

The frames of tenders with rigid wheelbases are generally made in a similar manner to locomotive main frames, being angled to the buffer and drag beams. The wheels and axles generally need a little end-play, especially if sharp radius curves are to be negotiated, in which case the end-play of the centre axle should be made greater than that of the outer axles. Where bogies are used, the axles should only have sufficient end-play to allow of free running.

The tender springs may be either solid castings, the actual spring being a coil spring concealed in a recess in the casting, or built up from spring steel or hard phosphor-bronze leaves. A built-up or laminated spring may be made less stiff by slotting out every leaf except the top and bottom ones. Another method is to use Tufnol leaves for all except the top and bottom leaves, which gives a nice flexible spring that is not too stiff.

As tenders used with the larger 1½ in. scale locomotives (and larger scales) are generally used for carrying the driver, the frames of these should be made of stout material, say ³/16 in. thick mild steel, well braced between the buffer beams and the springs made entirely of spring steel of thicker section than "scale". Ball races could be used with great advantage in the axleboxes, though if plain bronze bearings are used, the journals should not be smaller than ¹¹/16 in. diameter by about 1⅛ in. long (for a 1½ in. scale tender).

A problem often encountered in tender construction is the fouling of the buffer shanks or spindles by the ends of the frames. This can be avoided by the adoption of buffers in which the extension of the buffer body or stock does not protrude through the buffer beams.

The interior of the model tender may be built up in a similar way to the full-size tender, though some modification will be needed to accommodate the usual fittings such as an emergency hand pump, bypass pipe if an axle-driven or crosshead pump is fitted, and pipes and filters for the water supply to the injectors. The

Top and bottom of a tender bogie on Basil Palmer's 2-8-0 Indovu.

front coal plate will also require modification, bearing in mind that the "fireman" on the model locomotive will be shovelling forwards, whereas the full-size fireman has to fill his shovel in a backward direction before turning to feed the coal into the furnace.

The top of the tender water tank may be made removable so as to give access to the hand pump and the filters. The filters, especially when these are for use with injectors, should be made as large as possible and arranged so that they are not uncovered by the water until the water level in the tender is quite low; this will help to prevent air being drawn into the water supply to the injectors.

The water filler or manhole may be fitted with a removable filter while on some tenders, where the prototype had a large water pickup dome, this dome can be used in place of the filler (which is then made as a dummy) as the water pickup dome is usually of much larger diameter than the water filler.

The bypass from the pumps, if fitted, can be brought into the tender tank from underneath and then upwards towards the manhole; this enables the driver to see at a glance whether the pumps are working properly.

At the front end of the tender, there are usually two vertical columns with handles, which in full-size practice are used to control the hand brakes and the water pickup scoop. As the latter is not required in a model (except for a scale "glass-case" type of model), it is generally used as a control valve for the water supply to the injectors.

The pipes from the tender carrying the water supply to the injectors may be coupled up to the engine by rubber or plastic tube, but the water pipe from the

emergency hand pump should be fitted with a union with a coarse thread (such as 26t) placed so that it is not too difficult to adjust between the engine and the tender. To assist flexibility in the pipe from the hand pump, two or three coils may be put in it, underneath the tender.

ENGINE TO TENDER COUPLING

An engine-to-tender coupling for a passenger-hauling locomotive must be substantial. The pin on the engine is best made a fixture, while the pin on the tender should be quickly removable but so arranged that it cannot work loose in service, otherwise an accident could easily be caused. If flexibility is desired, the amount of movement allowed between engine and tender should not be too great or trouble may arise from the various water pipes etc. Spring buffers between engine and tender are often fitted, these being fitted to the tender drag beam, the heads of the buffers bearing on the locomotive beam.

SMOKEBOX SADDLES

In most locomotives, the smokebox saddle is a strong casting in gunmetal or cast-iron as in addition to supporting the front end of the boiler, it acts as a main frame stretcher at an important point, usually between or adjacent to the cylinders. To carry the weight of the boiler better, the saddle may be machined so that its edges on each side bear directly on the top of the frames.

As the steam and exhaust pipes normally pass through the base of the saddle, it is important to make the necessary holes quite air-tight. This can be done by wrapping around the pipes with asbestos string and plumber's jointing, or some asbestos "putty" made by kneading some scraps of asbestos up with a little water; this can be applied like putty and will set fairly hard when dry. Although asbestos has recently been given a bad name, the small amount involved here is not likely to cause any trouble health-wise, and once in the smokebox will be out of harm's way!

The saddle is generally fixed to the smokebox, or rather the smokebox is held down on top of the saddle, by a row of small hexagon-headed screws along the side flanges, and the whole held down to the main frames by means of screws put through clearing holes in the frames, into tapped holes in the saddle. The position of these holes must be carefully chosen at an early stage in the design so that the screws can be put in without having to disturb the cylinders.

Many locomotive builders have difficulty in machining smokebox saddles. If the casting used is really clean, it is of course possible to dispense with machining, relying on filing, but it is not easy to file the sides to a good fit between the frames. On medium-sized or large lathes, it is possible to machine the concave top surface of a saddle by flycutting. If the saddle is too wide to allow of it being set up on the cross-slide (the top-slide being removed) it can be held to one side of the cross-slide if two substantial angle-plates are available. This involves drilling two holes in the front (or rear) of the saddle to take bolts to hold the saddle to one angle-plate, which is then bolted to the second angle-plate clamped on the cross-slide. The holes drilled can be plugged afterwards and after painting will be practically invisible.

To machine the sides of the saddle, a milling machine is really the answer, but this can be done on the lathe if a little ingenuity is used. The method is to set the saddle up on the cross-slide with sufficient packing to bring the sides to be machined to lathe centre-height, for which purpose, several pieces of plate of uniform thickness will be required. A clamping bar is then put right across the top of the saddle, held down by the usual long bolts into the tee slots of the cross-slide. End-mills of various sizes are then used in the 3-jaw chuck or in collets.

LAGGING AND CLEADING

The author believes that the boilers of all model steam locomotives, of whatever size, should be properly lagged. This is done not so much for any gain in heat insulation, but so that fittings such as handrails can be fitted to the cleading sheet, rather than having to drill the boiler itself. In the smaller scales, only very thin lagging can be fitted, without having to make the finished boiler much oversize on its outside diameter. In this case, a sheet steam packing material such as "Hallite" can be used; this can be obtained in thicknesses from $1/64$ in. upwards. In the larger scales, other lagging materials may be considered such as fibreglass matting, or "Kaowool" blanket, which can be recommended.

The lagging is held in place by the cleading which may be made from hard brass sheet. 30 SWG sheet is about right for $1/2$ in. scale models, 26 SWG for $3/4$ or 1 in. scale locomotives. Before cutting the cleading sheet to size, a pattern can be made up from thick paper or thin cardboard, cutting the necessary holes in this for safety valves, domes, etc., so that when the metal is cut, there will be no mistakes and wasted metal.

Boiler bands are often made of too thick a metal. To look right, they should not be thicker than 26 SWG in $3/4$ in scale. The width of boiler bands varies to some extent in full-size practice, but an average width for $3/4$ in scale would be about $5/32$ in, or $7/32$ in. for 1 in. scale. While rustless steel would be an ideal material for boiler bands, as this is difficult to cut, hard brass or nickel-silver is often used. To strengthen the ends of the boiler bands to take the securing bolts, a short piece of thicker metal may be riveted or silver-soldered to each end of the band. Steel screws and nuts are then used to pull the ends of the boiler bands in tight. On most locomotives, it is correct to arrange the fixing bolt of the boiler band underneath the boiler barrel, but those around the firebox are usually placed on top. The ends of the boiler bands around the firebox can be held by small bronze screws into tapped holes in the firebox wrapper – where possible

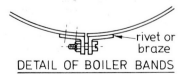

rivet or braze

DETAIL OF BOILER BANDS

FIG. 186

into the foundation ring. These screws should be treated with plumbers' jointing before screwing home, to prevent leakage. Brass or steel screws should not be used here.

SANDING GEAR

Working sanding gear is sometimes fitted to locomotives of 3/4 in. scale and above; in fact it is quite possible to make sanding gear work even on such a small scale as 1/2 in. to the foot. However, many model engineers regard sanding equipment as of doubtful value. The motion work of small locomotives is so close to track level that it is very difficult to prevent the sand from eventually finding its way on to the bearings, axleboxes, etc. with disastrous results.

There is no doubt that the proper application of sand to the rails does assist the locomotive in starting or in dealing with steep gradients, but it must also be remembered that some sand will inevitably find its way under the wheels of the passenger cars, and this will cause extra friction and drag, so that some of the advantage of additional adhesion of the locomotive may be lost.

A gravity sanding gear can be built up using sandboxes of the usual shape and fitting them with sand valves under-

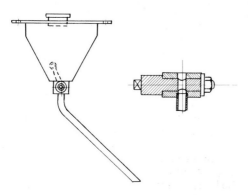

FIG. 187   GRAVITY SANDING GEAR

neath of the usual "plug-cock" type; the bore of the valves should be about 3/32 in. and the pipes down to the wheels can be thin-walled 5/32 in. dia. copper tube. The ends of the pipes should be about 1/8 in. above rail level and as close to the wheels as practicable. A short lever on the sand valves can be operated by a lever in the cab with operating rodding arranged in a similar manner to that used with cylinder drain cocks.

Most full-size locomotives were fitted with steam sanding gear, and this can be made to operate on model locomotives, although great care should be taken to keep the sanding under control. A sand "trap" is required, arranged between the sandbox and the pipe to the wheels. This is provided with an air-hole. Into the pipe carrying the sand, another pipe to

FIG. 188

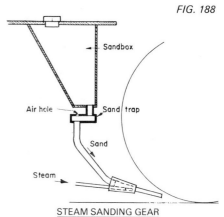

STEAM SANDING GEAR

carry the steam is introduced. If the sand pipe is 5/32 in. dia., even 1/16 in. dia. pipe will carry enough steam. The end of the steam pipe should be provided with a fine jet.

In use, the sand falls into the sand-trap but it will not pass through this until the steam is applied. The sudden rush of steam from a steam valve in the cab causes a rush of air down the end of the sand pipe and this draws the sand down from the trap. The sand-trap should be provided with plugs at each end so that if the sand should get damp, it can be easily cleaned out.

In both gravity and steam sanding, it is most important that the sand be very fine and kept quite dry, otherwise the equipment will fail.

LOCOMOTIVE DETAILS

To give a proper finish to the edge of cabs, tanks and tender sides, etc. half-round brass wire is often used. In the smaller scales, this can be soft-soldered to the brass superstructure, while on the larger scales, brass rivets can be used. Sometimes, the beading used on full-size locomotives was of rather an elaborate section. For instance, on Great Western locomotives, the beading was of an inverted tee section, with the base of the tee slightly rounded. This would be rather difficult to copy on the model,

A spun G.W.R. safety valve casing (Roy Amsbury)

but a fair representation would be a slightly rounded flat section of brass laid on edge.

The glazing of cab spectacles and side windows may be achieved by using Perspex sheet about 1/16 in. thick, a thin "window-frame" of brass sheet being arranged on the inside, the two being held in place by small round-head brass screws put through the frame and the Perspex into tapped holes in the cab sides, the screws being filed flush afterwards.

Footsteps can be built up from sheet steel and angle. As nothing looks worse on a model locomotive than steps hanging down at all angles, it is a good plan to provide additional stiffening at the back of the plate. Ready-made chequer plate, suitable for footsteps, can be obtained from the trade, but can also be made by soldering sheet metal of suitable thickness to some thicker metal and using a small slitting saw, working at a suitable angle to form the usual diamond shape.

Mileometer of Geoff Cashmore's L.N.W.R. tender

The chequer plate so made is then unsoldered and cut to size for soldering on the footsteps.

Handrails on model steam locomotives are sometimes made over scale size for the sake of strength, but this is not really necessary and being rather prominent, spoils the appearance of the locomotive. The handrails on full-size locomotives vary in size from 1 1/8 in. dia. to 1 1/2 in. dia., so that 15 SWG would be about right for a 3/4 in. scale model, and 3/32 in. to 1/8 in. for 1 in. scale. The handrail knobs can be turned from nickel-silver and should not be screwed directly into the boiler. After lightly marking out the position of the handrail knobs on the cleading sheet, this is removed and a thickening piece of brass soldered inside at each spot, the handrail knob can then be securely attached to the cleading with a thin nut on the inside.

BUFFERS

Even highly skilled model engineers seem to get the shape of locomotive buffers wrong! The usual fault is to omit the radius at the back of the head of the buffer, where it blends into the shank. The mouth of the stock should also be internally radiused to match the radius at the back of the head.

Locomotive buffers may have parallel or tapered stocks, the former being more usual on modern engines. On models, the stocks are generally iron or gunmetal castings, in which case, the small footstep which is often fitted on the top in full-size practice (with a chequered surface) can be made integral with the casting. The heads are usually turned from mild or stainless steel and may be round or ovaL. Oval heads must of course be prevented from turning either by the end of the shank being made of a square section, this working in a square cut in the stock, or a key and keyway may be used in the stock.

The springs in the buffers fitted to the front end of a passenger-hauling locomotive may be such that about one-third of the weight of the engine would be required to close the head right up. The springs fitted to the rear or tender buffers may be a little lighter. Rubber buffers (insets that is) are sometimes used, or a combination of a steel spring and a rubber buffer may be used with success.

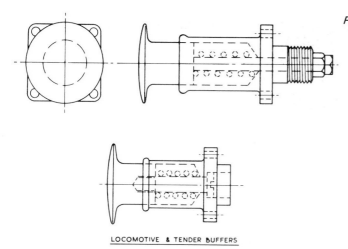

LOCOMOTIVE & TENDER BUFFERS

FIG. 189

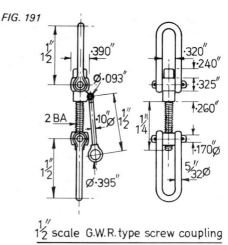

FIG. 191

$1\frac{1}{2}$ scale G.W.R. type screw coupling

In some model designs, the buffer beam is shown as tapped with a fine thread and the buffer stock turned down and threaded to suit. This is a very poor practice. For one thing, it is impossible to thread the stock right up to the base, an undercut being essential, and as the buffer beam may not be thicker than 1/8 in., this means that the effective length of thread may be no more than 1/16 in. or so. A much better method is to have a plain hole in the buffer beam, large enough to take a plain extension of the stock, and to rely on fitting four small hex-head bolts in the corners of a square base to the stock.

COUPLINGS

While screw couplings give a most realistic finish to a model locomotive, they should not be used for "live" passenger hauling except in the largest scales. A strong single link can be fitted to the hook on the passenger car and this made to suit the hook on the rear of the locomotive. Even then, some kind of safety device is advised, to prevent the link from jumping off the hook.

A G.W.R. style screw coupling by Keith Wilson.

Below, an American style auto-coupler by Jack Kerr.

Difficulty is often encountered in bending up the links of screw couplings. One method in common use is to turn the links from mild steel rod of large enough section to form the eyes, then bend the rod on a simple jig. consisting of a pin of suitable diameter pressed into a plate with two levers on each side pivoted at one end so as to bend the ends of the rod evenly inwards to the centre-line.

FIG. 190

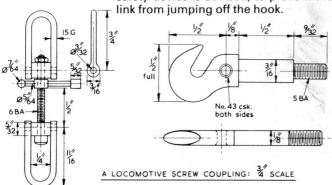

A LOCOMOTIVE SCREW COUPLING: $\frac{3}{4}$" SCALE

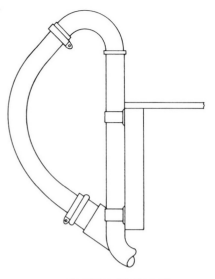

VACUUM BRAKE PIPE

FIG. 192

1in. scale locomotive lamps by Keith Wilson.

The drawhook is generally made from mild steel, though sometimes from stainless steel, the hook itself being well rounded and tapered in plan towards the outer end. The shank, where it passes through the buffer beam, can be of either square or rectangular section, to prevent it turning. For operation on sharp curves, the slot in the beam can be well radiused on each side.

When plain three-link couplings are being made, the ends of the links should always be brazed, otherwise they may be pulled open in service.

BRAKE PIPES

Even if working vacuum or air brakes are not being fitted, a model locomotive looks much better with the usual brake pipe fitted to the buffer beams. A dummy pipe can be bent up from brass rod and rubber tubing used for the hose, the hose clips being made from brass or nickel-silver wire.

A fine 3½in. gauge L.M.S. 0-6-0T by the late H.A. Taylor.

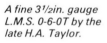

CHAPTER TWENTY ONE

Painting, nameplates, fuels, feed water, raising steam, driving

PAINTING

Many model engineers find the painting and lining of their locomotive the most difficult part of the whole job. The author's method is to paint as many parts of the locomotive as possible as construction proceeds. This applies particularly to the frames and parts between the frames. Most full-sized British locomotives painted the inside of main, bogie and tender frames a bright red or vermilion, (an exception was the old Great Eastern Railway, which used yellow) and generally such parts as frame stretchers, horn castings and eccentric rods were similarly painted, though there were exceptions.

There is no doubt that the best finish of all for a working model is a stove enamel, but this calls for not only the correct stoving enamel but a proper place in which to carry out the stoving, with the maintenance of the correct temperature according to the instructions of the manufacturers of the enamel.

If stove enamelling is not possible, the next best thing is some kind of spraying equipment. A proper high-pressure spray gun, with adequate clean air, is the

Another of H.A. Taylor's excellent locomotives, a 3½in. gauge L.M.S. Class 5 before and after painting.

obvious answer, but such equipment is expensive. A more modest set-up, such as a Badger air-brush, can give good results. Some model engineers have obtained quite good results with one of the "aerosol" sprays, as used for motor-car "touch-ups", though the author confesses that he has never had much luck with these; in any case, the colours available do not usually correspond with the liveries of the railways of Great Britain!

As to the paints to be used, as much of the external surfaces of the model locomotive are likely to be of brass, a "self-etch" primer may be applied first, followed by several thin coats of the chosen colour. The black parts should be painted in a semi-matt finish and the

An unpainted 5in. gauge Simplex. *A* Simplex *won the 1977 New Zealand efficiency competition.*

FIG. 193

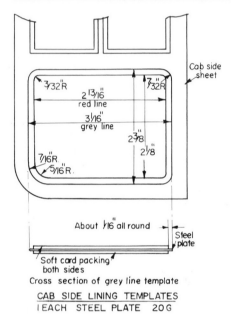

3/32"R 2 13/16" red line 7/32"R 3/16" grey line 2 3/8" 2 7/8" 7/16"R 5/16"R

Cab side sheet

About 1/16" all round

Soft card packing both sides

Steel plate

Cross section of grey line template

CAB SIDE LINING TEMPLATES
1 EACH STEEL PLATE 20 G

FIG. 194

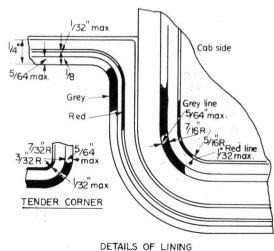

1/32" max. 1/4" 5/64 max. 1/8 Grey Red

Cab side

Grey line 5/64"max. 7/16R 5/16R Red line 1/32 max.

7/32"R 5/64" max. 3/32"R 1/32" max

TENDER CORNER

DETAILS OF LINING

smokebox usually looks better with a dull or matt surface. After any lettering and lining has been applied, one or two thin coats of varnish can be used.

One of the "secrets" of getting the professional finish on the locomotive is to prepare the job properly first. It is not the slightest use trying to paint metal which is not absolutely clean: the slightest trace of oil or grease will cause trouble. The locomotive should be washed thoroughly in petrol, preferably out of doors, and then kept strictly away from dust, and the surfaces should not be touched with the hands. After this, every effort should be made to keep dust at bay. It is worth making up some kind of drying cabinet or booth in which the model can be placed while the paint is drying; this need not be anything very elaborate, it can be made up from wood and stiff cardboard.

When painting, choose a day when there is little or no wind, but also when the atmosphere is fairly dry. Try not to disturb the workshop floor which would raise the dust, and wear an overall of some kind, avoiding any clothing made of wool. If spraying the locomotive, a simple turntable is a great help, enabling the model to be turned round without touching it and making it easier to get the spray gun into the right attitude to the part being dealt with.

If it is decided to paint the locomotive entirely with brushes, do not despair. If the brushes are right, quite good results can be obtained if the job is not hurried. Good brushes are expensive, but only the best sable are suitable for the best work. A flat sable about ½ in. wide plus two fine brushes such as "0" and "00"

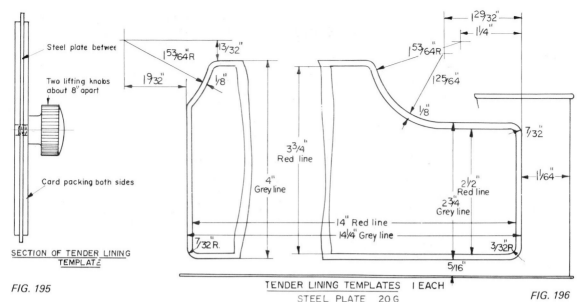

SECTION OF TENDER LINING TEMPLATE

FIG. 195

Steel plate betwee

Two lifting knobs about 8" apart

Card packing both sides

$1\frac{53}{64}$R

$\frac{13}{32}$"

$1\frac{9}{32}$"

$\frac{1}{8}$"

$3\frac{3}{4}$" Red line

4" Grey line

$\frac{7}{32}$R.

$1\frac{29}{32}$"

$1\frac{1}{4}$"

$1\frac{53}{64}$R

$1\frac{25}{64}$"

$\frac{1}{8}$"

$\frac{7}{32}$

$1\frac{1}{64}$

$2\frac{1}{2}$" Red line

$2\frac{3}{4}$" Grey line

14" Red line

$14\frac{1}{4}$" Grey line

$\frac{3}{32}$R.

$\frac{5}{16}$"

TENDER LINING TEMPLATES I EACH
STEEL PLATE 20 G

FIG. 196

FIGS 193 – 197 show lining on a ¾ in. scale L.M.S. locomotive using templates.

should be obtained from a proper art dealer. Brushes should be rinsed in the appropriate thinners immediately after use, and then carefully washed in warm water with a little soap; then they will last a long time.

In brush prainting, each coat should be allowed to dry really hard before lightly rubbing down, until the final finishing coat is applied. Up to eight coats of THIN paint should be applied for the best results, followed by two thin coats of varnish after all lettering and lining have been completed.

If transfers are to be used, note that as received they will be in duplex form, that is to say there is a very thin transparent paper which actually carries the "paint" and this is closely attached to a thicker plain white paper; so the first operation is to separate the two, which can be done by carefully inserting a razor blade at one corner. Next, coat the actual letter or numeral with a quick-drying varnish (called a "quick-jobbing" varnish in the trade) trying as far as possible not to get the varnish outside the letter. Allow 5 to 10 minutes for the varnish to get "tacky" (a trial should be made first on a piece of scrap metal painted in a similar way to the locomotive) then press the transfer firmly down in the desired position. As the backing paper is transparent, it is not difficult to see if the letter has been placed properly. Leave the job to dry for several hours, then place the model under the cold tap (or in a large model, pour the water over the transfer from a small jug) allowing a gentle stream of water to wash the paper away, leaving the letter or crest firmly on the model. On no account attempt to pull the backing paper away by hand, or the job will be damaged.

Lining is best done with a spring-bow pen and templates, plus the use of the finest brushes. Painting, and especially lining, is a difficult art, but it can be acquired in time, given much practice and a great deal of patience!

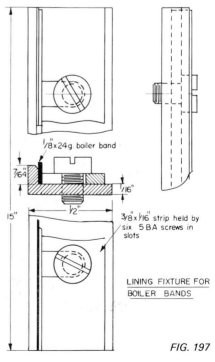

$\frac{1}{8}$x24g. boiler band

$\frac{7}{64}$"

15"

$\frac{1}{2}$"

$\frac{1}{16}$"

$\frac{3}{8}$"x$\frac{1}{16}$" strip held by six 5 BA screws in slots

LINING FIXTURE FOR BOILER BANDS

FIG. 197

201

FIG. 198

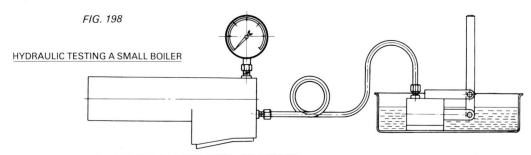

HYDRAULIC TESTING A SMALL BOILER

MINIATURE NAME AND NUMBER PLATES.

On many full-size locomotives, name and number plates, often made as brass castings, though sometimes in steel, were fitted, particularly on express locomotives and on the late Great Western Railway.

The majority of nameplates had characters raised above a plane background and one way of reproducing these to small scale is by photo-etching. The characters are produced by chemically etching away the metal between them; unfortunately the sides of the characters are also attacked to some extent, which limits the depth of etch which is acceptable. A reasonable depth of etch is about 12 thou; for plates where the characters are required considerably thicker than this, it is better to adopt castings in brass.

The etching process starts with a plate of brass of thickness equal to the finished plate and somewhat larger in area. On this is deposited a layer of material capable of resisting the chemical action of the etchant. This layer is called the resist. In order to remove the resist selectively, it is exposed to light through a photographic film which has been prepared in such a way that those areas where the resist must remain are clear areas on the film, thus allowing the light to pass to the resist and harden it. On the other areas, the film is intensely black, so blocking the path of the light and allowing the resist to remain soft, so that it can be dissolved away.

The film is prepared by photographing an enlarged drawing of the desired nameplate. The drawing is made with indian ink on thin white cardboard, bristol board or good quality cartridge paper. A rectangle should be drawn around the lettering. The photographic process calls for a camera having a format large enough to accommodate the size of the finished plate or plates. For very small plates, a 35 mm. camera can be used, but generally a larger camera is called for.

Model engineers who do not wish to carry out the photographic process and the etching process can prepare the black and white drawing and have the remainder of the process carried out by one of the trade firms specialising in this work.

FUELS

Welsh steam coal is undoubtedly the best solid fuel for model steam locomotives. It is a good coal because not only is its steam-raising capacity high, but it burns with very little smoke and if the boiler is a good one, leaves very little residue or ash. Unfortunately, at the time this book was being written, it was very difficult to obtain!

FIG. 199

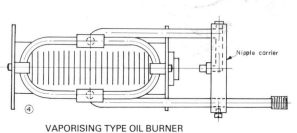

VAPORISING TYPE OIL BURNER

FIG. 200

*Burner for Propane
suitable for 3/4 – 1 in.
scale locomotives.*

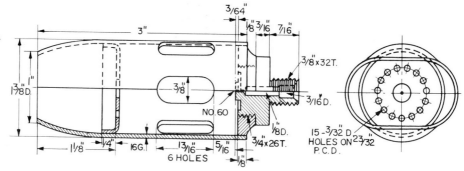

Anthracite is a useful fuel for model locomotives, but its use requires a very strong blast, as it consists of something near 92 per cent of carbon. It is therefore better used with steam coal, in the approximate proportion of 2 parts steam coal to 1 part anthracite.

Where good steam coal cannot be obtained, some of the "patent" fuels may be considered, such as Phurnod, Coalite, etc.

Whatever coal is to be used, it should be carefully sifted and broken up to size according to the size of the locomotive's firebox. For most 1/2 in. scale engines, the coal may be broken up to the size of peas, for 3/4 in. scale about the size of broad beans, and for large 1 in. scale locomotives about the size of walnuts.

Charcoal is good for raising steam, but burns away far too quickly to be used once steam has been raised.

Some model engineers favour oil firing. There are various types of burners available using paraffin (kerosene) and these work on the principle of the atomising of the fuel by means of a jet of steam from the boiler, or by means of a pressure jet; the oil reservoir, which is fitted with a non-return valve, is pumped up with air to a pressure of anything between 15 and 40 lbs. per sq. in., according to the type of burner.

Fig. 199 shows a vaporising type of oil burner designed by the late Edgar T. Westbury. This is of the diffused flame type and burns almost silently. The Blakeney burner is of the pressure atomising type, using steam or air pressure, according to the diameter of the nozzles used. In all types of oil burners, a lot of noise does not mean that the flame being emitted is a very hot one; on the contrary, it may indicate that too much air is being consumed in proportion to the fuel being burnt.

Oil and gas burners should always be made of brass, with any joints silver-soldered. Primus nipples can generally be obtained for use with paraffin, or if home

A Rob Roy *with a
bottled gas burner by
E.N. Kimberley of
Australia.*

203

A ³/₄in. Scale propane-fired locomotive by F. Grosse-Holtfort (Germany).

working pressure is lower and re-filling of the gas container (which may be carried in the locomotive's tender) can be done from a commercial gas bottle such as the well-known "Camping Gaz".

The author has used propane burners in locomotives as small as Gauge "0", the burner being adapted from one of the smaller "Sievert" burners, the burner tube being flattened to splay the flame out. The flame from such burners should not be allowed to play directly on the tubeplate of the boiler, but on to firebrick or other incandescent material.

In large fireboxes of 1 inch scale locomotives, two or four small burners would be advisable, rather than one large one. As mentioned for oil firing, the gas container for propane must be built up as for steam boilers, with proper silver-soldered joints and properly stayed.

Although water-tube boiler are sometimes used with gas firing, the author believes that the best results are obtained by adopting the normal locomotive type boiler, but with tubes of smaller diameter than would be used for coal firing. Unlike the coal-fired boiler, the gas-fired boiler does not suffer from the building up of solid matter, ash etc., in the tubes. Wide firebox boilers for gas-firing do not require combustion chambers, the rather long tubes usually found on these boilers being no real disadvantage. The normal firedoor may still be fitted and this should be provided with a means of adjusting the amount of air drawn in to maintain good combustion; this applies also to the space normally occupied by the grate in coal-fired boilers.

made, they should be drilled with a drill not larger in diameter than No. 78 drill size.

Fuel containers for oil burning must be designed in a similar manner to a boiler as they have to withstand a considerable pressure. The cylindrical shape is therefore convenient and the flat ends should be properly stayed. A motor-car tyre valve can be used for pumping up to obtain the desired pressure.

Perhaps a better alternative to oil firing is bottled gas firing. Bottled gas can be obtained as Butane or Propane. These gases are very similar though Propane has a slightly higher heat value. Butane is generally used in Gauge "1" and "0" locomotives, as its normal

The burner dominates the cab on this German 4-6-4.

FEED WATER

It is seldom that absolutely pure water can be obtained for model steam locomotives, as there are always some impurities present, varying in quantity and character, according to the locality.

Water used for locomotive purposes may be classed as follows:-
1. Surface drainage.
2. River or stream water.
3. Well water.
4. Domestic tap water.
5. Distilled water.

Distilled water is clearly the best for the model boiler, but in most cases will be ruled out on the grounds of both cost and availability. Water from surface

A double propane burner for a 5in gauge locomotive.

obtained from many reputable firms which specialise in water treatment.

Further information on the treatment of water for locomotive boilers can be found in the author's "Model Locomotive Boilers".

RAISING STEAM

drainage is probably the next best as its impurities have been absorbed if the district is one of limestone or chalk, where the impurities settle in the form of scale. This can be removed by frequent washing out and periodical descaling.

River water is generally not too good for model boilers as the type of impurities are influenced by the gathering grounds of the districts through which the water flows. Many works, particularly chemical or iron works, contribute a great deal of matter detrimental to the water. Organic matter, sewage, etc, may also be present in river water.

Well waters vary a great deal; some well water is excellent for drinking purposes, but this does not mean that it is equally good for steam boilers!

The treatment of raw water to make it suitable for model boilers can only be decided upon after a proper chemical analysis; expert advice can however be

Before steam can be raised in a model locomotive fired by solid fuel, an induced draught up the chimney must be provided. There are several ways of providing this draught. One method is to use the locomotive's own blower, air being pumped into the boiler via a non-return valve from some outside source such as a foot pump. Another method is to use an extension chimney and to create a draught by means of a compressor or rotary blower. If a compressor is used for this purpose, an air reservoir will be required between the compressor and the jet in the extension chimney. A rotary blower, which can be driven by an electric motor of about ¼ h.p., does not need an air reservoir, but the jet in the chimney should be larger in the bore as a rotary blower supplies a larger quantity of air at a lower pressure than a compressor.

But the most convenient type of steam-raising blower is probably the small electric motor combined with a rotary fan which can be placed directly on the locomotive's chimney. Such motors are generally available from Government surplus stores; although they are usually designed for 24 volts, they run well enough on 12 volts and being for D.C. current may be run from a motor-car battery. Similar steam-raising blowers are also available from the model engineering trade.

The usual method of lighting the fire in small locomotives is to use charcoal, broken up into small pieces and soaked in paraffin. The firebars are covered by a layer of the soaked charcoal or wood and the external blower started; a match can then be thrown in and the firedoor closed. If the charcoal does not light up immediately, a further teaspoon or two of paraffin can be put in. When the charcoal is properly alight, more charcoal can be fed in until a reasonable depth of fire has been built up, when coal can be fed, a little at a time, until a good depth is burning nicely; by this time, there should be enough steam in the boiler to

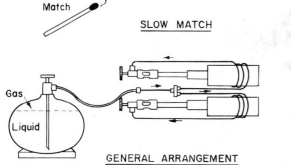

PROPANE BURNER

SLOW MATCH

GENERAL ARRANGEMENT

FIG. 201

work the locomotive's own blower, so that the external auxiliary blower can now be removed.

Another method for lighting the fire is to use cotton-waste soaked in methylated spirit. As methylated spirit is highly volatile, the cotton-waste must be kept in an air-tight container until it is required for use. The soaked cotton-waste is placed on the firebars, a lighted match thrown in and charcoal added immediately. This method is favoured by some model engineers as it is cleaner than using paraffin.

PREPARATION FOR THE RUN

When there is enough steam in the model locomotive boiler to work the engine's own blower, it should not be long before working pressure is reached. Any undue delay here should be investigated. It may be due to a leak of air into the smokebox, thus destroying the effect of the blower, or it may be that the blower jet has not been properly lined up with the petticoat pipe and chimney.

On reaching working pressure, the blower should be turned down a little, so that the various fittings can be tested, without excessive blowing-off from the safety valves. Blowing-off can also be checked by opening the firehole door, or by closing the damper doors if fitted. The safety valves too should be checked for correct operation.

The injectors, if any, should next be tested. If these do not work immediately, the water supply to them should be checked, while it should be seen whether the injectors themselves are cool. The water level must of course be kept under close scrutiny, remembering that the actual level of the water in the boiler is always a little lower than shown on the gauge glass, due to capillary attraction. Operation of the water gauge blowdown valve should ensure a clean glass.

The lubricator/lubricators should be filled, using a proper grade of steam cylinder oil such as Shell Valvata or Vacuum 600W, and all moving parts lubricated with a good quality medium grade lubricating oil (but be sparing with this as we do not want to get it all over the track!).

To start the locomotive, the cylinder drain cocks should be opened, and the regulator opened very slightly, after which the blower can be closed or left open very slightly. The locomotive can now be allowed to move very slowly in full gear to warm up the cylinders and clear condensed water from them. At the same time the action of the pumps, if fitted, can be observed by opening the bypass and noting the return of the bypassed water to the tender or side tanks.

DRIVING

The driving of a model locomotive should follow the same principles as are observed in full-size practice. In starting, the cylinder cocks are always opened, the regulator opened very slightly with the reverser in the full gear position and the blower closed. If the engine wheels take hold, the train will move off smoothly, but if, as so often happens, the locomotive slips at the start, the regulator should be shut promptly and a more gradual opening tried. As the train gathers way, the regulator may be gradually opened up and the reversing gear brought back a notch or two, according to the weight of the train, the gradient of the track and so on.

The water gauge should be watched — this is extremely important with small locomotives with little water capacity — and if the engine is fitted with pumps, the bypass may be adjusted so that the water level in the boiler is kept as near as possible constant. Where injectors are being used, the time to put these on is when the safety valves are about to blow off and when the fire is showing bright.

As for firing, the general principle should be that immediately the safety valves show signs of lifting, further coal should be added so that unnecessary waste of steam is avoided. If this method still allows of frequent blowing-off, the firehole door can be partially opened or the damper doors partly closed and the fire kept to a somewhat smaller size. Coal should, in any case, be fed little and often, rather than a lot at infrequent intervals.

While the train is running, a watch should be kept on the lubrication to the cylinders. When oil is being fed regularly to the cylinders, a certain amount may be thrown out by the blast, and this should wherever possible to kept to the minimum. A slightly oily appearance around the top of the chimney will indicate that the cylinders are not being starved of oil, while the amount of oil left

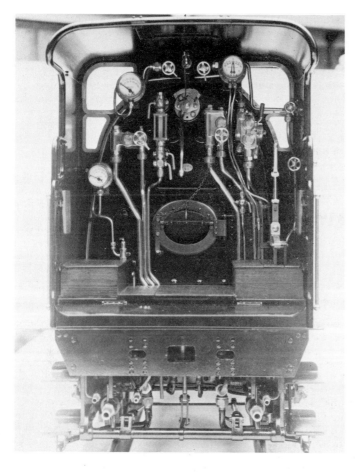

in the lubricator tank at the end of the run will give an indication of how much has been used. There may also be a slight seepage of oil from the piston rod and valve rod glands; this may be corrected by slightly tightening the gland nuts but this should not be over-done as a slight loss of oil from these parts is not important, while unnecessarily tight glands will cause excessive friction and wear.

Should the lubrication to the cylinders fail, this is sometimes indicated by a different note from the pistons (sometimes a squeak will he heard) and if this is suspected, the locomotive must be stopped immediately for investigation or the pistons may seize up.

AFTER THE RUN

As soon as a locomotive is taken out of service, the ashpan and grate should be dropped and the boiler allowed to cool gradually until the pressure indicated is about 30 p.s.i., when the blowdown valves should be opened and the boiler blown down. After this, the smokebox door is opened and the ashes cleaned out, taking great care that no ash or grit falls on the lubricator or its driving mechanism. The tube and flues are then swept out (suitable brushes can be obtained from model engineering suppliers) and any cinders choking the tubes or flues carefully dislodged.

While the locomotive is still warm, it should be thoroughly cleaned down with oily rags and the motion examined and oiled. If it is desired to pack the locomotive in a crate or box for transport or to put it into a motor-car boot, this should never be done until it is quite cold, otherwise condensation will set in and all bright parts will quickly become covered with rust.

A little care taken over the maintenance of the model steam locomotive will be amply repaid. An engine which has been well designed and carefully built, and driven only in a railway-like manner, should give years of service and pleasure to its owner and to all who follow this most fascinating hobby.

Top, the cab of Bill Carter's 5in. gauge G.N.R. "Atlantic" and, left, a driver's view of a smaller saddle tank locomotive by R.W. Fenwick.

Index